Stop Dieting AND
Lose Weight

Stop Dieting AND Lose Weight

The **easiest way** to a slimmer you!

With **175** delicious recipes

Anne Egan and Regina Ragone, M.S., R.D.

RODALE

© 2003 by Rodale, Inc.

Printed in the United States of America
Rodale Inc. makes every effort to use acid-free ∞, recycled paper ♺ .

Book design: Carol Angstadt and Joanna Williams
Cover Photographs: Mitch Mandel
Cover Food Stylist: Diane Simone Vezza

Photo Credits
Stop Dieting and Lose Weight
Fruit and nut cereal, citrus fruit, apple skillet cake, multigrain blueberry waffles, curried sweet potato and apple soup, ginger vegetable broth, moroccan salad, sweet potato salad, tomato pepper balsamic vinaigrette, mexican pork stew, barbecued leg of lamb, swordfish, tabbouleh fruit, quinoa and pepper, baked stuffed potato, root mash, stir fried broccoli, cauliflower and red pepper, roasted beet salad, grilled tomato and cheese sandwiches, pork and pepper stir fry, penne with salmon and roasted vegetables, fish stew with couscous, ginger pumpkin pie, apple crumble with toasted oat topping:
Interior Photographs: Mitch Mandel/Rodale Images; Kurt Wilson/Rodale Images
Food Stylist: Melissa DeMayo

Berry, berry smoothie and banana-orange smoothie, apple skillet cake, cornmeal flapjacks, florentine omelets, pasta e fagioli, mushroom barley soup, mediterranean chickpea salad, fruited turkey salad, potato salad with warm onion dressing, orange beef and broccoli, orange roughy vera cruz, five alarm shrimp, linguine with clams, baked scallops newburg, spaghetti squash casserole, fresh strawberry shortcake:
Interior Photographs: Kurt Wilson/Rodale Images
Food Stylist: Diane Simone Vezza
Prop Stylist: Debrah Donahue

Asian slaw
Interior photograph: Mitch Mandel/Rodale Images
Food Stylist: Diane Simone Vezza
Prop Stylist: Debrah Donahue

Library of Congress Cataloging-in-Publication Data

Egan, Anne.
    Stop dieting and lose weight : the easiest way to a slimmer you / Anne
Egan and Regina Ragone.
        p.   cm.
    Includes index.
    ISBN 1–57954–885–7 hardcover
    1. Reducing diets—Recipes. I. Ragone, Regina. II. Title.
    RM222.2.E32 2003
    641.5'635—dc22   2003014986

2   4   6   8   10 9   7   5   3   1   hardcover

WE **INSPIRE** AND **ENABLE** PEOPLE TO IMPROVE
THEIR LIVES AND THE WORLD AROUND THEM

FOR MORE OF OUR PRODUCTS
WWW.**RODALESTORE**.COM
(800) 848-4735

contents

acknowledgments

Many thanks to everyone involved in bringing this book to fruition, especially:

Eric Metcalf, for writing that brought shape to many ideas

Shea Zukowski, for editing and imagination in menu planning

Lois Hazel, for diligent attention to the editing details

Kathy Everleth, for editorial advice and thoughtful insights

Wendy Hess, for her talents in layout

Miriam Rubin, for developing delicious recipes

Carol Angstadt and Joanna Williams, for their fresh and lively design

How to Use
This Book

Often, when you buy a cookbook, you may flip through
the pages looking for great-tasting recipes. You will find
plenty of them here—this book contains more than 175
delicious, enticing recipes divided by dishes. But preceding
the recipe pages are three chapters of very useful information about weight loss that may help you achieve permanent
results and see things in a whole new light.

The first chapter, "Use Your Mind, Lose Your Weight,"
explains why we shouldn't approach weight loss with a
rigid "I'm going on a diet" mentality. Most diets require
too many radical shifts in our eating habits. And as we are
largely creatures of habit, we simply can't make so many
long-term changes all at once. Instead, the experts we
talked to recommend focusing your efforts one step at a
time on a simple, sensible, rewarding way of eating that

will guide you for the rest of your life. This chapter walks you through all the steps you need.

Next, you'll learn the top ten secrets of successful weight loss winners. We cover all the bases, showing you what is best to eat, and when to eat it. These expert-recommended changes can help rev up any weight loss effort; plus you'll find dozens of ideas you can use to make the changes real in your own life.

In chapter three, we put this weight loss philosophy into action and show you how to use your plate at every meal to achieve the slow, steady weight loss you want. By imagining your plate divided into three parts and filling each section with a different food group, you'll know that you're getting the right combination of foods to ensure long-term results.

And to make it even easier, each recipe in this book will show you at a glance how its ingredients count toward covering the different regions of your plate. You'll find a picture of a plate divided into the following color-coded sections:

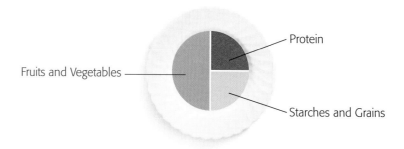

And you'll know right away if the recipe you're reading doesn't fill out your plate completely—one section will not be filled out. If that's the case, you'll find great suggestions for dishes to serve with each recipe. Just open the book to any recipe and you're on your way to a truly satisfying meal in minutes. No calorie counting, no measuring, no kidding!

In the back of this book, you'll find a variety of delicious dessert recipes that won't derail your weight loss efforts. According to the experts we talked to, working the occasional treat into your plans can help you avoid other temptations more successfully. Because these treats are reserved for special situations, they're not interchangeable with the other recipes in this book—you won't see a plate next to them to tell you how it fits into a daily menu. Even so, most of these sumptuous desserts provide around 200 calories or less per serving, so go ahead and enjoy!

Overall, variety is an important key to success with this plan because these recipes are designed to fill your plate with delicious food, not to reach a specific calorie goal. But because some recipes have more calories than others, the more recipes you incorporate into your weekly menu, the better your results should be. And if you prefer to search just for recipes by plate, you'll find all of them in the Plate Index in the back of the book (page 343).

In the end, our goal was simply to do all of the hard work for you so that you can get to the fun part easily and effortlessly. What is the fun part? Cooking and eating delicious food, of course!

Use Your Mind, Lose Your Weight

Monika Woolsey had brought two apples to work to enjoy during the day, and she was growing hungry for one. But she couldn't find them anywhere, no matter where she looked.

She dug through her bag. No apples.

She scanned around her desk. Still no apples.

"Eventually I looked up," she recalls, "and found two apple cores on my keyboard." She'd gnawed two apples to the core without even realizing or remembering that she'd eaten them!

"That was really my introduction to mindless eating," she adds.

Fortunately, apples rank high on the list of healthy

foods that won't wreck a diet or pack on pounds easily. But what if she'd brought a sleeve of miniature doughnuts and only meant to eat two? Or a bag of chips from which she only meant to eat a small handful? She could have consumed far more calories than she needed or wanted—and if she were trying to lose weight, she could have suffered a real setback that day.

Woolsey, a registered dietitian, exercise physiologist, and consultant, shares this story with the clients she works with through After The Diet Network, her Glendale, Arizona-based company.

She sees our sped-up, overscheduled culture as a big factor in why so many of us are overweight and have trouble slimming down. "There are only so many brain cells to devote to your daily life," she says. Too often we feel we must eat on the run—in our cars, in our offices, and on the way out the door. As a result, we focus our limited attention on driving or working, and wind up eating mindlessly.

The food industry has readily complied with this need to eat while multi-tasking by providing us with an array of snacks that will easily fit into our hands, purses, and our cars' nooks and crannies.

Unfortunately, it's usually after eating yet another bag of chips, or package of cookies, or meal with a plate that's been filled too full that we realize we've taken another step away from healthy eating or the healthy weight we desire. After that, we too often become upset with ourselves, Woolsey says.

"How could I be so weak-willed?" we may think. "Why can't I just control myself?" These thoughts just add to the emotional stress that is another major problem that gets in the way of healthy eating, she says.

The answer?

Forget about going on a diet to lose weight. That's merely a short-term bandage for a long-term issue, a quick fix that will likely stop working in a few weeks or months when you can't stand the artificial constraints of a diet, Woolsey points out. Instead, focus your efforts on putting together a simple, sensible, rewarding way of eating that will see you through your lifetime.

Nor should you plan to change "30 things all at once" in your life, Woolsey says. Unless you make changes slowly, you won't have any way of knowing what is working and what isn't. When too many changes occur at once, people become more inclined to drop them all at once, too.

Instead, you merely need to become more aware of the way you eat and steer your eating habits, step by step, toward a lifestyle that encourages good nutrition and a healthy weight.

This includes developing an eye for truly satisfying food instead of picking foods because they "look" healthy or have a label proclaiming "low-fat" or "low-calorie." You'll also need an easy way to fill your plate day in and day out with foods that do your body—and your figure—good, without having to carry around confusing lists of calorie content or food exchanges. And, of course, you need plenty of delicious, easy-to-follow recipes for meals that fill all these needs.

Stop Dieting and Lose Weight will teach you how to do just that. In the following pages, you'll find the best advice from the country's leading nutritional experts on how to shed pounds simply by changing your approach to food. You'll also encounter real people who have lost weight and kept it off by simply making small changes in how they look at food and eat it.

No longer will you look down at the scale and ponder how many long-forgotten snacks, second helpings, and repeated trips to the buffet table are hidden in that number you're seeing. Nor will you suffer through tiny portions, radical changes to your lifestyle, or outlandish diets.

As Socrates said, "An unexamined life is not worth living." Along the same lines, an unexamined approach to food is often not worth eating. So let's start by talking about how to become more aware of the food you eat.

The Power of Mindful Eating

Mindless eating is a sneaky enemy. You may think you're vigilant about watching what you eat. But new research shows that "eating amnesia," or forgotten nibbling, could undermine your weight-loss success. Stolen bites and tastes (such as handfuls of a friend's popcorn at the movies, or tasting the dough while baking cookies) can rack up a few hundred uncounted calories, which can put on pounds quickly.

Eating while distracted can cause this amnesia too. When women who normally watch their portions had lunch in different situations, researchers reported in a study in the *American Journal of Clinical Nutrition* that the women ate 15 percent more (72 additional calories) when they ate while listening to a detective story compared with when they ate alone and free of any distractions. Instead, if food is going into your mouth, you want to make sure that your mind is focused on it and not elsewhere (while on the computer, for example). Whenever you put food in your mouth, you should peel it, unwrap it, set it on a plate, and sit. Engage all of the senses in the pleasure of nourishing your body. Obviously you can't do this when you're driving in the car, or working under deadline.

So eliminate unnecessary distractions when you're eating. Perhaps all you need to do is turn off the radio or set aside your book for a few moments. But other situations may require more creative interventions to get your mind on what you're doing.

At the office: A coworker bakes a delicious banana bread for your morning meeting. Take one slice, and set it aside to savor when you have a moment of quiet time back at your desk. If you eat during the meeting, it would be easy to have two slices, or even more.

Making dinner: Chew gum. Besides offering your mouth another flavor to enjoy, you have to take it out every time you sample your cooking—try it and you'll soon realize how much food you're taking in with each little taste.

Cleaning up from the kids' lunch: If you regularly snack on your kids' leftovers, don't serve them as much to start, and offer seconds later if needed. The minute they're finished, wrap up or toss what's left.

Watching TV: Keep your hands busy by knitting, filing your nails, or playing a game of solitaire. If you truly need a snack, get up and go to a quiet place to enjoy it.

Another important part of mindful eating is listening to your body and knowing when it *really* needs food, and that's a balancing act. While you don't want to let yourself get *ravenously* hungry (that's a perfect setup for overeating), you should always perform a quick reality check before you put food in your mouth. Make sure your need for food is real, and try to avoid the rationalizations if it's not.

For example, imagine you just ate lunch, when a birthday cake for a coworker suddenly appears in your area. As you take a slice, you think, "I'll eat less later." But according to weight-loss researchers, that's not necessarily the way things will happen. In a study reported in the *American Journal of Clinical Nutrition*, when researchers fed 11 lean men a 250-calorie snack soon after lunch, they

Use Your Brain to Outsmart Advertising

Eating snack foods is fun and sexy and cures every mood—or so advertisers would have you believe. The truth is, all that fat or sugar won't make you vibrantly healthy. Many of these products may not even satisfy your hunger!

Here are some examples of recent food promises, along with slimming alternatives that really give you what you're craving. Unlike cookies, candy, potato chips, or soda, these feel-good indulgences won't ruin your waistline.

The Product: Hershey's Nuggets (4 pieces, 210 calories)
The Sell: "One of life's little rewards"
Better Solution: Reward yourself with a manicure, a new CD, or a new gadget for your kitchen.

The Product: Coca-Cola (20 oz, 250 cal)
The Sell: "You can't beat the feeling"
Better Solution: You *really* can't beat the feeling of a beautiful walk outdoors.

The Product: Keebler Fudge Shoppe Clusters (2 cookies, 140-200 cal)
The Sell: "Take time to indulge in some fudge therapy"
Better Solution: Soak in a bubble bath, or curl up with a good book.

The Product: Doritos (2 oz or 22 chips, 280 cal)
The Sell: "Be bold, be daring"
Better Solution: Be bold or daring by trying a new sport or fitness activity

The Product: General Foods International Coffees (12 oz, 100 cal)
The Sell: "Take a moment" "Unplug"
Better Solution: Relax with chamomile tea; it's caffeine- and calorie-free.

didn't feel more satisfied, delay dinner, or eat less later on. Instead, they simply tacked an extra 250 calories onto their day's total .

How does that happen? When you eat because you're hungry, blood glucose levels rise, which signals satisfaction and an end to the meal. But if you eat simply because food is there, or because you're upset or stressed, you're more likely to gain weight. That's because when your energy stores are already replenished from your meal, your body immediately stores any extra calories it receives as fat. To avoid this, eat only when you feel hungry. It could be 2 hours after a small meal or 5 hours after a huge one.

Need a simple tool to know when to eat and when to pass? Listen to Joanne Pekrul. When she was diagnosed with diabetes, she knew she had to lose weight, so she enrolled in a weight management program. "I learned that a lot of times when I thought I was hungry, I was really eating for emotional reasons, for comfort," says Pekrul, who lost 17 pounds during the 12-week program.

She uses a scale to help her identify when it is time to eat. The scale goes from 0 (famished) to 10 (completely stuffed). Her goal is to stay between 3 and 7 at all times: 3 is reasonable hunger and a good time to eat; 7 is comfortably full, but not stuffed.

Her story brings us to another important part of mindfulness: learning to separate your desire for food from your emotions.

Could You Have a Thinking Problem?

Eight years ago, working mother Pat Cherry, of Sacramento, California, carried 165 pounds on her 5'3" frame and a host of worries in her heart. Two years later, without following any special diet or exercise plan, she had dropped 40 pounds. Today, still weighing a trim 125, Pat is happy to share her weight loss secret: "My twice daily meditations keep me slim."

She proves that it's possible to melt away pounds with your mind, particularly if you deal with emotional distress by eating. In fact, say some experts, unless you come to grips with what's going on in your head, no weight-loss plan will ever work.

Pat's pound-shedding odyssey actually began when she joined a program for emotional eaters and started seeing a therapist. She battled long-buried issues from a painful childhood, but gradually she began to feel more in control of her life. Daily meditation helped her relax. And as her self-worth grew, her food cravings miraculously disappeared. "Every time I dealt with a new issue, I lost three pounds," she says.

Many people struggling with their weight are what Stephen P. Gullo, Ph.D., a prominent weight loss expert in New York City, calls food therapists, people who use food to deal with stress and the problems of life.

"They have developed a one-word response to any and all problems: Eat!" says Dr. Gullo.

It's not surprising that so many people use food as a tranquilizer, says Dori Winchell, Ph.D., a psychologist in private practice specializing in eating disorders in Encinitas, California. "From the time you're a baby through childhood, whenever you're unhappy, someone soothes you with a cookie. We've been pairing emotions with eating for so long that it's little wonder we know anything else." What's more, admits Dr. Winchell, food works. "Food can create soothing changes in brain chemistry, and even the simple act of chewing will increase endorphins and ease your pain."

You eat for relief, which, unfortunately, lasts only as long as the last bite. Then the problems you were trying to solve with food suddenly reappear. And you feel like a failure: Not only didn't you solve your problems, you created a new one, right there around your waist!

The solution? Find tools besides a fork to attack emotional angst. In the time it takes to forage for your favorite quick-fix food, you can take steps to break the cycle, beat stress, eliminate emotional eating, and yes, finally drop that excess weight for good without even trying.

Play detective. Keep a food journal, suggests eating expert Joan Chrisler,

Ph.D., professor of psychology at Connecticut College in New London. "Every time you reach for food, write down what you eat and how you were feeling. Bored? Frustrated? Happy? Before long, you'll see a pattern. Then you can start to break it."

But skip the part where you look up and log the food's every vital statistic. That's more of a chore than we'd recommend. To see eating patterns you can change, just write down what you've eaten (Doritos), the circumstances (by self at home), and your hunger level or feelings (not very; bored).

Shop for some stimulants. Do you eat when you're bored? Time to make a new "grocery" list, says Dr. Chrisler. Buy inexpensive, accessible things such as books, CDs, and tapes or DVDs of favorite films that provide the emotional lift you're seeking from food. Keep them handy, and turn to them when you're down.

Make a human connection. "For some people, food is love," says *Prevention* magazine columnist Edward M. Hallowell, M.D., a psychiatry instructor at Harvard Medical School. "You may be hungry for feeling, closeness, and companionship. Make a human connection instead," suggests Dr. Hallowell. "Call your best friend." Make sure you pick someone who makes you feel good. If you have issues with a parent or friend, calling them could lead you to finish off an entire row of cookies.

Create new habits. Many people eat every time there's a lull, such as during TV commercials, says eating disorders expert Sandra Haber, Ph.D., adjunct associate clinical professor at Adelphi University's Derner Institute in New York City. Be prepared for those lulls. "Keep manicure supplies, stacks of empty photo albums, or a cross-stitch project by the TV for something to do," she suggests. Even better, find a hobby. When you're engrossed in something you love, you forget all about eating, especially if you're active.

Confront the here and now. "If dwelling on the past burned calories, no woman would be overweight," says Pamela M. Peeke, M.D., M.P.H., assistant clinical professor of medicine at the University of Maryland School of Medicine in Baltimore and author of the bestselling book *Fight Fat After Forty* (Viking Press, 2000). "Instead of ruminating, take action." If your mother was abusive, resolve to be a better mother yourself. If certain relatives upset you, limit your time with them. And if you need help, get therapy, as Pat Cherry did.

Learn to relax. To completely conquer emotional eating, you need to trump stress, the source of anxiety and artificial food cravings. "I was amazed to learn that all my pangs didn't mean I was really hungry," says Naomi Henderson, 58, an entrepreneur in Bethesda, Maryland, who found herself growing along with her new company. "I'd eat a full meal and be ravenous 45 minutes later! All my cravings were from stress." Stress-taming tricks such as beginning each day with a 20-minute blissful bath instead of a hurry-up shower helped her drop from a size 18 to a 12.

Of course, tried-and-true stress-blasters such as steamy baths and good books help douse stress for the moment. But to really give it the heave-ho, you need to stress-proof your body with lasting relaxation exercises. Two of the best are yoga and meditation. These practices use deep breathing and mental concentration to make you more aware of your body and emotions. Deep-breathing relaxation exercises also affect your body's physiology, lowering blood pressure and slowing heart rate, making it easier to distance yourself from the everyday worries that trigger stress and overeating.

Monika Woolsey is also a proponent of yoga, as well as the relaxing art of tai chi. These offer exercises to "keep your mind in the present and away from feeling guilty about what you've eaten in the past."

Of course, your emotions aren't the only way that your mind interacts with how you deal with food. Another way you should "change your mind" about eating is by changing the way you perceive the healthfulness of the foods around you.

Let's Get Critical

Things are not always what they seem.

You may have heard that nuts are rich in heart-healthy vitamin E and mononounsaturated fat. Does that mean a handful of them is better than a handful of microwave popcorn if you're trying to lose weight? Er, probably not. Nuts *are* healthy but—and this is crucial—they're dense with calories. Put those bowls away, and use nuts as a garnish instead of a snack.

What about ordering your salad dressing on the side and dipping into it instead of eating salad covered in dressing? That's a sure-fire way to lose weight, right? Sorry, but again, not necessarily.

Ordering salad dressing "on the side" may not be saving you calories. In one survey, some restaurants served three times the recommended amount of dressing (equal to 600 calories) on the side.

So even if you eat only half, you may be getting more calories than you thought. For about 60 to 100 calories, you should spoon out no more than 1 tablespoon (half-dollar size) of dressing or butter, or 2 tablespoons of sour cream or guacamole.

If the numbered wheel in your bathroom scale seems to be nailed down and won't budge, maybe errors in judgment like these are to blame. Perhaps you should pick out and discard some of the entries in your mental Rolodex of what's healthy. Or perhaps you're assuming that a healthy snack offers a blank check to eat as much as you want. Some do. Some don't.

Try the following quiz comparing tempting duos to see how you fare in picking today's skinny snacks.

What's Skinnier?
Energy Bar or Chocolate Bar?
The Winner . . . Energy Bar (but not by much)

A Balance Gold Rocky Road energy bar (1.76 oz) contains 210 calories, while a Hershey's Milk Chocolate bar (1.55 oz) contains 230 calories. Surprised that the energy bar is almost as high-cal as the candy bar? "Even though the calories are roughly the same, the energy bar has only half as much artery-clogging saturated fat as the candy bar. And the fortified vitamins and minerals in most energy bars do constitute a plus," says Kathryn Miller, R.D., nutritionist at The Cooper Aerobics Center in Dallas.

What's Skinnier?
High-Fiber Cereal or Doughnuts?
The Winner . . . Doughnuts

Stunned, shocked, and chagrined? Many would be. Two Hostess plain doughnuts register in at 300 calories and 16 g of fat. Compare that with the 380 calories and 6 g of fat in 2 cups of Kashi GoLean Crunch! cereal, a popular snack that dieters are munching by the boxful lately. "Portion size is everything," says Karen Miller-Kovach, R.D., chief scientist for Weight Watchers in Woodbury, New York. "Limit the calories of the cereal snack by eating only 1 cup for 190 calories versus 2 cups for 380."

What's Skinnier?
Granola Bar or Apple?
The Winner . . . Granola Bar (Sort of)

If calories are your only measure, a 10-oz apple (the size of a baseball on steroids) has about 165 calories, while a Quaker Chewy Chocolate Chip Granola Bar (the size of a Pez dispenser) has 120 calories.

But that apple is going to last much longer as a snack than the three-bite granola bar. Plus, the apple has 8 g of fill-you-up fiber; the granola bar has only 1 g of fiber.

What's Skinnier?
36 Cashews or 12½ Cups of Popcorn?
The Winner . . . 12½ Cups of Popcorn (by a Nose)

Honestly speaking, most people who eat microwave popcorn do so with one goal in mind: to wolf down the entire bag in one contented sitting. But even so, a whole bag of popped Orville Redenbacher's Reden-Budders Light Movie Theater Butter popcorn (12-½ cups' worth) contains only 312 calories and 6 g of fat.

Compare that with 36 cashews (barely 2 handfuls), which contain 340 calories and 28 g of fat. True, the monounsaturated fat in cashews is a good fat, the kind that helps lower cholesterol. But nuts are easy to eat by the handful, so unless you have tons of willpower, it's best to eat nuts only when they're a part of a salad or other mixed dish.

But eat them you may. And that's a radical departure from the rules that most "diets" hold you to. Many may even require you to abandon all the foods you love for a grueling regimen of grapefruit and dry toast, complicated by endless counting of fat grams and fiber. That's why the concept of this cookbook is to give you choices so you can live a normal lifestyle, without sacrificing the foods you love or remembering complicated formulas.

So what about those foods that speak to the dark side of our desires, the foods we love, even though we know they aren't good for us—or our waistlines? As if you didn't know what they are already, the fattening foods that pose the biggest problems for most people are the foods that might be considered the "old faithfuls" of our national menu—hot dogs, hamburgers, fried chicken, french fries, and bacon and eggs—according to research from the University of Minnesota. And the answer to how to live with them is actually quite simple: cutting back on these diet offenders—**not cutting them out totally**— can help you lose up to 23 pounds a year without doing anything else.

Sound too good to be true? Try switching your favorite fattening dish for a lower-calorie alternative just a few days a week and see how much weight you can lose. Replace two favorites, and shed even more. The following examples illustrate how much these simple substitutions can add up over the course of a year.

Fattening favorite: French fries, large (533 calories).

Tasty alternative: Potato chips, 1-oz snack-size bag (150 calories). If you regularly have fries four times a week, try the alternative half the time and you can save 766 calories a week - over the course of a year, you'll lose 12 pounds. Have the alternative four times a week, and you can save 1,532 calories a week and lose 23 pounds in a year.

Fattening favorite: Fried chicken, breast and wing (494 calories).

Tasty alternative: Roasted chicken breast and thigh without skin (251 calories). Have your fave twice a week and the alternative twice, and you can save

486 calories a week and lose 7 pounds in a year. Choose the alternative altogether and you'll save 972 calories a week and lose 15 pounds in a year.

Fattening favorite: Burger (306 calories).

Tasty alternative: Meat-style veggie burger (90 calories). Have your fave twice a week and the alternative twice, and you can save 432 calories a week and lose 7 pounds in a year. Have the alternative four times a week, and you can save 864 calories a week and lose 13 pounds in a year.

Fattening favorite: Bacon (3 slices) and eggs (2, any style) (299 calories).

Tasty alternative: Deli-style ham (2 slices) and egg substitute (100 calories). Have your fave twice a week and the alternative twice, and you can save 398 calories a week and lose 6 pounds in a year. Have the alternative four times a week, and you can save 796 calories a week and lose 12 pounds in a year.

Fattening favorite: Hot dog (180 calories).

Tasty alternative: Light (95% fat-free) beef hot dog (55 calories). Have your fave twice a week and the alternative twice, and you can save 250 calories a week and lose 4 pounds in a year. Have the alternative four times a week, and you can save 500 calories a week and lose 8 pounds in a year.

Hey, this switching one tasty treat for another even extends to dessert!

Instead of a Snickers candy bar (2.07 oz, 280 calories), have a Milky Way Lite (1.57 oz, 170 calories) and save 110 calories. Make that switch twice a week and lose three pounds a year.

Instead of . . . 2 chocolate-chip cookies (2-½ inches diameter, 280 calories), have 2 sugar cookies, (2-½ inches diameter, 130 calories) and save 150 calories. Make that switch twice a week and lose four pounds a year.

Instead of . . . 20 Peanut M&Ms (202 calories), have 20 Plain M&Ms (68 calories) and save 134 calories. Make that switch twice a week and lose four pounds a year.

Instead of . . . ½ cup Haagen-Dazs Chocolate Ice Cream (270 calories), have ½ cup Breyers chocolate ice cream (160 calories) and save 110 calories. Make that switch three times a week and lose *five* pounds a year!

These are the kind of changes you need to make in order to be a more

Compromise With Your Favorites

Don't say goodbye to your favorite food friends . . . just learn how to enjoy them differently!

Guilty Pleasure: Pizza

Downside: A 12-inch double sausage and pepperoni pizza delivers more than 2,000 calories and 60 grams of saturated fat.

Healthy Indulgence: Two slices of thin-crust veggie pizza weigh in at just 300 calories and 2.5 g of saturated fat.

Avoiding Temptation: Order a small pizza with extra tomato sauce. While you wait, have a salad (a mostly veggie antipasto) or a mug of minestrone or pasta e fagioli soup, followed by those two slices of pizza. Patronize shops that pile on the sauce and veggies, but just lightly oil the pan. (Place your slice on a napkin to detect pizza with a greasy bottom.) For takeout, order plain cheese pizza with extra tomato sauce, then add veggies at home. Or make your own pizza with reduced-fat cheese. Gotta have meat? Precook pepperoni or sausage, and then blot the grease on paper towels before adding the meat to the pizza. Add anise seed or hot pepper seasonings to low-fat Canadian bacon if you want to mimic sausage.

Guilty Pleasure: Ice cream

Downside: Premium brands drip with calories and saturated fat. A ½-cup serving of coffee flavor Haagen-Dazs packs a whopping 275 calories and 11 g of saturated fat.

Healthy Indulgence: Officially, one serving of ice cream is ½ cup—the size of a tennis ball. Stick to this amount if you're eating calorie- and fat-loaded premium ice cream (one with 250 calories or more per ½ cup). But if you're eating regular or low-fat brands, one cup is a more realistic serving size.

Avoiding Temptation: If you can't keep a "high vulnerability" half-gallon on hand, go to an ice cream shop, and buy just one scoop. At home, have an ice cream on a stick, or buy just enough so that everyone in your family gets one scoop. Or save the real deal for birthdays or other occasions when guests can help prevent leftovers.

Guilty Pleasure: Cheese

Downside: Cheese has lots of cholesterol-raising saturated fat; 1½ ounces of cheddar packs 9 grams of the stuff. For most women, that's more than half of the saturated fat than you should have in a day.

Healthy Indulgence: 1 ½ ounce, max, in any one day. Eyeballing it? It's equal to about six dice.

Avoiding Temptation: Choose strong-flavored cheeses like extra-sharp cheddar or gorgonzola, and you'll be satisfied with less. Prevent overindulgence: Take what you need, then wrap and refrigerate the rest immediately. Or use proportioned string cheese, cheese slices, or mini-cheese wedges.

Guilty Pleasure: Beef

Downside: Plate-size portions of fatty meats such as hamburger and prime rib are loaded with saturated fat, which raises cholesterol and heart disease risk. A restaurant-size 14-oz sirloin steak has 27 grams of saturated fat—nearly twice the saturated fat that women should have in a day.

Healthy Indulgence: When it comes to beef, portion size is everything. Stick with a 3-ounce portion, about the size of a computer mouse. A 3-oz sirloin steak has 6 grams of saturated fat, well within a woman's saturated fat maximum of 14 grams.

Avoiding Temptation: Choose the select grade, and stick with lean cuts such as round (top, bottom, eye) and loin (sirloin, tenderloin). These don't raise cholesterol any more than poultry or fish, a recent study shows. Use small portions as flavor enhancers for stir-fries. When you eat out, pass on the huge steaks and burgers. Instead, get dishes containing beef with plenty of veggies, like stir-fries or kebabs.

Guilty Pleasure: Peanut butter

Downside: Peanut butter is chock-full of calories, at 180 to 200 per 2-tablespoon serving, and it's so easy to overeat.

Healthy Indulgence: According to the American Diabetes Association, two level tablespoons of peanut butter provide as much protein as an ounce of lean meat.

Avoiding Temptation: Spread your peanut butter on small slices of dense, whole grain bread or crackers to get more out of your two tablespoons. Once you permit yourself to indulge on a regular basis, the urge to pig out should pass. Then use peanut butter instead of cream cheese on your bagel, or use it in place of butter on English muffins, waffles, and pancakes.

mindful eater. Not bad, huh? Trading one kind of ice cream for another doesn't seem like much of a dietary hardship.

They're not big changes, either. Which gets us back to Monika Woolsey's comment that people shouldn't make a ton of changes at one time in order to lose weight. It's hard to maintain that much change, and it's hard to know which ones are working when you want to drop some of them. Just resolve that you're going to make one new little change each week, and see how they add up - and your weight subtract.

Let's look at some more small changes you can make for the sake of mindfulness.

Keep Those Fixes Small

Don't believe that just one little change can help you lose weight? You might if you saw how one woman accidentally *gained* 15 pounds with just one tiny little change.

Laura Kiesling, a 29-year-old stay-at-home mom, worked very hard to lose the 90 pounds she'd gained while pregnant with her two children. Daily 3-mile walks, weight training, and calorie counting helped her drop from 200 pounds to 112. Then one day, her mother told her about spray margarine.

"It tasted great, and the label said no calories, so I started using it pretty liberally on popcorn, steamed vegetables, and lots of other things," she recalls. "I hate scales and don't weigh myself, but after awhile, I started to notice that my pants were getting tight." Since she hadn't changed her diet, Kiesling feared the weight gain might have come from an underlying health problem. "I went to my doctor and had a blood test to check my thyroid and hormones," she says. "Everything was fine, except I'd gained 15 pounds and couldn't figure out why."

Then she read in *Prevention* magazine that products with fewer than 5 calories per serving can claim to have zero calories, even though an entire bottle of spray margarine contains 900 calories and 90 g of fat. "When I discovered that spray margarines weren't as calorie-free as I thought, I stopped using them," says Kiesling, who switched to calorie-free and low-calorie alternatives such as cheese powder, basil, and pepper. "In 3 months, I was back to 112 pounds."

One little fix brought on the pounds, and one little fix can take them off.

Just add one fix a week. Cut out a few calories from one habit, and a few more from another habit. (Of course, tiny changes to *burn* more calories will help, too. Find some new ways to add bits of physical activity to your schedule and you'll certainly see a boost in your weight loss.)

If you like a change, keep it and add on another later. If not, drop it and try a different one. You've seen plenty of potential changes in this chapter— read the following scenarios for more food-based choices to fit into your lifestyle:

At the Mall

Endless food peddlers and long lines can make the mall a diet disaster. Here's how to avoid stress and keep your waistline in check.

Start late. Avoid hectic weekend crowds. Shop during late weekday holiday hours, after you've eaten at home.

Dress casually. Wear comfortable walking shoes, and leave your coat in the car. You won't be as tired—or need a snack to revive you.

Nix the mall. Shop downtown or at an open-air plaza where you can stroll the streets and stop for a healthy bite at a local cafe.

Dine first. Instead of waiting until you're crazed with hunger, start your trip energized from a nice lunch at a sit-down restaurant.

De-stress. Stop for a sample of soothing bath lotions or a chair massage. You'll be less likely to eat from stress.

Hit the drugstore. Save calories (and money) by grabbing a bottled drink and a snack bag of pretzels for later so you won't be tempted by the overpriced food court.

Indulge—a little. A single, decadent truffle (0.4 oz) is just 60 calories. If you must eat a bigger meal or snack at the mall, steer away from the usual burgers-and-fries outlet, and toward one of these:

- Chick-fil-A: 4 Chick-n-Strips (230 calories)
- Smoothie King: Slim & Trim Orange-Vanilla smoothie (20 oz) (200 calories)
- Au Bon Pain: English Toffee Cookie (220 calories)
- Starbucks: Cappuccino with fat-free milk (16 oz) (110 calories)
- Auntie Anne's: 4 Kidstix (227 calories)

At the Medicine Cabinet.

If you started a new prescription weeks or months ago—and then began to notice the needle on the scale going in the wrong direction—it's probably not a coincidence. Weight gain is an often-overlooked side effect of many common medications, but you can do something about it.

"Most medicines can easily be switched for alternatives that are less prone to cause appetite and weight changes," says Lawrence Cheskin, M.D., director of the Johns Hopkins Weight Management Center in Baltimore and author of a study that identified the drugs most likely to cause weight gain. Obviously, you should talk to your doctor before you stop taking any medication. For a look at the most common offenders and tips on what to do (besides asking your doctor about an alternative), see below.

Antihistamines

Cause of weight gain: Increased appetite; plus, these medications can possibly dry out your nose and throat.

Action plan: Time your medication to when you're most prone to allergies. You may feel the need to drink more, so beware of high-calorie beverages.

Diabetes meds

Cause of weight gain: Better regulation of blood sugar enables you to retain vital nutrients (as well as calories) that your body used to excrete.

Action plan: Eat a low-fat diet and balance your calories throughout the day.

Psychiatric meds (such as certain antidepressants)

Cause of weight gain: Increased appetite, possibly because you're in a better mood

Action plan: Practice portion control, and eat smaller meals throughout the day.

Steroid hormones (corticosteroids)

Cause of weight gain: Fluid and salt retention; increased appetite.

Action plan: Ask your doctor about taking the med less frequently.

In Your Married life

When he grabs a third slice of pizza, it's tempting to do the same. "Many women put on 10 pounds or more soon after they marry or start living with a man," says Ellen Albertson, RD, co-host with her husband of *The Cooking Couple Show*. In general, men can eat more than women without gaining weight. And you don't have to be a newlywed to suddenly find yourself mimicking your partner's eating habits.

To keep manly meals in check, try these tips next time.

He brings home junk food. Ask him to keep the chips and ice cream out of your sight. Take a trip together to the supermarket, so when he goes solo next time, he can identify the whole-wheat crackers and sorbet you'd choose. Go over take-out menus, and circle healthy entrées; if he wants something else, get him to order a small portion of the marked item for you.

You start matching his portions. You only need two-thirds of his helping, according to Albertson. Serve your meal on a salad plate and his on a dinner plate. To keep from finishing before he does (and going back for seconds), give him a head start while you sip half a glass of wine or ice water. (For more on using plates to lose weight, see the tips beginning on page 42.)

He cooks fattening meals. Tell him how much you appreciate his cooking. Then every few weeks, make it a point to suggest one change, such as leaving butter off the veggies or serving his rich favorites as side dishes. Small changes apply to spouses, too!

At the Table

Slice first. Don't just put the platter on the table and dig in. Divvy up that lasagna, frozen pizza, meat loaf, or cake into individual servings before you serve it. You'll save 200 calories by cutting banana bread into 12 servings (200 calories each) instead of slicing off a chunk that could equal ⅙ of the loaf (400 calories).

Grab a handful. Limit your snacking on chips, crackers, and other finger foods to whatever you can fit into the palm of one hand. A handful of pretzels (roughly one serving) is 110 calories versus 440 calories if you munch through half of the 8-ounce bag.

Add more for less. Cut beverage calories in half by filling up the entire glass with ice. Savings in a tall glass of presweetened iced tea: 135 calories.

Always share. Don't reserve dessert splitting just for dining out. At home, dish out the frozen yogurt into one bowl, split it, then put half into a second bowl (about 1 cup each) for your spouse. Save 240 calories.

Pull a switch. Instead of whole milk, switch to 1 percent. If you drink one 8-oz glass a day, you'll lose 5 pounds in a year.

Have it whole. Juice has as many calories, ounce for ounce, as soda. Set a limit of one 8-oz glass of fruit juice a day if you must. Dilute it with water. Better yet, get calories from foods you chew, not beverages. Have fresh fruit instead of fruit juice.

Make it low-cal. Cut back on or cut out caloric drinks such as soda, lemonade, etc. Plenty of people have lost weight by making just this one change. If you have a 20-oz bottle of Coca-Cola every day, switch to Diet Coke. You should lose 25 pounds in a year.

During Holiday Season

The month-long cookie fest from Thanksgiving to Christmas leaves so many of us with 5 added pounds that it's almost a holiday tradition. So break tradition next November!

Munch mindfully. At a party, rather than munch carelessly, prepare a single plate just as you would for any substantial meal. Choose lots of veggies and small portions of one entrée and one dessert—and no going back! As obvious as it sounds, don't stand near the food at parties. Make the effort, and you'll find you eat less.

Pass along rich food gifts—still in their original wrappers—to a local food bank. Find one in your area by calling America's Second Harvest at (800) 771-2303.

Get into scrapes. You can scrape lots of calories off treats and still enjoy them. Scrape two tablespoons of icing off a piece of carrot cake, and you save 137 calories. Eat pie without the crust, and save 120 calories. Pizza cleared of cheese saves about 90 calories.

Spit it out. Sometimes you pop a high-cal treat into your mouth, only to realize that it's just not worth the extra calories. Don't be embarrassed—just spit it out discreetly into a napkin.

Get undressed. A daily glimpse of yourself naked in a full-length mirror can be revealing in more ways than one—try it and you may inspire day-long restraint.

Deny permission. Don't tell yourself, "It's okay, it's the holidays." That opens the door to splurging all the way through.

At a buffet? Eating a little of everything guarantees high calories. Decide on three or four things, only one of which is high in calories. Save that for last so there's less chance of overeating.

Tighten your belt. For the duration of the holidays, wear your snuggest clothes that don't allow much room for expansion. Wearing sweats is out until January.

What Successful Weight Losers Know

Boy meets girl, boy loses girl. So goes the familiar plot of so many movies and novels. People embarking on hastily planned weight-loss endeavors often follow a common story line, too:

Person meets reflection in mirror and decides to lose weight. Person stops eating to lose weight fast.

Unfortunately, that's a story destined to have an unhappy ending.

"People think 'To lose weight I need to eat less, so I'll skip breakfast and skip lunch.' But they slow their metabolism down, which makes weight loss difficult," says Heidi Reichenberger, M.S., R.D., a Boston-based dietitian, consultant, and spokesperson for the American Dietetic Association.

Not only do their bodies burn fewer calories to protect themselves from starvation, but "now they get into a position where they're overly hungry," she says. And a hungry dieter isn't in the position to think clearly enough to avoid the next tempting food.

And when it comes to weight loss, people take their cues from our sped-up times—from fast food to the Internet—and want those pounds off *now*, Reichenberger says.

Unfortunately, a diet's results tend to be quick, too. The weight may vanish, but it tends to come back rapidly. That's why this book is called *Stop Dieting and Lose Weight*.

If you keep the following nine simple suggestions in mind, you won't be confined to a diet that you feel you must escape from in a few weeks. And you won't find yourself trapped in that age-old story of "person loses weight, weight comes back."

1. Go for the Garden Goods

If you were to ask a group of the country's leading registered dietitians about the single best way to lose weight and improve your long-term health, they'd tell you what they told *Prevention* magazine: Eat more fruits and vegetables, every single day.

You didn't realize that fruit and vegetables could do that? They sure can.

Your stomach speaks the language of *volume*, not calories. On a day-to-day basis, it expects the same volume of food. So you could feed it a quantity of snack cakes and hamburgers and fries. Or you could fill it with a greater volume of fruits and veggies, which are less calorically dense and higher in water content. Eating more vegetable-based meals and snacks can automatically reduce the number of calories you eat by up to 20 percent, without making you feel hungry.

The Mayo Clinic Healthy Weight Pyramid advocates eating *unlimited* quantities of these foods—which is a word not often heard in conjunction with weight loss! You can crunch all day on veggies like string beans, broccoli, cauliflower, tomatoes, spinach, and cabbage. They fill up your stomach but never show up on the scale.

You don't have to eat them all day, though. Just focus on getting at least **nine**

How Much is a Fruit or Veggie Serving?

- **A medium piece of fruit**
- **½ cup cooked or raw fruit or vegetable**
- **¾ cup (6 ounces) 100-percent juice**
- **1 cup raw leafy greens**
- **¼ cup dried fruit**
- **½ cup cooked beans or peas (such as lentils, pinto beans, and kidney beans)**

servings of fruits and vegetables each day. This may sound like a lot, but it really isn't. For example, one lightbulb-size portion (or about one cup) of broccoli counts as two of those servings, or nearly a quarter of your daily quota.

Maybe it's not the amount of nine servings that keeps you from being a produce fan. Maybe it's the image of eating nine bowls of cooked spinach. Or the thought of peeling and cutting a bundle of carrots. If so, the following suggestions will remind you of the rainbow of different colors and textures you can stuff into your grocery cart and the many ways you can prepare them easily.

- **Add just one fruit or veggie serving daily.** Once you get comfortable with that, add another serving until you reach 9 or 10 a day. You should wind up eating at least two servings of a fruit or veggie at every meal.

- **Branch out your preparation.** Just eating vegetables raw and plain or boiled into submission will make them grow boring. In reality, the healthiest way to eat vegetables is by fixing them by any means that make them attractive to you . . . with the exception of deep-fat frying. Sprinkle them with low-fat cheese, olive oil, or nuts to make them taste seductively rich. By adding a bit of fat, you'll also absorb tons more of the fat-soluble nutrients they contain.

- **Hide them.** Frozen veggies can slip easily into any soup, chili, casserole, pasta sauce, or stir-fry. Shred carrots into coleslaw, meat loaf mix, or banana bread. Or use prebagged baby spinach on sandwiches, heated in soups, wilted in hot pasta, and added to salads. You (and your family) won't even notice they're there.

- **Shop for convenience.** Given the luxury of a perpetually stocked salad bar, we could snack on veggies all day long. So if you're pressed for time, go ahead and pick up pre-chopped broccoli spears, cucumbers, and cauliflower from your supermarket's in-store salad bar. Pick up grape tomatoes, prewashed celery stalks, and baby carrots, put them into resealable plastic bags at home, and carry them with you in the car, at work, and at the mall.

- **Stuff your freezer.** Mix any combination of your favorite frozen vegetables, pop them into your microwave, and top with your favorite low-fat dressing. You'll have several of your daily servings in minutes.

- **Prep them ahead of time.** After you get your groceries into the kitchen, wash and chop all the veggies before they go into the fridge. You can also bag meal-size portions for the freezer, ready to be tossed into a stir-fry, soup, or pasta dish.

- **Be sneaky.** Your vegetable servings don't have to scream "vegetable!" You can disguise them. Instead of a Diet Coke, have a V8 or tomato juice. Doctor your veggies to make them delicious: drizzle maple syrup over carrots, or sprinkle chopped almonds on green beans. And don't forget that vegetable soup counts as a vegetable.

- **Chunk them.** Cutting carrots, celery, zucchini, cucumbers, red and green peppers, and other veggies into crunchy chunks—instead of shredding or slicing them thinly—will give you the sensation of eating more because you use more effort to eat them.

- **Fall back on fruit.** Are you still unswayed by these ideas? Do you really hate veggies and nothing will change your mind? Relax. If you love fruits, eat plenty of them; they are just as healthy (especially colorful ones such as oranges, mangoes, and melons).

2. Fill up on Fiber

Odds are, you've never uttered the following words: Mmmm . . . fiber. This underappreciated food component tends to stay in the background, doing favors that you know are good for you, but that you rarely discuss (you know - like the "keeping you regular" thing.)

Now that you're losing weight, it's time to let fiber play a larger role in your life. By increasing the fruits and vegetables you eat, you'll be taking in more fiber every day. And switching to whole-grain foods will open another door to fiber.

How does fiber help in weight loss? Let's count the many ways.

For starters, consider its main claim to fame: It alleviates constipation.

Studies have found that people who switch to high-fiber diets and leave constipation in the dust feel more energetic, possibly because they feel lighter and more comfortable. Having extra energy certainly helps you stay more interested in getting exercise.

And since fiber is found only in plant foods, if you eat a lot of fiber, you're making better food choices automatically. Experts estimate that for each gram of fiber you eat instead of simple carbohydrates, like candy or white bread, you drop 7 calories from your diet. That means if you tripled your fiber intake from 13 grams per day—the amount most Americans eat—to 40 grams, you'd displace 200 calories daily. And that adds up to 20 pounds of weight loss in the course of a year!

Fiber "crosses out" calories by speeding them through your digestive system before they can be absorbed and stored as fat.

It also takes up a lot of room in your stomach, so when you start to eat more fiber, you'll get full more quickly. After your stomach signals to your brain that you're full, your appetite drops off dramatically, regardless of how good the meal tastes.

Fiber also helps regulate blood sugar, which is especially important for people with diabetes. Though bowel regularity depends on insoluble fiber, the kind found in many whole grain breads, cereals, and vegetables, researchers suspect that soluble fiber—found in oats, beans, and fruits such as oranges, cantaloupes, and strawberries—plays an important role in controlling blood sugar. Soluble fiber slows the movement of your food through the small intestine, tempering spikes in

Fiber Content

Food and Serving Size	Grams
Barley (1 cup)	13.6
General Mills Fiber One (½ cup)	13
Kellogg's All-Bran with Extra Fiber (½ cup)	13
Baked acorn squash (1 cup)	10
Black bean soup (1 cup)	10
Bulgur wheat (1 cup)	8.2
Navy beans (½ cup)	8
Wheatena hot cereal (1 cup)	6.5
Fresh figs (4)	6.5
Large baked apple (1)	5
Large pear (1)	5
Roasted pumpkin seeds (¼ cup)	5
White corn (½ cup)	4.7
Acorn squash (½ cup)	4.5
Wheat berry (1 cup)	3.5
Blackberries (½ cup)	3.1

blood sugar. Some studies have found that people with type 2 diabetes who ate a high-fiber diet improved their blood-sugar control by an average of 95 percent.

So increase your fiber intake to at least 25 to 35 grams a day—or even more. Here's how to do it easily.

- **Choose wisely.** Start by reaching for fruits and veggies like zucchini, beans, apples, and blackberries, and whole grains like whole wheat, brown rice, oatmeal, and popcorn.

- **Go slow.** If your body's not accustomed to a fiber-rich diet, you may experience some normal, unpleasant gastric side effects when starting up. (They should go away once your intestinal tract is used to the new demands.) To minimize problems in the beginning, gradually increase the amount of fiber you're eating, and drink at least eight glasses of water a day.

- **Go natural.** The less processed a food is, the more fiber it contains. For example, a whole apple has 3.7 grams of fiber; refined applesauce has less than half that (1.5 grams).

- **Save your skins.** Don't throw away perfectly good fiber in your favorite foods—keep skins on potatoes, shred unpeeled carrots into salads, and resist the urge to trim all the white strings off your orange or grapefruit. Every little bit helps.

- **Read the label carefully**. Some "wheat" bread is actually heavily processed white bread with a caramel coloring. A true whole-grain bread should list "whole wheat" or a combination of whole-grain ingredients as the first items on its list of ingredients.

  When you read the label, you should also see that each slice contains 3 to 5 grams of fiber, and you should see buried bits of grain or seeds in the bread.

- **Know your oats.** Stay away from flavored instant oatmeal packages—most provide only 2 grams of fiber per 140-calorie serving, with a tablespoon of added sugar per packet. Buy a big container of instant oats—it's cheaper pound for pound, with no added sugar.

3. Get Up and Go . . . Eat Breakfast

Research has found that if you skip breakfast, your resting metabolic rate—in other words, the calories your body burns just keeping itself going—may dip by 5 percent. That's a small decline, but one that could creep up to a 10-pound weight gain in a year's time. As we learned in the first chapter, those little changes mean a lot.

And what's a crucial component to the perfect breakfast? Why, one that lets you start your day the fiber way: A bowl of crunchy cereal.

People who regularly enjoy ready-to-eat breakfast cereal with fruit weigh less than those who either skip breakfast or eat other breakfast foods such as eggs and bacon or bagels, according to research presented at the North American Association for the Study of Obesity meeting in 2001.

Ideally, your cereal should contain at least 7 grams of fiber per serving. But don't just settle for plain bran flakes—make your cereal even more appealing by adding fresh fruit (a good idea anyway) or a small handful of nuts.

4. Eat Regularly the Rest of the Day

Heidi Reichenberger—who, remember, speaks for the American Dietetic Association—sometimes tells people to go eat a snack. It's true.

"I tell people to certainly eat breakfast, lunch and dinner. Then depending on how long it goes between those meals, possibly a snack between meals as well," she says.

Going too long without eating is a major setup for overeating at night, and it's a fairly common problem. Traditional weight-loss plans had you wear hunger like a badge of honor—but also set you up to devour the next calorie-laden snack put in front of you, the first slip on a rebound slope to weight gain.

In the first chapter, you learned to only eat when your body tells you it needs food. But that doesn't mean you should skip meals to make yourself hungry. Eating a small meal or snack every three to four hours can be a useful tool in your weight-loss arsenal.

People who spread their food intake over the course of the day tend to take in fewer calories overall and eat more nutritious foods. In one study, a group of obese men were fed a specially prepared meal, and another group were served the same food split into five mini-meals throughout the day. When permitted to eat whatever they liked at a later meal, researchers found that the men who had eaten the small meals throughout the day continued to eat smaller portions and consumed 27 percent fewer calories than the men who hadn't.

When large meals dump huge amounts of sugar into your system, your pancreas has to work overtime to produce enough insulin to get the sugar ushered into its proper places. It usually produces too much, and you end up even hungrier before your next meal. Repeated intense fluctuations like this can lead to insulin resistance, the precursor to diabetes, and also intensify sugar cravings. We tend to reach for sweets because our bodies instinctively know sugar is processed quickly. By keeping blood sugar levels on an even keel, eating regularly wipes out cravings.

And, since your body—including your brain—needs glucose for fuel, when you don't eat for long periods, your mental energy and stamina dip, primarily because your brain isn't getting nourishment. That doesn't help motivate you to enjoy your normal exercise routine.

However, that doesn't mean you can snack on just anything.

"Make snacks nutritious foods you miss during meals, such as fruits and yogurt," suggests Anna Maria Siega-Riz, Ph.D., R.D., assistant professor at the University of North Carolina at Chapel Hill.

Or perhaps chicken . . .

French researchers found that high-protein snacks keep you full longer than high-carb snacks (like pretzels or popcorn) and may reduce the amount you eat at your next meal. "High-carbohydrate snackers got hungry as quickly as subjects who had no snack at all," says researcher Jeanine Louis-Sylvestre, Ph.D., "but protein eaters, who snacked on chicken, stayed full nearly 40 minutes longer." Since it takes longer for protein to break down, you stay satisfied longer. (Note: Snackers ate 200-calorie snacks.)

So try these ideas to spread your food out:

- **Two's better than one.** Wrap your sandwich in two pieces, and eat one half at lunchtime and the other during the midafternoon energy slump.

- **Skip the sugar.** Most people find that abstaining from refined sugar for a month cuts their cravings for candy entirely. Satisfy your sweet tooth with a midafternoon apple, or pile a half-cup of fresh strawberries and blueberries into a cup of fat-free cottage cheese.

- **Do like the French do**—or at least those in the aforementioned study— and try prebaked chicken strips, such as a cup of Perdue's chicken strips

(38 g protein, 180 cal); a 3-oz can of white chicken (14 g protein, 70 cal); or a fast-food grilled chicken sandwich, minus the bun, mayo, and toppings (28 g protein, 160 cal). Other options: one cup of low-fat cottage cheese (28 g protein, 164 cal) or two string cheese sticks (14 g protein, 160 cal).

5. Serve Yourself Some Soup

You should always keep a bowl at the ready so you can serve yourself some soup. This filling, satisfying food can play an important role in your weight-loss plan.

When 24 women ate three different snacks that contained the same ingredients and calories—chicken rice casserole, the casserole with a glass of water, or a soup made with the casserole and water—the soup curbed their appetite the best. They reported less hunger and ate 80 fewer calories at a meal two hours later.

Part of the satisfaction you get from having broth-based soup is that you can eat a large portion while still sparing calories. "Your mouth likes the extra food, your brain is turned on by knowing you're having more, and now it seems that your stomach stays full longer than we expected. All work together to keep you satisfied," says study author Barbara Rolls, Ph.D., Guthrie chairperson of nutrition at Pennsylvania State University in State College.

So for a fast and filling snack, keep a 100-calorie cup of instant beef noodle or vegetable soup in your briefcase. When the weather gets warmer, try chilled soups such as strawberry and gazpacho. They seem to work just as well as hot versions, says Dr. Rolls.

Also, be sure to try the full range of soup recipes starting on page 84.

6. Fats: Bump Up The Good, Lose the Bad

In spite of the fat-free mantra spouted for years, fat may not be the pound-packing devil it was once suspected of being. A little unsaturated fat from olive or canola oil can help increase our level of satiety—food's "staying power"—making us less likely to overeat later.

However, saturated fats, found in animal products like beef and dairy, and hydrogenated fats, found in many baked and fried processed foods, may be even more dangerous than previously believed. Some evidence shows that changes in blood triglyceride levels from just one high-fat meal could increase your chance of having a heart attack for 8 to 12 hours afterward. And hydrogenated oils are being linked to everything from high cholesterol to immune-system malfunction.

However, by allowing "good" unsaturated and polyunsaturated fats, like canola, olive, flaxseed, and fish oils, to provide 30 percent of your calories while drastically decreasing "bad," or saturated and hydrogenated fats, you can reap many weight-loss benefits. (Remember, though, that any fat, even the good ones, has calories. If you add some fat in one place, you need to lose some calories from another place. Be ruthless about cutting empty-calorie foods.)

- **Increase food's staying power.** Unsaturated fat can help food stick around longer, which fat-free foods generally cannot do.

  Marshall Goldberg, M.D., an endocrinologist at Thomas Jefferson University Medical College in Philadelphia, has found that a concentrated dose of olive oil—2 teaspoons on half a slice of bread, eaten 15 to 20 minutes before a meal—helps his patients control their cravings.

  Researchers think olive oil may slow stomach contractions, which creates a sense of fullness, and it stimulates the release of cholecystokinin (CCK), a gut hormone that signals the brain to stop eating.

- **Maintain weight loss.** In a study at Brigham and Women's Hospital in Boston, 101 overweight people were divided into two groups. One group limited fat to a very low 20 percent of calories. The other group ate plenty of unsaturated fats from foods such as peanut butter, nuts, olive oil, and avocados, for 35 percent of their calories. Both groups got the same overall number of calories, and both lost weight, but twice as many people on the 35-percent diet maintained their weight for 18 months.

A good way to increase your good fats is to have small servings of nuts. A small handful of shelled walnuts or cashews will easily stem your hunger, and studies show that people who regularly eat nuts have less heart disease. Try to work about two tablespoons of nuts a day into your meals—but because they're so high in calories, steer clear of eating them by the handful.

Also, eat plenty of monounsaturated fats in foods such as olives, olive oil and avocados, and omega-3 fats, found in flaxseed, walnuts, salmon, and white albacore tuna. Omega-3s are credited with health benefits ranging from preventing irregular heartbeats to improving mood and memory. And, although more research needs to be done, animal studies suggest omega-3s may even help the body use more energy to burn the same number of calories. Canola oil, containing monos and omega-3s, can help you reach both goals.

7. Be Sensible with Protein

When kept to reasonable proportions, protein plays a critical role in weight loss. A small Yale University study found that women who ate a mix of carbohydrate and protein at lunch ate 20 percent less at dinner than those who had eaten pure-carbohydrate meals. Researchers pointed to protein's effect on satiety hormones to blunt appetite and decrease food intake.

Steer clear of the greasy ribs, though, and get your protein the following ways:

- **Beans:** These have protein, carbohydrate, calcium, B vitamins, and a little bit of unsaturated fat. They're also the highest fiber foods you can find, with the exception of breakfast cereals made with wheat bran.

  Handy canned beans have the same nutritional benefits as dried, but be sure to rinse them to remove their excess sodium. There are plenty of satisfying meals that feature beans or legumes as the main ingredient, like vegetarian chili. Slip cannellini beans or chickpeas into pasta dishes and marinara sauce. Spread hummus onto a thick wedge of ripe tomato inside a whole wheat tortilla or pita.

- **Soy:** Low in saturated fat, soy contains no cholesterol, and its beneficial compounds may directly lower blood cholesterol and help prevent certain kinds of cancer. Your best bet is to sneak soy into foods you already love.

Start by mixing up a delicious smoothie with silken tofu instead of yogurt. For snacks, try replacing pretzels or rye crackers with soy nuts, or crunch on edamame, which are fresh soybean pods with a satisfying snap. Look for veggie burgers with textured soy protein.

- **Fish:** In a study of almost 70 overweight people, adding one serving of fish a day helped participants lose more weight and increase their good cholesterol (HDL) more than those who ate fish once a week or less.

- **Eggs:** Long maligned as a source of dietary cholesterol, eggs are getting a better reputation these days, and for good reason. They're inexpensive, individually portioned, portable, and completely satisfying. Egg protein is also one of the most complete and digestible of all proteins.

  With its 75 calories and 6 grams of protein, one egg's staying power can stem the mightiest midafternoon hunger attack. Boil a dozen at once and store them on the top shelf of the fridge for a quick breakfast on the run or a hunger-blasting counterpart to whole wheat crackers. They can last a week.

- **Chicken and Turkey:** Broiled, grilled, sautéed, baked, ground and pounded into patties or crumbled into chili, chicken and turkey make nice accompaniments to almost every grain and veggie on the planet.

  Skinless cuts help you avoid most of chicken's fat, but breasts can be pricey - buy an economy pack and portion it out into individual bags when you get home. Ground turkey makes an excellent stand-in for ground beef. If you like the stronger flavor of beef, brown the turkey with a tablespoon of beef stock, and then drain it before adding it to your spaghetti sauce or lasagna.

- **Beef:** While the aroma of a steak sizzling on the grill may be one of life's top 10 smells, the sad fact is that beef is a mixed blessing. True, it is high in protein, iron, zinc, and niacin—but it's also very high in saturated fat and cholesterol. In a 10-year study of nearly 80,000 people, women who ate more than seven servings of meat a week were 1-½ times more likely to gain weight than women who ate two or less.

Save beef for special occasions and make it a great cut, like a 3-ounce sirloin steak or a few slices of fresh lean roast beef from the deli. Or substitute ground turkey or brown rice for half the ground beef in meat loaf, and add shredded carrots and chopped broccoli stems for extra fiber. Limiting yourself to one serving of meat every two or three days (or less) and making up the difference in fruits or vegetables will help you shed pounds quickly.

8. Drink Water

Making sure you get eight 8-ounce glasses of water a day—almost the amount in a 2-liter bottle—can help you look and feel thinner immediately, as well as speed long-term weight loss, for many reasons.

When cells get dehydrated, the body seeks water from other sources, including fat cells. After your fat cells give up their water, their ability to turn fat into energy is hampered; essentially, this is like having a broken fuel gauge in your car. Even though your tank is half full, your body thinks it's running on fumes and you start feeling hungry. Overall, dehydration can slow your metabolism by 3 percent. At a weight of 150 pounds, that would be 45 fewer calories a day, or five extra pounds a year.

Water also fills empty space in your stomach with no calories. And it helps your intestinal tract adapt to the high-fiber diet you enthusiastically adopted several pages ago.

Plus, without water, your kidneys can't remove toxic wastes and salt from your blood, and your liver is forced to pitch in with the kidneys' work, preventing them from metabolizing as much fat as they should. Your body also will have trouble transporting nutrients to your brain, leaving you dizzy, confused, and irritable—definitely not the state for energizing workouts.

Finally, drinking water reduces the "empty" calories you get from sweetened drinks. Added-sugar juice drinks and sodas, as well as alcoholic beverages, are a tremendous source of extra calories for Americans.

If you just aren't interested in drinking plain ol' water, try the following tricks:

- Pick club soda or seltzer as your first drink at a restaurant or bar so you can savor your next drink (alcoholic or not), instead of sucking it down to relieve dehydration.

  If water tastes better, you'll be tempted to drink more. Invest in a water filter pitcher or consider renting a water cooler. Drink a full glass of water as soon as you wake up and before each meal, and sip water between bites.
- Make water a refreshing treat by squeezing cut limes into your glass of water or seltzer for extra flavor. Keep a bowl of the limes on the top shelf of your fridge to remind you to keep drinking.
- Combine half of your normal amount of cranberry or orange juice with seltzer water to cut up to 85 calories per glass, which can help you trim five pounds or more per year. To get the flavor without sugar, try seltzer waters with essence of cherry or mandarin orange.
- Get a sports bottle with a water filter for your walks, and keep a case of small water bottles in your trunk for emergencies, picnics, and soccer games.

9. Boost Your Metabolism

We've shown you several ways already that sensible eating can lift your metabolism. Here are more foods that can give your body a calorie-burning kick, too:

- **Hot red pepper.** Early studies show that capsaicin, the active ingredient in hot peppers, may increase the body's fat-burning abilities, boost metabolic rate, and even cut appetite. In one study, Japanese women who ate red pepper with a high-carbohydrate breakfast decreased their desire to eat before lunch. What's more, they ate less fat at their midday meal.
- **Coffee.** The amount of caffeine (about 135 milligrams) in an 8-ounce cup of brewed coffee is enough to raise your metabolism for more than two hours. Drinking it before a workout may give you an extra kick, too. And caffeine may help free stored fat, so your body can burn it for energy as you exercise. (If you have high blood pressure, avoid caffeine before exercise.)

Avoid This Metabolism Booster

Contrary to what you might hear on radio advertisements, ephedra isn't safe for weight loss. While some studies of ephedrine—the active compound in ephedra, also called ma huang— have reported modest weight-loss success, there have also been deaths associated with the herb. It is believed that most of these were due to improper use, such as taking too much, using it on a regular basis, or taking it at inappropriate times.

Because the herb has been linked to increased risk of heart attack and stroke, people with heart disease or hypertension *absolutely* should not use ephedra. You should also avoid it if you have diabetes or thyroid disease. And while ephedra has been shown to help with some health problems (asthma, for example), you should use it only under a doctor's supervision. Even then, watch for possible side effects, which include seizures, heart palpitations, headaches, dizziness, skin flushing, and vomiting.

- **Tea.** In a study from Switzerland, 6 out of 10 men who took a green tea supplement (the equivalent of one cup of green tea) three times a day with their meals burned about 80 more calories during the following 24 hours than those who took a caffeine pill or a dummy pill. The researchers believe that flavonoids in the tea were responsible for the metabolism boost.

  In another study, at the Beltsville Human Nutrition Research Center in Maryland, men who drank five cups of oolong tea a day also burned 80 more calories over 24 hours. That's enough to lose eight pounds in a year! Researchers believe that caffeine and polyphenol compounds in the tea work to promote weight loss in two ways: by speeding up metabolism and turning on your body's fat burners.

- **Gum:** Researchers at the Mayo Clinic found that volunteers who chewed sugar-free gum at the rate of 100 chomps per minute burned significantly more calories than they did at rest.

Look at Your Plate, Lose Your Weight

Thus far, you've learned that losing weight should be a simple, natural journey. It's about paying attention to the foods and drinks that go into your mouth. It's about common-sense choices like eating your fruits and vegetables and whole grains, and choosing good sources of fat.

You shouldn't have to eat only from unusual food groups, or count calories or multiply fat percentages. You should just eat like humans are supposed to eat.

Even so, life moves quickly, and it can be hard to remember even simple suggestions when you're hungry, rushed, and need to fill a plate quickly. So here comes the best idea in this whole weight-loss plan—the trick that lies at the heart of the recipes you're about to find. And it boils the suggestions of the previous chapters down into a very simple formula.

Tricks to Complement the Plate Method

- When dining out, make it automatic: Order one dessert to share.
- Use a salad plate instead of a dinner plate.
- See what you eat. Plate your food instead of eating out of the jar or bag.
- Eat the low-cal items on your plate first, then graduate. Start with salads, veggies, and broth soups, and eat meats and starches last. By the time you get to them, you'll be full enough to be content with smaller portions of the high-calorie choices.
- The American Institute for Cancer Research, which recommends a similar plate technique for cancer prevention, recommends that you think of meat as a side dish or condiment rather than the main ingredient. For example, prepare your favorite store-bought brown rice or grain mix and top it with steamed green beans, carrots, yellow squash and an ounce or two of cooked chicken, instead of making a pile of chicken with the vegetables on the side.
- When your vegetables are covered in cheese sauce, gravy, regular salad dressing, full-fat sour cream or any other high-fat topping, they start losing their value on your plate as vegetables. Keep them healthy by baking, steaming, microwaving or stir-frying in a small amount of oil, suggests the AICR. Cooking them with herbs and spices, or a dash of lemon juice, is also recommended.

Look at your plate. Divide it with an imaginary line into two equal sides. Fill one side—or more—with vegetables and/or fruits. Fill the remaining side with roughly equal amounts of starch (carbohydrate) and a high-protein food. Then watch the weight come off.

As far as the *height* of the food on the plate, the rule is to go sky-high with fruits and veggies if you like, but keep the portions of starch and protein to no more than ¾ to 1 inch high.

When *Prevention* magazine readers tried this plan, they dropped pounds, got fitter, and felt better after just two months of following this simple strategy. Even better, they may have reduced their risk of cancer, heart disease, and other common killers. You can, too.

By using your plate as a weight loss tool, you no longer have to remember confusing details about portions and servings, says Netty Levine, R.D., a nutritionist at Cedars-Sinai Medical Center in Los Angeles.

"I recently worked with a client for an hour, hammering out a fabulous, detailed weight loss plan," recalls Levine. "When we finished, he looked up, and I could see it in his eyes: We'd both just wasted our time. He didn't want to remember all that information on servings and portions and food groups." So Levine took out a fresh piece of paper and drew a big, round circle with a line through the middle. "This is your plate; fill the top half with fruits and vegetables, and divide the bottom half in two. In one quarter put your protein, such as meat, poultry, or fish, and in the remaining quarter put your starch, such as whole grains, potatoes, or pasta," she advised.

Four months later, that client, Bill Knapp, was 28 pounds lighter and loving his plate plan. "I still go to my favorite restaurants, but now I know what to order to get the right amount of food," he says.

This divided-plate concept also offers another beautiful bonus: built-in portion control. "You fill the divided plate once. If you're still hungry, have another plate of vegetables, and then you're done. It's that simple," says Levine. And with a plate half filled with vegetables, there's no room for the megacalorie, gigantic burgers and pasta "hills" notorious for contributing to the obesity epidemic.

"Everything today is supersized, and people are confused about how much they really should eat," says Nancy Vuckovic, Ph.D., investigator at Kaiser Permanente Center for Health Research in Portland, Oregon. "The overweight people coming into my office are not eating a cheeseburger, they're eating supersized meals with giant burgers, mounds of fries, and huge sodas," says Levine. The divided plate strategy eliminates this problem, since there's simply not room for all that meat and starch when half the plate is filled with veggies and/or fruits. It brings out-of-control portions back down to size. And you're still eating enough food to feel full and satisfied.

Not only are dietitians using divided-plate plans for weight loss, but the

American Institute for Cancer Research (AICR) in Washington, D.C., also recommends harnessing the power of plates to fight cancer!

The AICR recommends portions similar to the ones described above with some slight variation: Its dietitians recommend covering at least two-thirds of your plate with plant-based foods (vegetables, fruits, whole grains, and beans), with the remainder left for meat, fish, poultry, or low-fat dairy.

These plate strategies fight disease because of all the fruits and vegetables they include, says James Shikany, D.P.H., assistant professor of medicine, division of preventive medicine, University of Alabama at Birmingham. While he's a big fan of all produce, he suggests making the following your staples: cruciferous vegetables such as broccoli and cabbage; spinach, kale, and other dark leafy greens; and orange-fleshed fruits and vegetables such as sweet potatoes, carrots, peaches, and citrus fruits. "Each of these groups contains its own disease-fighting compounds," he explains.

We'll show you throughout the rest of the cookbook how each recipe's ingredients will count toward covering the different regions of your plate. Plus, we'll offer some great suggestions for what dishes to serve with each recipe to make sure you're getting a perfectly full plate that will help you reach your weight loss goals. But so you can see how truly easy and flexible this plan is, here are some general ways to use your plate throughout the day.

Using Your Plate at Breakfast

You still think in terms of fruits/veggies, starch (whole grains), and protein (milk or eggs), but they don't always fit neatly on a plate. Remember: You're still aiming for half or more of the meal to be fruits and veggies.

Here are some sample meals.

- Fruit-topped whole grain cereal with milk and a small glass of orange juice
- Vegetable-stuffed three-egg-white omelette with whole grain toast and fruit

Pump Up the Volume

Now that you're learning how to use your eyes to fill a plate the right way, here's an optical illusion you can use to make the plate look fuller than it really is, and save yourself some calories: Eat inflatable foods.

In one study, researchers asked 28 men to drink a strawberry milkshake before a buffet lunch on three different days. The shakes contained exactly the same ingredients and number of calories, but they were blended differently to incorporate more or less air so that each one had a different volume, filling half, three-quarters, or a full glass. After drinking the "biggest" shake, the men ate 100 fewer calories at lunch and reported less hunger compared to when they drank the "smallest" shake. And they didn't make up for it at dinner, so they trimmed 100 calories off their day's total.

"Pumping up the volume of foods means you get to eat more, and making food look bigger satisfies your desire to have a filling portion," says study author Barbara Rolls, Ph.D., Guthrie chair of nutrition at Pennsylvania State University in State College and co-author of *Volumetrics* (HarperCollins, 2000).

So try to choose foods that fill more of your plate with air, such as:

Angel food cake
* Fruit smoothies
* Low-calorie breads
* Mousses and meringues
* Popcorn
* Puffed or flaky cereals
* Tubular-shaped pastas

* Two whole grain waffles smothered in chopped fruit with yogurt or milk
* Fruit or juice with a small bran muffin and low-fat milk

Using Your Plate at Lunch

The rule remains: At least half of your meal should be vegetables and fruits. (When using a plate, opt for a traditional 8-inch luncheon plate.) Consider bread, tortillas, potatoes, or beans as your starch (beans double up for both starch and protein). Make a pledge to always finish your veggies or fruits first. If you have room, you can finish the rest of your meal.

Sample meals:

- A sandwich filled with two or three slices of lean meat, poultry, a few spoonfuls of reduced-fat tuna salad, or a veggie burger patty, with a salad, fruit salad, or vegetables

- Black bean, lentil, or other bean-based soup with a salad or side dish of vegetables or fruits

- Baked potato with a cup of broccoli or other vegetable and reduced-fat cheese

- Large salad topped with grilled chicken/lean beef/seafood (a portion the size of a deck of cards) and one or two slices of whole grain bread

- One tortilla stuffed with beans and chicken with a salad or large side dish of vegetables or fruits

Using Your Plate at Dinner

You're in luck when you've got the good ol' meat/vegetables/starch offering, but casseroles and other mixtures take some imaginative dissection. Just think of the ingredients, remember the half fruits and veggie rule, and you're good to go. Some sample meals:

- **Traditional meat and potatoes.** About half of the plate should contain salad or cooked vegetables. Cover another one-third to one-quarter of the plate with deck-of-cards-size fish, poultry, or lean meat. The final quarter can go toward brown rice, a whole-wheat roll, polenta, or other starch

- **Stir-fry.** Make the stir-fry three-quarters vegetables and one-quarter meat, poultry, or seafood. Then fill the plate three-quarters full with stir-fry and one-quarter with rice.

Learn to Recognize Healthy Portions

Eating too much undermines a top goal of healthy living: keeping your body trim. And yet whenever you eat out, the average restaurant meal has become so huge that you're actually being set up to gain. In a recent survey by the American Institute for Cancer Research (AICR), 26 percent of diners say that they eat all of what's put in front of them when they eat out—a clear recipe for expanding middles, says the AICR's Melanie Polk, R.D.

Instead, learn what a healthy portion is, and save the excess for the next day—or share it with your dining companion.

Size-up Your Portions

Outback Steakhouse

How Much You Get:	14-oz steak	1,213 calories
How Much is Healthy:	3-oz steak; size of a deck of cards	260 calories

Olive Garden

How Much You Get:	25-oz pasta with meat sauce	725 calories
How Much is Healthy:	8-oz pasta with meat sauce, size of two tennis balls	232 calories

McDonald's

How Much You Get:	44-oz cola	555 calories
How Much is Healthy:	8-ounce cola, size of a yogurt container	101 calories

Perkins Restaurant

How Much You Get:	2.3-oz chocolate chip cookie	318 calories
How Much is Healthy:	Two 0.5-oz chocolate chip cookies, size of a yo-yo	138 calories

- **Pasta.** Mix 1 or 1-½ cups of pasta with an equal amount or more of vegetables. Throw in a few pieces of shrimp, chicken, or soy "meat" for protein and flavor. Sprinkle Parmesan or low-fat cottage or ricotta cheese on top.

Using Plate Power at Restaurants

The key here is communication with the server.

- Bring in a quick sketch of the ideal plate; let the waiter guide your choice. In fast-food restaurants and diners where the staff may not be helpful, order a la carte or side dishes in the proportions you want.

- Inquire about portion size; if it's huge, ask the waiter to split yours in half in the kitchen and refrigerate the doggy bag. That way it'll never show up on your plate. Or split it with your dinner partner. A typical restaurant entrée has 1,000 to 2,000 calories, not counting the bread, appetizer, beverage, and dessert.

- Rotisserie chicken establishments are easy in terms of plate division, but beware the creamed spinach and roasted potatoes, which are loaded with fat. Get the mixed vegetables or corn (unless it's creamed).

breakfasts

The most important meal of the day, breakfast jump-starts your energy level and keeps your blood sugar stable, which helps prevent overeating later. To make rushed mornings easier, prepare "cook-ahead" breakfasts earlier in the week. If you make waffles or pancakes on the weekend, for example, prepare extra and freeze them for a quick reheat. Accompanying fruit sauces will keep in the refrigerator for up to 5 days. If eating on the run is more your style, opt for a breakfast shake or a hearty whole grain muffin.

In this chapter . . .

citrus fruit bowl *quick*

4	medium navel oranges
3	large pink grapefruit
1/3	cup dried sweetened cranberries
	Fresh mint leaves (optional)

Cut off the peel and pith from the oranges and grapefruit. Working over a large bowl, cut out the sections of fruit from between the membranes, letting the sections fall into the bowl. Squeeze the juice from the membranes over the fruit; discard the membranes.

Add the cranberries and stir to combine. Garnish with the mint, if using.

Makes 8 servings
Per serving: 78 calories, 1 g protein, 21 g carbohydrates, 0 g fat, 0 g saturated fat, 0 mg cholesterol, 5 g fiber, 0 mg sodium

plate power

pair with . . .

apple skillet cake, page 67

or

fiesta cornmeal pudding, page 83

plate ∿ power

pair with . . .

toasted oat muesli,
page 58

or

one egg, a slice of canadian bacon, and an English muffin

honeyed summer fruit bowl

¼	cup honey
1	tablespoon lemon juice or lime juice
	Pinch of ground cinnamon
1½	pints strawberries, quartered
½	large cantaloupe, cut into chunks or balls
2	medium nectarines, cut into thin wedges
2	medium peaches, cut into thin wedges
2	large or 3 small plums, cut into thin wedges
1	cup blueberries

In a large bowl, combine the honey, lemon juice or lime juice, and cinnamon. Add the strawberries, cantaloupe, nectarines, peaches, plums, and blueberries. Toss just until the fruit is well-mixed and coated with the honey mixture.

Let stand for 30 minutes before serving to allow the flavors to blend.

Makes 6 servings
Per serving: 150 calories, 2 g protein, 38 g carbohydrates, 1 g fat, 0 g saturated fat, 0 mg cholesterol, 5 g dietary fiber, 11 mg sodium

banana-orange smoothie

1	cup orange juice
1	banana
2	tablespoons flaxseeds, ground

photograph on page 56

In a blender, combine the orange juice, banana, and flaxseed. Blend until smooth and frothy.

Makes 1 serving
Per serving: 338 calories, 8 g protein, 62 g carbohydrates, 9 g fat, 1 g saturated fat, 0 mg cholesterol, 10 g dietary fiber, 114 mg sodium

plate power

pair with . . .

a hard boiled egg

or

a ½ cup of soft tofu blended into the smoothie

the power of
FLAX
For centuries, flaxseed (and the plant from which it comes) was used for just about everything except food. Flax is one of the oldest sources of textile fiber, used in making linen. Its seed, also know as linseed, is used for making paint. Through the 20th century, the seed has been used for livestock feed but not human "feed." Until recently. Flaxseed is one of the best sources of plant-provided omega-3 fatty acids, and is very high in fiber. Since it is so new to the kitchen, here are some simple tips when using flaxseed products.

- Grind whole flaxseeds in a clean coffee grinder. Always grind only as much as you plan to use because it turns rancid faster when ground.
- Store flaxseeds in the freezer to keep them fresh longer.
- Sprinkle ground flaxseeds on cereal, yogurt, or salads. Start with 1 teaspoon and see how your intestines react. Since they are a great source of fiber, too much can cause gas.
- Add 2 tablespoons of ground flaxseeds to muffin and quick bread batter or cookie dough.

berry, berry smoothie (quick)

½	cup frozen unsweetened raspberries
½	cup frozen unsweetened strawberries
¾	cup unsweetened pineapple juice
1	cup 1% milk or fat-free milk

In a blender, combine the raspberries, strawberries, and pineapple juice. Add the milk and blend until smooth.

Makes 2 servings
Per serving: 132 calories, 5 g protein, 26 g carbohydrates, 2 g fat, 1 g saturated fat, 5 mg cholesterol, 3 g dietary fiber, 63 mg sodium

the power of
BERRIES
Adding more berries to your meals can help prevent cataracts, cancer, and constipation. Berries contain fiber, vitamin C, and the antioxidant ellagic acid.

To get the most nutrients, buy or pick berries at peak freshness and eat them raw. To store for later use, freeze them raw. Do this by placing unwashed berries in a single layer on a baking pan. Freeze completely. Place in a zip-top freezer bag, seal, and freeze for up to 8 months. To use, rinse the frozen berries quickly, then add directly to a recipe.

plate power

pair with . . .

breakfast burritos, page 82

or

orange-bran muffin, page 62, *a banana, and a hard-boiled egg*

plate 〜
power

pair
with . . .

*honeyed summer
fruit bowl, page 54*

or

*a banana and a
small glass of juice*

toasted oat muesli

6	cups old-fashioned oats, preferably thick-cut
1¼	cups sliced natural almonds
1	package (7 ounces) dried fruit bits
1	cup toasted wheat germ
½	cup unsalted raw pumpkin seeds
½	cup unsalted raw sunflower seeds

Preheat the oven to 325°F.

Spread the oats out on a jelly-roll pan. Spread the almonds in a small baking pan. Place the oats and almonds in the oven and bake, stirring often, until the oats are lightly browned and the almonds are toasted. The oats will take 30 to 35 minutes; the almonds will toast in 20 to 25 minutes.

Place the oats and almonds in a large bowl and cool completely.

Add the fruit bits, wheat germ, pumpkin seeds, and sunflower seeds. Toss to combine. Store in an airtight container.

To serve, place ½ cup of the cereal mixture in a bowl. Top with soy milk, fat-free milk, or yogurt.

Makes twenty-two ½-cup servings
Per serving: 300 calories, 12 g protein, 40 g carbohydrates, 11 g fat, 1 g saturated fat, 0 mg cholesterol, 7 g dietary fiber, 2 mg sodium

multigrain cereal

2	cups rolled oats
2	cups wheat flakes
2	cups malted barley flakes
2	cups rye flakes
1	box (1 pound) dark or golden raisins
1½	cups flaxseeds, ground
¾	cup sesame seeds

In an airtight container, combine the oats, wheat flakes, barley flakes, rye flakes, raisins, flaxseeds, and sesame seeds. Store in the freezer until ready to use.

To cook: For 1 serving, bring 1 cup water to a boil in a small saucepan. Add a pinch of salt. Add ⅓ cup of the cereal, cover, and cook, stirring occasionally, for 25 minutes, or until thickened and creamy.

For 4 servings, use 3 cups water, ¼ teaspoon salt, and 1½ cups cereal. Cook for 25 to 30 minutes.

Makes thirty-six ⅓-cup servings
Per serving: 160 calories, 5 g protein, 29 g carbohydrates, 4 g fat, 0 g saturated fat, 0 mg cholesterol, 5 g dietary fiber, 4 mg sodium

plate ﹨
power

pair
with . . .

asparagus and leek frittata, page 80, and a small glass of juice

or

a cup of sliced canteloupe and 8 ounces of fat-free vanilla yogurt

fruit and nut cereal

2	cups rolled oats
1	cup wheat flakes
2	tablespoons sunflower seeds
1 1/2	tablespoons sesame seeds
1/4	cup frozen apple juice concentrate, thawed
1/4	cup packed brown sugar
2	tablespoons canola oil
1/2	teaspoon ground cinnamon
1/4	cup chopped dried figs
1/4	cup chopped dried apple rings
1/4	cup chopped dried apricots
1/4	cup slivered toasted almonds

Preheat the oven to 250°F. Coat a jelly-roll pan with cooking spray.

In a medium bowl, combine the oats, wheat flakes, sunflower seeds, sesame seeds, apple juice concentrate, brown sugar, oil, and cinnamon.

Spread the oat mixture in the prepared pan. Bake, stirring occasionally, for 45 to 60 minutes, or until golden brown. Cool completely.

Place the cereal, figs, apples, apricots, and almonds in an airtight container.

To serve, place 2/3 cup of the cereal mixture in a bowl. Top with soy milk, fat-free milk, or yogurt.

Makes about 18 1/3-cup servings
Per serving: 117 calories, 3 g protein, 19 g carbohydrates, 4 g fat, 0 g saturated fat, 0 mg cholesterol, 2 g dietary fiber, 4 mg sodium

plate power

pair with . . .

a scrambled egg topped with 1/2 cup sautéed red peppers and mushrooms, and small glass of juice

or

2 links turkey sausage and 1 cup of strawberries

orange-bran muffins   *quick*

plate ɣ power

pair with . . .

asparagus and leek frittata, page 80, and small glass of juice

or

berry, berry smoothie, page 57, one banana, and a hard-boiled egg

2	cups shredded all-bran cereal
¾	cup hot water
¼	cup canola oil
1	orange
¾	cup buttermilk
2	tablespoons light molasses
2	tablespoons honey
1	egg
1¼	cups whole grain pastry flour
⅓	cup + 2 teaspoons rolled oats
2	teaspoons baking soda
½	teaspoon salt
1	cup raisins
¼	cup chopped toasted walnuts (optional)
¼	cup sugar
¼	cup orange juice

Preheat the oven to 400°F. Coat a 12-cup muffin pan with cooking spray.

In a medium bowl, combine the cereal, water, and oil. Stir until the cereal is softened.

Grate 1 tablespoon of the peel from the orange into another medium bowl; cut the orange in half and squeeze ¼ cup juice into the bowl. Stir in the buttermilk, molasses, honey, and egg until well-blended. Stir into the cereal mixture.

In a large bowl, combine the flour, ⅓ cup of the oats, baking soda, and salt. Add the cereal mixture and stir just until blended. Stir in the raisins and walnuts, if using.

COOKING TIP
Most recipes for 12 muffins baked in a 12-cup muffin pan can also be baked in an 8" × 4" loaf pan. Bake at the specified temperature, but add 10 to 12 minutes to the baking time.

Divide the batter evenly among the prepared muffin cups. Sprinkle with the remaining 2 teaspoons oats. Bake for 15 minutes, or until a wooden pick inserted in the center of a muffin comes out clean. Place the pan on a rack.

Meanwhile, combine the sugar and orange juice in a small saucepan. Bring to a boil over medium heat and stir until the sugar dissolves. Using a wooden pick, poke holes in the muffin tops. Brush with the orange syrup.

Cool on the rack for 5 minutes. Remove to the rack to cool completely.

Makes 12 muffins
Per muffin: 220 calories, 5 g protein, 42 g carbohydrates, 6 g fat, 1 g saturated fat, 18 mg cholesterol, 6 g dietary fiber, 353 mg sodium

the power of
FIBER
Getting the recommended 25 to 35 grams of fiber every day is an easy task with the help of these top 10 fiber-packed cereals. Some give you more than half of your daily fiber in one serving. All are low in fat and added sugar.

Cereal and Serving Size	Fiber (g)	Calories
Kellogg's All-Bran Bran Buds (⅓ cup)	13	80
Kashi Go Lean (¾ cup)	10	120
Kellogg's Original All-Bran (½ cup)	10	80
Kashi Good Friends (¾ cup)	8	90
Post 100% Bran (⅓ cup)	8	80
Kashi Seven Whole Grains and Sesame (¾ cup)	8	90
Post Raisin Bran (1 cup)	8	190
Post Shredded Wheat 'N Bran (1¼ cups)	8	200
Kellogg's Raisin Bran (1 cup)	8	200
General Mills Multi-Bran Chex (1 cup)	7	200

nutty fruit muffins quick

1¾	cups whole grain pastry flour
1½	teaspoons baking powder
1½	teaspoons ground cinnamon
½	teaspoon baking soda
¼	teaspoon salt
1	cup (8 ounces) fat-free vanilla yogurt
½	cup packed brown sugar
1	egg
2	tablespoons canola oil
1	teaspoon vanilla extract
½	cup drained crushed pineapple in juice
⅓	cup currants or raisins
¼	cup finely shredded carrots
¼	cup chopped walnuts, toasted

Preheat the oven to 400°F. Coat a 12-cup muffin pan with cooking spray.

In a large bowl, combine the flour, baking powder, cinnamon, baking soda, and salt.

In a medium bowl, combine the yogurt, brown sugar, egg, oil, and vanilla extract. Stir into the flour mixture just until blended. Stir in the pineapple, currants or raisins, carrots, and walnuts. Divide the batter evenly among the muffin cups. Bake for 20 minutes, or until a wooden pick inserted in the center of a muffin comes out clean.

Cool on a rack for 5 minutes. Remove to the rack to cool completely.

Makes 12 muffins
Per muffin: 174 calories, 5 g protein, 30 g carbohydrates, 4 g fat, 0 g saturated fat, 18 mg cholesterol, 2 g dietary fiber, 178 mg sodium

plate ι power

pair with . . .

florentine omelette, page 76, and ½ cup rapberries

or

8 ounces low-fat yogurt and honeyed summer fruit bowl, page 54

COOKING TIP
For a more hearty muffin, replace ¼ cup of the whole grain pastry flour with ¼ cup oat bran or wheat bran. You can also try adding ¼ cup chopped dried apricots and ¼ cup semisweet chocolate chips.

southwestern (quick) double-corn muffins

1	cup yellow cornmeal
1	cup whole grain pastry flour
¼	cup soy flour (sifted if lumpy)
2	teaspoons baking powder
¼	teaspoon ground cinnamon
⅛	teaspoon salt
1	egg
1	egg white
¾	cup milk
¼	cup canola oil
1½	cups frozen corn kernels
½	cup golden raisins

Preheat the oven to 400°F. Coat a 12-cup muffin pan with cooking spray.

In a large bowl, combine the cornmeal, pastry flour, soy flour, baking powder, cinnamon, and salt.

In a small bowl, combine the egg, egg white, milk, oil, corn, and raisins. Add to the flour mixture and stir just until blended. Divide evenly among the prepared muffin cups.

Bake for 18 minutes, or until the muffins are firm to the touch and lightly browned at the edges. Cool on a rack for 5 minutes. Remove to the rack to cool completely.

Makes 12 muffins
Per muffin: 178 calories, 5 g protein, 26 g carbohydrates, 7 g fat, 1 g saturated fat, 20 mg cholesterol, 3 g dietary fiber, 121 mg sodium

plate power

pair with . . .

scrambled eggs topped with 1 tablespoon salsa and ½ cup melon chunks tossed with 1 teaspoon finely chopped jalapeno pepper

or

½ cup pineapple chunks, 1 slice of Canadian bacon, and small glass of juice

COOKING TIP
Store any leftover muffins in the freezer for a breakfast on the go.

apple skillet cake

1	tablespoon butter
4	apples, peeled and sliced
2	tablespoons packed brown sugar
½	teaspoon ground cinnamon
½	cup raisins
¾	cup whole grain pastry flour
⅓	cup sugar
⅛	teaspoon salt
1½	cups 1% milk
2	eggs
1	egg white
2	teaspoons vanilla extract

Preheat the oven to 375°F.

Melt the butter in a medium ovenproof skillet over medium-high heat. Add the apples and cook for 2 minutes. Add the brown sugar, cinnamon, and raisins. Cook, stirring, for 5 minutes, or until the apples are tender. Remove from the heat and spread the apples evenly over the bottom of the skillet.

Meanwhile, in a large bowl, combine the flour, sugar, and salt.

In a medium bowl, combine the milk, eggs, egg white, and vanilla extract. Add to the flour mixture and stir just until blended. Pour over the apple mixture in the skillet.

Bake for 40 minutes, or until golden brown and puffed. Remove to a rack to cool for 5 minutes. To serve, cut into wedges.

Makes 4 servings
Per serving: 400 calories, 10 g protein, 79 g carbohydrates, 7 g fat, 3 g saturated fat, 118 mg cholesterol, 8 g dietary fiber, 219 mg sodium

plate ↘
power

pair
with . . .

berry, berry smoothie, page 57

or

½ cup honeydew melon

pair
with . . .

*2 slices Canadian
bacon and small
glass of juice*

or

*2 turkey sausage
links and ½
grapefruit*

cornmeal flapjacks (quick)

1	cup cornmeal
¾	cup whole grain pastry flour
1	teaspoon baking soda
½	teaspoon salt
1¼	cups buttermilk
1	egg
1	tablespoon vegetable oil
2	tablespoons maple syrup
3	cups berries such as blueberries, raspberries, and blackberries

Preheat the oven to 200°F. Coat a baking sheet with cooking spray.

In a large bowl, combine the cornmeal, flour, baking soda, and salt.

In a medium bowl, combine the buttermilk, egg, oil, and maple syrup. Add to the flour mixture and stir just until blended.

Coat a large nonstick skillet with cooking spray and warm over medium heat. Pour the batter by scant ¼ cupfuls into the skillet. Cook for 2 minutes, or until tiny bubbles appear on the surface and the edges begin to look dry. Flip and cook for 2 minutes, or until golden. Place the flapjacks on the prepared baking sheet and place in the oven to keep warm.

Coat the skillet with cooking spray. Repeat with the remaining batter to make a total of 18 flapjacks.

Serve the flapjacks with the berries.

Makes 6 servings
Per serving: 218 calories, 7 g protein, 40 g carbohydrates, 5 g fat, 1 g saturated fat, 37 mg cholesterol, 6 g dietary fiber, 477 mg sodium

plate 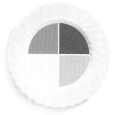 power

pair
with . . .

citrus fruit bowl,
page 53

or

*½ cup melon
chunks*

oat-berry pancakes with vanilla ricotta cream

Sauce

2	teaspoons cornstarch
1	cup orange juice
1	tablespoon lime juice
1	tablespoon honey

Ricotta Cream

²/₃	cup fat-free ricotta cheese
2	tablespoons fat-free cream cheese
1	tablespoon honey
	Grated peel of 1 lime
1	teaspoon vanilla extract

Pancakes

1	cup oat bran
1	cup whole grain pastry flour
1½	teaspoons baking powder
½	teaspoon baking soda
3	egg whites
2	cups buttermilk
2	cups mixed berries

To make the sauce: Place the cornstarch in a cup. Add 2 tablespoons of the orange juice and stir until smooth.

Place the remaining orange juice in a small saucepan. Add the lime juice and honey and cook, stirring constantly, over medium heat for 1 minute, or until the honey is dissolved. Add the cornstarch mixture. Cook, stirring constantly, for 1 minute, or until thickened. Remove from the heat and set aside to cool. Cover and refrigerate for at least 3 hours before serving.

To make the ricotta cream: In a food processor or blender, process the ricotta until smooth. Add the cream cheese, honey, lime peel, and vanilla extract. Process until smooth. Refrigerate until ready to use.

To make the pancakes: Preheat the oven to 200°F. Coat a baking sheet with cooking spray.

In a large bowl, combine the oat bran, flour, baking powder, and baking soda.

In a medium bowl, combine the egg whites and buttermilk. Add to the flour mixture and stir just until blended.

Heat a large nonstick skillet coated with cooking spray over medium heat. For each pancake, spoon about 3 tablespoons batter into the skillet and spread to form a 3" pancake. Cook for 2 minutes, or until tiny bubbles appear on the surface and the edges begin to look dry. Flip and cook for 2 minutes, or until golden. Place the pancakes on the prepared baking sheet and place in the oven to keep warm. Repeat with the remaining batter to make a total of 8 pancakes.

For each serving, spread a pancake with the ricotta cream and top with a second pancake. Drizzle with the sauce and top with the berries.

Makes 4 servings
Per serving: 370 calories, 22 g protein, 72 g carbohydrates, 4 g fat, 1 g saturated fat, 9 mg cholesterol, 10 g dietary fiber, 602 mg sodium

multigrain blueberry waffles

1 ½	cups whole grain pastry flour
½	cup rolled oats
½	teaspoon baking powder
½	teaspoon baking soda
½	teaspoon salt
1 ⅔	cups fat-free milk
2	egg whites
3	tablespoons packed brown sugar
1	tablespoon vegetable oil
2	cups blueberries
2	cups sliced strawberries
½	cup maple syrup

Preheat the oven to 200°F. Coat a baking sheet with cooking spray.

In a large bowl, combine the flour, oats, baking powder, baking soda, and salt.

In a medium bowl, combine the milk, egg whites, brown sugar, and oil. Add to the flour mixture and stir just until blended. Fold in 1 cup of the blueberries.

Coat a nonstick waffle iron with cooking spray. Preheat the iron.

Pour ½ cup of the batter onto the center of the iron. Cook for 5 minutes, or until steam no longer escapes from under the waffle-iron lid and the waffle is golden. Place the waffles on the prepared baking sheet and place in the oven to keep warm. Repeat with the remaining batter to make a total of 8 waffles.

Meanwhile, in a small saucepan over medium heat, combine the remaining 1 cup blueberries, the strawberries, and maple syrup. Cook for 5 minutes, or until the berries are softened and the mixture is hot. Serve with the waffles.

Makes 8 waffles
Per waffle: 219 calories, 7 g protein, 45 g carbohydrates, 3 g fat, 0 g saturated fat, 1 mg cholesterol, 4 g dietary fiber, 301 mg sodium

COOKING TIP
This batter also makes excellent pancakes. To create your own nutritious convenience mix, double or triple the recipe for the dry ingredients and store in an airtight container in a cool cupboard. To make pancakes, measure 2 cups of the dry mix into a bowl and then add the liquid ingredients from the recipe.

plate ↄ power

pair with . . .

small glass of mulled cider

or

citrus fruit bowl, page 53

whole grain french toast with nutmeg-scented fruit

Fruit

½	cup apricot all-fruit spread
¼	cup water
2	teaspoons lemon juice
½	teaspoon freshly ground nutmeg
3	pears (about 1¼ pounds), unpeeled, cored, and cut into 1" slices
⅓	cup dried apricot halves, halved

French Toast

2	eggs
2	egg whites
1	teaspoon vanilla extract
¼	teaspoon freshly ground nutmeg
¼	cup fat-free milk
8	slices whole wheat or multigrain bread, cut diagonally in half

To make the fruit: In a large skillet over medium heat, combine the all-fruit spread, water, lemon juice, and nutmeg. Bring to a boil.

Add the pears and apricots. Reduce the heat to low, cover, and simmer, stirring occasionally, for 10 minutes, or until the pears are tender. Cover to keep warm.

To make the French toast: Preheat the oven to 425°F. Coat a large baking sheet with cooking spray.

In a shallow bowl, beat the eggs, egg whites, vanilla extract, and nutmeg with a fork. Beat in the milk.

Dip the bread slices, one at a time, into the egg mixture, letting the slices soak briefly. Arrange the soaked slices on the prepared baking sheet, fitting them together tightly if necessary. Spoon any remaining egg mixture over the bread.

Bake, without turning, for 20 to 25 minutes, or just until the outside slices are lightly golden.

Serve with the fruit.

Makes 4 servings
Per serving: 395 calories, 11 g protein, 80 g carbohydrates, 5 g fat,
1 g saturated fat, 107 mg cholesterol, 7 g dietary fiber, 332 mg sodium

florentine omelette

plate ↄ
power

pair
with . . .

*rosemary roasted
potatoes, page 280,
and small juice*

or

*nutty fruit muffin,
page 64, and ½ cup
raspberries*

2	eggs
2	egg whites
3	tablespoons water
1	teaspoon dried Italian seasoning, crushed
¼	teaspoon salt
8	ounces mushrooms, sliced
1	onion, chopped
1	red bell pepper, chopped
1	clove garlic, minced
4	ounces (2 packed cups) spinach leaves, chopped
¾	cup (3 ounces) shredded low-fat mozzarella cheese

Preheat the oven to 200°F. Coat a baking sheet with cooking spray.

In a medium bowl, whisk together the eggs, egg whites, water, Italian seasoning, and salt.

Coat a large nonstick skillet with cooking spray and place over medium-high heat. Add the mushrooms, onion, pepper, and garlic and cook, stirring often, for 4 minutes, or until the pepper starts to soften. Add the spinach and cook for 1 minute, or until the spinach is wilted. Place in a small bowl and cover.

Wipe the skillet with a paper towel. Coat with cooking spray and place over medium heat. Pour in half of the egg mixture. Cook for 2 minutes, or until the bottom begins to set. Using a spatula, lift the edges to allow the uncooked mixture to flow to the bottom of the pan. Cook for 2 minutes longer, or until set. Sprinkle with half of the reserved vegetable mixture and half of the cheese. Cover and cook for 2 minutes, or until the cheese melts. Using a spatula, fold the egg mixture in half. Place on the prepared baking sheet and place in the oven to keep warm.

Coat the skillet with cooking spray. Repeat with the remaining egg mixture, vegetable mixture, and cheese to cook another omelette. To serve, cut each omelette in half.

Makes 4 servings
Per serving: 128 calories, 13 g protein, 7 g carbohydrates, 7 g fat, 3 g saturated fat, 115 mg cholesterol, 3 g dietary fiber, 346 mg sodium

pair
with . . .

*honeyed summer
fruit bowl, page 54*

or

*1 cup mixed
berries and melons*

frittata with red-pepper sauce

Sauce

1	large red bell pepper, cut into chunks
½	cup water
1	tablespoon tomato paste
1	clove garlic, sliced
¼	teaspoon sugar
⅛	teaspoon salt
2	tablespoons chopped fresh basil

Frittata

2	large red potatoes, halved
1	tablespoon extra-virgin olive oil
½	teaspoon salt
½	teaspoon freshly ground black pepper
6	scallions, thinly sliced
4	eggs
2	egg whites
2	tablespoons chopped fresh basil
½	cup (2 ounces) shredded reduced-fat Jarlsberg cheese

To *make the sauce:* In a medium saucepan, combine the pepper, water, tomato paste, garlic, sugar, and salt. Bring to a boil over high heat. Reduce the heat to low, cover, and simmer, stirring occasionally, for 18 minutes, or until the pepper is very tender. Place in a food processor or blender and process until very smooth. Return to the saucepan. Stir in the basil and cover to keep warm.

CONVERSION CHART

Liquid Measure

8 ounces =	1 cup
2 cups =	1 pint
16 ounces =	1 pint
4 cups =	1 quart
1 gill =	1/2 cup or 1/4 pint
2 pints =	1 quart
4 quarts =	1 gallon
31.5 gal. =	1 barrel
3 tsp =	1 tbsp
2 tbsp =	1/8 cup or 1 fluid ounce
4 tbsp =	1/4 cup
8 tbsp =	1/2 cup
1 pinch =	1/8 tsp or less
1 tsp =	60 drops

Conversion of US Liquid Measure to Metric System

1 fluid oz. =	29.573 milliliters
1 cup =	230 milli liters
1 quart =	.94635 liters
1 gallon =	3.7854 liters
.033814 fluid ounce =	1 milliliter
3.3814 fluid ounces =	1 deciliter
33.814 fluid oz. or 1.0567 qt.=	1 liter

Dry Measure

2 pints =	1 quart
4 quarts =	1 gallon
8 quarts =	2 gallons or 1 peck
4 pecks =	8 gallons or 1 bushel
16 ounces =	1 pound
2000 lbs. =	1 ton

Conversion of US Weight and Mass Measure to Metric System

.0353 ounces =	1 gram
1/4 ounce =	7 grams
1 ounce =	28.35 grams
4 ounces =	113.4 grams
8 ounces =	226.8 grams
1 pound =	454 grams
2.2046 pounds =	1 kilogram
.98421 long ton or 1.1023 short tons =	1 metric ton

Linear Measure

12 inches =	1 foot
3 feet =	1 yard
5.5 yards =	1 rod
40 rods =	1 furlong
8 furlongs (5280 feet) =	1 mile
6080 feet =	1 nautical mile

Conversion of US Linear Measure to Metric System

1 inch =	2.54 centimeters
1 foot =	.3048 meters
1 yard =	.9144 meters
1 mile =	1609.3 meters or 1.6093 kilometers
.03937 in. =	1 millimeter
.3937 in.=	1 centimeter
3.937 in.=	1 decimeter
39.37 in.=	1 meter
3280.8 ft. or .62137 miles =	1 kilometer

To convert a Fahrenheit temperature to Centigrade, do the following:
a. Subtract 32   b. Multiply by 5   c. Divide by 9

To convert Centigrade to Fahrenheit, do the following:
a. Multiply by 9   b. Divide by 5   c. Add 32

2014

✝ **AMERICAN LUNG ASSOCIATION**®
Fighting for Air

JANUARY

SUN	MON	TUES	WED	THU	FRI	SAT
			1	2	3	4
5	6	7	8	9	10	11
12	13	14	15	16	17	18
19	20	21	22	23	24	25
26	27	28	29	30	31	

FEBRUARY

SUN	MON	TUES	WED	THU	FRI	SAT
						1
2	3	4	5	6	7	8
9	10	11	12	13	14	15
16	17	18	19	20	21	22
23	24	25	26	27	28	

MARCH

SUN	MON	TUES	WED	THU	FRI	SAT
						1
2	3	4	5	6	7	8
9	10	11	12	13	14	15
16	17	18	19	20	21	22
23	24	25	26	27	28	29
30	31					

APRIL

SUN	MON	TUES	WED	THU	FRI	SAT
		1	2	3	4	5
6	7	8	9	10	11	12
13	14	15	16	17	18	19
20	21	22	23	24	25	26
27	28	29	30			

MAY

SUN	MON	TUES	WED	THU	FRI	SAT
				1	2	3
4	5	6	7	8	9	10
11	12	13	14	15	16	17
18	19	20	21	22	23	24
25	26	27	28	29	30	31

JUNE

SUN	MON	TUES	WED	THU	FRI	SAT
1	2	3	4	5	6	7
8	9	10	11	12	13	14
15	16	17	18	19	20	21
22	23	24	25	26	27	28
29	30					

JULY

SUN	MON	TUES	WED	THU	FRI	SAT
		1	2	3	4	5
6	7	8	9	10	11	12
13	14	15	16	17	18	19
20	21	22	23	24	25	26
27	28	29	30	31		

AUGUST

SUN	MON	TUES	WED	THU	FRI	SAT
					1	2
3	4	5	6	7	8	9
10	11	12	13	14	15	16
17	18	19	20	21	22	23
24	25	26	27	28	29	30
31						

SEPTEMBER

SUN	MON	TUES	WED	THU	FRI	SAT
	1	2	3	4	5	6
7	8	9	10	11	12	13
14	15	16	17	18	19	20
21	22	23	24	25	26	27
28	29	30				

OCTOBER

SUN	MON	TUES	WED	THU	FRI	SAT
			1	2	3	4
5	6	7	8	9	10	11
12	13	14	15	16	17	18
19	20	21	22	23	24	25
26	27	28	29	30	31	

NOVEMBER

SUN	MON	TUES	WED	THU	FRI	SAT
						1
2	3	4	5	6	7	8
9	10	11	12	13	14	15
16	17	18	19	20	21	22
23	24	25	26	27	28	29
30						

DECEMBER

SUN	MON	TUES	WED	THU	FRI	SAT
	1	2	3	4	5	6
7	8	9	10	11	12	13
14	15	16	17	18	19	20
21	22	23	24	25	26	27
28	29	30	31			

To *make the frittata:* Place a steamer basket in a large saucepan with ½" of water. Place the potatoes in the steamer. Bring to a boil over high heat. Reduce the heat to medium, cover, and cook for 20 minutes, or until the potatoes are very tender. Cool briefly under cold running water and drain. Cool completely. Cut the potatoes into ¼"-thick slices.

Heat the oil in a large nonstick skillet over medium heat. Add the potatoes. Sprinkle with ¼ teaspoon each of the salt and pepper and toss to coat well. Cook, turning often, for 8 minutes, or until golden and crisp. Add the scallions and cook, tossing gently, for 3 minutes.

Meanwhile, in a medium bowl, whisk together the eggs, egg whites, basil, cheese, and the remaining ¼ teaspoon each of the salt and pepper. Pour into the skillet over the potato mixture and reduce the heat to low. Cover and cook, without stirring, for 3 minutes, or until the eggs start to set at the edges. Using a spatula, lift the edges and tilt the skillet to allow the uncooked mixture to flow to the bottom of the pan. Cover and cook for 4 minutes longer, occasionally loosening the frittata at the bottom and shaking the pan until the eggs are set and firm.

Slide the frittata onto a plate. Cut into wedges and serve with the sauce.

Makes 4 servings
Per serving: 247 calories, 17 g protein, 27 g carbohydrates, 9 g fat, 3 g saturated fat, 217 mg cholesterol, 4 g dietary fiber, 534 mg sodium

asparagus and leek frittata

1	tablespoon extra-virgin olive oil
1	medium leek, white and some green parts, halved lengthwise, rinsed, and thinly sliced
¾	pound thin asparagus, tips left whole and stems sliced ¼" thick
2	tablespoons chicken broth
¼	teaspoon salt
¼	teaspoon freshly ground black pepper
2	tablespoons chopped flat-leaf parsley
1	tablespoon snipped fresh chives
6	eggs
2	egg whites
3	tablespoons crumbled feta cheese

Preheat the broiler.

Heat the oil in a medium nonstick skillet with an ovenproof handle over medium-high heat. Add the leek and cook, stirring often, for 3 minutes, or until soft.

Add the asparagus, broth, ⅛ teaspoon each of the salt and pepper, parsley, and chives. Cook, stirring often, for 3 minutes, or until the asparagus is tender-crisp and the broth has evaporated. Spread the asparagus mixture evenly in the bottom of the skillet.

Meanwhile, in a medium bowl, whisk together the eggs, egg whites, cheese, and the remaining ⅛ teaspoon each of the salt and pepper. Pour into the skillet with the asparagus. Shake the skillet to evenly distribute the egg mixture. Reduce the heat to low, cover, and cook, without stirring, for 3 minutes, or until the eggs begin to set at the edges.

With a spatula, lift up an edge of the frittata and tilt the skillet to allow the uncooked mixture to flow to the bottom of the pan.

Place under the broiler. Broil for 1 to 3 minutes, or until the eggs are set on the top and the frittata is lightly puffed.

Cut into wedges to serve.

Makes 4 servings
Per serving: 209 calories, 14 g protein, 8 g carbohydrates, 13 g fat, 4 g saturated fat, 325 mg cholesterol, 2 g dietary fiber, 528 mg sodium

breakfast burritos

4	fat-free honey-wheat tortillas (8" diameter)
1	tablespoon olive oil
1	medium zucchini, halved lengthwise and cut into ¼"-thick slices
1	small red bell pepper, chopped
¼	teaspoon freshly ground black pepper
¾	cup fresh or frozen and thawed corn kernels
3	eggs
3	egg whites
2	tablespoons 1% milk
½	avocado, cut lengthwise into 8 thin slices
1	cup mild or medium-spicy salsa

Preheat the oven to 350°F.

Wrap the tortillas in foil. Place in the oven to heat for 10 minutes. Turn the oven off, leaving the tortillas in the oven to stay warm.

Meanwhile, heat the oil in a large nonstick skillet over medium heat. Add the zucchini, bell pepper, and black pepper. Cook the vegetables, stirring often, for 5 minutes, or until tender. Add the corn and cook, stirring often, for 1 minute.

In a medium bowl, combine the eggs, egg whites, and milk.

Reduce the heat to low. Pour the egg mixture into the skillet and scramble gently until the eggs are cooked but still moist.

Evenly divide the eggs, avocado slices, and salsa among the tortillas. Roll up and serve immediately.

Makes 4 servings
Per serving: 255 calories, 13 g protein, 28 g carbohydrates, 11 g fat, 2 g saturated fat, 160 mg cholesterol, 10 g dietary fiber, 774 mg sodium

fiesta cornmeal pudding

2 1/4	cups water
1/2	teaspoon salt
3/4	cup yellow cornmeal
1	tablespoon extra-virgin olive oil
1	large red bell pepper, chopped
4	scallions, thinly sliced
2	large cloves garlic, minced
1	package (10 ounces) frozen chopped spinach, thawed and squeezed dry
2	egg whites
1/4	teaspoon hot-pepper sauce
1/2	cup (2 ounces) shredded sharp Cheddar cheese

Preheat oven to 350°F. Coat a 9" baking dish with cooking spray.

Bring the water to a boil in a large saucepan over high heat. Add the salt. Reduce the heat to medium-low. Add the cornmeal in a slow, steady stream, whisking constantly. Reduce the heat to low, cover, and cook, stirring frequently, for 10 minutes, or until very thick. Remove from the heat.

Meanwhile, heat the oil in a medium nonstick skillet over medium heat. Add the bell pepper; cook, stirring, for 4 minutes. Add the scallions and garlic; cook, stirring, for 2 minutes, or until the vegetables are tender. Add the bell pepper mixture, spinach, egg whites, and hot-pepper sauce to the cornmeal. Stir well. Place in the baking dish. Sprinkle with the cheese. Bake for 30 minutes, or until firm, puffed, and golden.

Makes 4 servings
Per serving: 214 calories, 10 g protein, 25 g carbohydrates, 9 g fat, 4 g saturated fat, 15 mg cholesterol, 5 g dietary fiber, 481 mg sodium

plate ⟍
power

pair
with . . .

1/2 grapefruit
or
small glass of juice

soups
and stews

A steaming bowl of soup or stew beckons with warmth and goodness. The blending of vegetables, broth, and often meat or fish can deliver a meal's worth of nutrients in one bowl. Soups and stews allow the cook to create low-fat meals flavored with nutritious garlic, ginger, chile peppers, and other aromatics without any added fat or sodium. So versatile, feel free to substitute your favorite vegetables, herbs, and spices for those listed in the recipes.

In this chapter . . .

plate ˻ power

pair with . . .

herbed chicken sandwiches, *page 152*

or

minted lamb chops with white beans, *page 190*

cold tomato and cucumber soup

2	pounds tomatoes, peeled and cut into chunks
1	large clove garlic
1	large cucumber, peeled, halved, seeded, and finely chopped
1	cup tomato juice
½	cup finely chopped fresh basil
1	tablespoon extra-virgin olive oil
1	tablespoon red wine vinegar (see note)
½	teaspoon salt
¼	teaspoon freshly ground black pepper

In 2 batches in a food processor, process the tomatoes and garlic until smooth. Place in a bowl.

Add the cucumber, tomato juice, basil, oil, vinegar, salt, and pepper to the bowl. Cover and chill for at least 3 hours, or until very cold and the flavors have blended.

Makes 4 servings
Per serving: 100 calories, 3 g protein, 16 g carbohydrates, 4 g fat, 1 g saturated fat, 0 mg cholesterol, 3 g dietary fiber, 410 mg sodium

cold beet borscht

1½	pounds beets, peeled and quartered
3½	cups vegetable broth
1	cup water
2	tablespoons lemon juice
1	tablespoon red wine vinegar
1	small cucumber, peeled and finely chopped
3	tablespoons reduced-fat sour cream
1	tablespoon snipped fresh dill

In a large saucepan or Dutch oven over high heat, combine the beets, broth, and water. Bring to a boil. Reduce the heat to low, cover, and simmer for 30 minutes, or until the beets are very tender.

With a slotted spoon, place the beets in a large bowl and allow to cool to room temperature. Pour the cooking liquid into another large bowl and refrigerate.

Finely chop the cooled beets and add to the cooking liquid. Cover and refrigerate until cold.

Add the lemon juice and vinegar to the soup. Place half of the soup in a blender or food processor and blend or process until smooth. Add to the soup with the cucumber.

Ladle the soup into bowls. In a cup, combine the sour cream and dill. Dollop onto each serving.

Makes 6 servings
Per serving: 67 calories, 5 g protein, 13 g carbohydrates, 1 g fat, 1 g saturated fat, 3 mg cholesterol, 4 g dietary fiber, 484 mg sodium

plate power

pair with . . .

roast beef and charred vegetable sandwiches, page 153

or

pork tenderloin with vegetables, page 184

curried sweet potato and apple soup

1	tablespoon olive oil
1	large onion, sliced
2	cloves garlic, sliced
1	tablespoon finely chopped fresh ginger
1	teaspoon curry powder
¾	teaspoon ground cumin
½	teaspoon salt
¼	teaspoon ground cinnamon
4	cups water
1¼	pounds sweet potatoes, peeled and cut into chunks
3	large Granny Smith apples, peeled, cored, and cut into chunks
½	cup chopped fresh cilantro

Heat the oil in a large saucepan or Dutch oven over medium heat. Add the onion and garlic and cook, stirring occasionally, for 5 minutes, or until tender.

Add the ginger, curry powder, cumin, salt, and cinnamon. Cook, stirring constantly, for 1 minute. Add the water, sweet potatoes, and apples and bring to a boil over high heat. Reduce the heat to low, cover, and simmer, stirring often, for 20 minutes, or until the sweet potatoes are very tender.

In a food processor or blender, puree the soup in batches until very smooth, pouring each batch into a bowl. Reheat if necessary. Stir in the cilantro.

Makes 8 servings
Per serving: 134 calories, 2 g protein, 29 g carbohydrates, 2 g fat, 0 g saturated fat, 0 mg cholesterol, 4 g dietary fiber, 162 mg sodium

plate power

pair with . . .

spiced pork scallops with fruit chutney, page 176, *and spiced brown rice with cashews,* page 248

or

indian-spiced potatoes and spinach, page 286, *and ½ a grilled chicken breast*

plate ~ power

pair with . . .

penne with salmon and roasted vegetables, page 223

or

shrimp with chard and red beans, page 238

turnip and carrot soup with parmesan ⟨quick⟩

1	pound white turnips, peeled and cut into chunks
4	large carrots, cut into chunks
2	large red or white new potatoes, peeled and cut into chunks
1	large onion, cut into chunks
5	cloves garlic, sliced
1½	cups chicken broth
1½	cups water
½	teaspoon dried thyme, crushed
½	teaspoon rubbed sage
¼	teaspoon salt
¼	teaspoon freshly ground black pepper
1	cup 1% milk
½	cup (2 ounces) freshly grated Parmesan cheese

In a large saucepan or Dutch oven, combine the turnips, carrots, potatoes, onion, garlic, broth, water, thyme, sage, salt, and pepper. Bring to a boil over high heat. Reduce the heat to medium, cover, and simmer for 20 minutes, or until the vegetables are very tender.

In a food processor or blender, puree the soup in batches until very smooth, pouring each batch into a bowl. When all the soup has been pureed, return it to the pan. Stir in the milk. Cook over low heat just until heated through (do not boil). Remove from the heat and stir in the cheese.

Makes 8 servings
Per serving: 108 calories, 6 g protein, 17 g carbohydrates, 2 g fat, 1 g saturated fat, 6 mg cholesterol, 3 g dietary fiber, 364 mg sodium

root vegetable soup

1	tablespoon olive oil
6	cloves garlic, minced
2	large onions, chopped
½	teaspoon dried marjoram, crushed
½	teaspoon dried sage, crushed
¼	teaspoon salt
½	teaspoon freshly ground black pepper
1	pound lean, well-trimmed beef round, cut into 1" cubes
3	cups low-sodium beef broth
3	cups water
1	can (28 ounces) whole tomatoes, drained and broken up
4	small turnips, peeled and cut into ½" chunks
3	medium beets, peeled and cut into ½" chunks
3	large carrots, cut into ½" chunks
2	medium parsnips, peeled and cut into ½" chunks

Heat the oil in a large saucepan over medium heat. Add the garlic and onions and cook, stirring, for 5 minutes, or until soft. Add the marjoram, sage, salt, and pepper. Add the beef and cook, stirring, for 5 minutes, or until browned.

Add the broth, water, and tomatoes. Bring to a boil over high heat. Reduce the heat to low, cover, and simmer, stirring occasionally, for 45 minutes, or until the beef is very tender.

Add the turnips, beets, carrots, and parsnips. Return to a simmer. Cover and cook, stirring occasionally, for 25 minutes longer, or until the vegetables are very tender.

Makes 8 servings
Per serving: 194 calories, 16 g protein, 22 g carbohydrates, 5 g fat, 1 g saturated fat, 31 mg cholesterol, 5 g dietary fiber, 630 mg sodium

plate ›
power

pair
with . . .

kasha with onions,
page 251

or

southwestern
double-corn
muffins, page 65

gingery vegetable broth with tofu and noodles

1	tablespoon canola oil
8	ounces cremini mushrooms, finely chopped
2	large carrots, finely chopped
2	ribs celery, finely chopped
1	medium onion, finely chopped
6	large cloves garlic, minced
2	tablespoons finely chopped fresh ginger
3	tablespoons dry sherry
4	cups low-sodium vegetable broth
1/4	teaspoon salt
1	cup snow peas, cut into julienne strips
4	ounces thin soba noodles, broken in half
8	ounces baked smoked tofu, cut into 1/4" cubes
4	scallions, thinly sliced on the diagonal

Heat the oil in a large saucepan or Dutch oven over medium-high heat. Add the mushrooms, carrots, celery, onion, garlic, and ginger and cook, stirring often, for 10 minutes, or until the vegetables are lightly browned.

Add the sherry and cook for 1 minute, stirring to loosen browned bits from the pan. Add the broth and salt and bring to a boil over high heat. Reduce the heat to low, cover, and simmer for 45 minutes, adding the snow peas during the last 3 minutes.

Meanwhile, prepare the soba noodles according to package directions. Drain and set aside.

Stir the tofu, soba noodles, and scallions into the broth and simmer for 3 minutes, or until heated through.

Makes 4 servings
Per serving: 297 calories, 17 g protein, 40 g carbohydrates, 8 g fat, 2 g saturated fat, 5 mg cholesterol, 6 g dietary fiber, 575 mg sodium

plate ~ power

pair
with . . .

linguine and clams, page 241

or

barbecued butterflied leg of lamb, page 187, with polenta with fresh tomato sauce, page 254

minestrone verde

2	teaspoons extra-virgin olive oil
2	small leeks, white and green parts, halved lengthwise, rinsed, and thinly sliced
2	large ribs celery with leaves, thinly sliced
2	cloves garlic, minced + 1 whole clove garlic, peeled
¼	teaspoon dried oregano, crushed
¼	teaspoon freshly ground black pepper
⅛	teaspoon salt
2	cups water
1	cup chicken broth
4	cups chopped Swiss chard
⅔	cup frozen baby lima beans
¼	cup ditalini or other small pasta
¼	cup chopped Italian parsley
½	cup frozen green peas
4	teaspoons shredded Parmesan cheese

Heat the oil in a large saucepan over medium heat. Add the leeks, celery, minced garlic, oregano, pepper, and salt. Cook, stirring frequently, for 4 minutes, or until the vegetables begin to soften.

Add the water, broth, Swiss chard, lima beans, and pasta. Bring to a boil over high heat. Reduce the heat to medium-low, cover, and simmer for 8 minutes, or until the vegetables are tender and the pasta is al dente.

Meanwhile, coarsely chop the remaining garlic clove, then mince it together with the parsley. Stir the garlic-parsley mixture and the peas into the soup. Cover and cook for 5 minutes, or until the peas are heated through.

Ladle the soup into 4 bowls and top each with 1 teaspoon of the cheese.

Makes 4 servings
Per serving: 145 calories, 6 g protein, 24 g carbohydrates, 3 g fat, 1 g saturated fat, 1 mg cholesterol, 5 g dietary fiber, 413 mg sodium

pasta e fagiole (quick)

2	teaspoons olive oil
2	onions, chopped
2	cloves garlic, chopped
4	cups low-sodium chicken broth
1	can (15 ounces) diced tomatoes
2	cans (14–19 ounces each) cannellini or white beans, rinsed and drained
½	cup ditalini or other small pasta
4	cups chopped Swiss chard or spinach

Heat the oil in a large saucepan over medium heat. Add the onions and garlic and cook, stirring occasionally, for 5 minutes, or until the onions are soft.

Add the broth, tomatoes (with juice), beans, and pasta and cook, stirring occasionally, for 15 minutes, or until the pasta is al dente. Add the Swiss chard or spinach and cook, stirring occasionally, for 3 minutes, or until the chard or spinach is wilted.

Makes 4 servings
Per serving: 255 calories, 15 g protein, 42 g carbohydrates, 5 g fat, 1 g saturated fat, 4 mg cholesterol, 13 g dietary fiber, 342 mg sodium

plate
power

pair
with . . .

tossed salad with tomato vinaigrette, page 133

or

summer squash with walnuts and parmesan, page 313

pair
with . . .

barley risotto,
page 267

or

*a slice of garlic
bread*

stracciatelle with (quick) escarole and chickpeas

1	tablespoon extra-virgin olive oil
5	cloves garlic, minced
2	large carrots, shredded
1	medium head escarole, shredded
⅛	teaspoon freshly ground black pepper
4	cups low-sodium chicken broth
2¾	cups water
1	bunch broccoli, cut into small florets
1	can (14–19 ounces) chickpeas, rinsed and drained
2	eggs
⅓	cup (1½ ounces) freshly grated Parmesan cheese

Heat the oil in a large saucepan or Dutch oven over medium-high heat. Add the garlic and carrots and cook, stirring constantly, for 3 minutes, or until tender.

Add half of the escarole; cook, stirring, for 2 minutes, or until the escarole is wilted. Add the remaining escarole and the pepper; cook, stirring, for 2 minutes, or until wilted.

Add the broth, 2½ cups of the water, the broccoli, and chickpeas. Bring to a boil over high heat. Reduce the heat to low, cover, and simmer for 8 minutes, or until the broccoli is tender.

In a small bowl, using a fork, stir together the eggs, cheese, and the remaining ¼ cup water. Slowly pour into the soup and stir briskly with the fork to create fine threads.

Makes 4 servings
Per serving: 318 calories, 19 g protein, 37 g carbohydrates, 13 g fat, 4 g saturated fat, 118 mg cholesterol, 11 g dietary fiber, 534 mg sodium

greek-style lentil soup

1	pound brown lentils, picked over and rinsed
9	cups water
6	cloves garlic, minced
3	large carrots, cut into ¼" pieces
2	large onions, chopped
1	teaspoon dried thyme, crushed
1	teaspoon freshly ground black pepper
½	teaspoon dried rosemary, crushed
1½	cups tomato puree
1	teaspoon salt
¼	teaspoon ground cinnamon
2	tablespoons extra-virgin olive oil
1	tablespoon red wine vinegar
3	tablespoons coarsely chopped fresh marjoram or oregano (optional)

In a large saucepan or Dutch oven, combine the lentils, water, garlic, carrots, onions, thyme, pepper, and rosemary. Bring to a boil over high heat. Reduce the heat to low, cover, and simmer, stirring occasionally, for 35 minutes, or until the lentils are tender. Stir in the tomato puree, salt, and cinnamon, and simmer for 20 minutes to blend the flavors.

Remove from the heat and stir in the oil, vinegar, and marjoram or oregano, if using.

Makes 6 servings
Per serving: 351 calories, 23 g protein, 55 g carbohydrates, 5 g fat, 1 g saturated fat, 0 mg cholesterol, 26 g dietary fiber, 434 mg sodium

plate power

pair with . . .

side salad of chopped onion, tomato, and cucumber tossed with 1 teaspoon of italian vinaigrette

or

balsamic tomato and roasted pepper salad, page 143

seven-bean soup with greens

1/3	cup black beans
1/3	cup red kidney beans
1/3	cup appaloosa or small red beans
1/3	cup cranberry or pinto beans
1/3	cup great Northern or navy beans
1/3	cup Steuben yellow-eye beans or black-eyed peas
3	tablespoons extra-virgin olive oil
10	cloves garlic, minced
2	large onions, coarsely chopped
2	ribs celery, sliced
2	teaspoons dried Italian herb seasoning, crushed
3/4	teaspoon freshly ground black pepper
1/3	cup green or yellow split peas
6	cups water
2	cans (28 ounces each) crushed tomatoes in tomato puree
1/4	cup tomato paste
2	packages (10 ounces each) frozen chopped greens, such as collard, turnip, or kale
1/2	teaspoon salt
1 1/2	cups chopped fresh basil

Pick over and rinse all the beans. Place in a large saucepot and cover with 3" of water. Cover and let stand overnight. Drain.

Rinse and dry the pot. Heat the oil in the pot over medium-high heat. Add the garlic, onions, and celery and cook, stirring frequently, for 5 minutes, or until soft. Add the Italian seasoning and pepper and cook, stirring, for 30 seconds.

Add the beans, split peas, and water. Bring to a boil over high heat. Reduce the heat to medium-low, cover, and simmer, stirring occasionally, for 1½ hours, or until the beans are tender. (The black beans will take the longest to cook, so use them as a guide.)

Add the tomatoes, tomato paste, greens, and salt. Bring to a boil over high heat. Reduce the heat to medium-low, cover, and simmer, stirring occasionally, for 30 minutes longer, or until the greens are tender. Stir in the basil.

Makes 8 servings
Per serving: 349 calories, 19 g protein, 56 g carbohydrates, 6 g fat, 1 g saturated fat, 0 mg cholesterol, 18 g dietary fiber, 688 mg sodium

the power of
TOMATOES

The press has had a field day with the latest studies on tomatoes, and the news has been great! One medium tomato contributes a mere 40 calories to your total daily intake, but is bursting with nutrients. Choose fresh, select ripe red tomatoes, not pale ones. The redder, the better!

plate ⌒ power

pair
with . . .

botana, page 257

or

*½ cup sliced
papaya or mango*

black bean soup

2	cans (14–19 ounces each) black beans, rinsed and drained
1¾	cups low-sodium chicken broth
1	cup water
1	teaspoon ground cumin
¼	teaspoon dried oregano, crushed
¼	teaspoon freshly ground black pepper
	Large pinch of ground red pepper
1	teaspoon olive oil
½	large red bell pepper, slivered
½	large green bell pepper, slivered
½	teaspoon grated lemon peel

In a large saucepan, combine the beans, broth, water, cumin, oregano, black pepper, and ground red pepper. Bring to a boil over high heat. Reduce the heat to low, cover, and simmer, stirring once or twice, for 15 minutes, or until the flavors are blended.

Meanwhile, heat the oil in a small nonstick skillet over medium heat. Add the bell peppers and cook, stirring frequently, for 4 minutes, or until tender.

Ladle half of the soup into a food processor or blender. Process or blend until pureed. Return the puree to the pan; add the lemon peel.

Ladle the soup into bowls and top each serving with the bell peppers.

Makes 4 servings
Per serving: 188 calories, 13 g protein, 39 g carbohydrates, 2 g fat, 1 g saturated fat, 2 mg cholesterol, 14 g dietary fiber, 616 mg sodium

COOKING TIP
To make this soup with dried beans, place 1 pound of beans in a large pot with cold water to cover and let sit overnight. Drain, cover with fresh water, and simmer for 1¼ hours, or until tender. You'll have enough for this recipe, plus leftovers for other dishes.

fresh chicken soup

4	whole bone-in chicken legs
4	cups chicken broth
2	cups water
5	cloves garlic, minced
2	tablespoons finely chopped fresh ginger
1/4	teaspoon freshly ground black pepper
3	carrots, sliced
1	large leek, white and green part, rinsed and cut into 1/2" slices
1	large sweet potato (12 ounces), peeled and cut into large chunks
6	cups packed torn spinach
1	large tomato, cut into 1/2" chunks
1/4–1 teaspoon hot-pepper sauce	

Divide the chicken legs into thigh and drumstick portions. Remove and discard the skin and any visible fat.

Place the chicken in a large saucepot or Dutch oven. Add the broth, water, garlic, ginger, and pepper. Bring to a boil over high heat. Skim off any foam. Reduce the heat to low, cover, and simmer for 15 minutes, skimming the surface occasionally.

Stir in the carrots, leek, and sweet potato. Cover and simmer for 20 minutes, or until the vegetables are tender and the chicken is cooked through.

Add the spinach and tomato and cook for 5 minutes. Add the hot-pepper sauce to taste.

Makes 4 servings
Per serving: 320 calories, 30 g protein, 39 g carbohydrates, 5 g fat, 1 g saturated fat, 91 mg cholesterol, 11 g dietary fiber, 525 mg sodium

mushroom-barley soup

1	ounce dried mushrooms
3	cups boiling water
4	carrots, chopped
2	large onions, chopped
2	ribs celery, chopped
12	ounces cremini or button mushrooms, stems removed, sliced
1½	teaspoons dried oregano, crushed
5	cups chicken broth
1	cup barley
¼	teaspoon salt

Place the dried mushrooms in a small bowl and cover with the water. Let stand for 15 minutes.

Meanwhile, coat a large saucepan or Dutch oven with cooking spray. Add the carrots, onions, and celery. Coat lightly with cooking spray and set over medium heat. Cook, stirring occasionally, for 3 minutes. Add the sliced mushrooms and oregano. Cook, stirring occasionally, for 6 minutes, or until the vegetables are soft. Add the broth, barley, and salt. Cook for 10 minutes.

Line a sieve with a coffee filter or paper towel. Strain the dried mushroom water into the pot. Remove and discard the filter or paper towel. Rinse the dried mushrooms under running water to remove any grit. Chop and add to the pot.

Cook for 20 minutes, or until the barley is tender.

Makes 4 servings
Per serving: 340 calories, 13 g protein, 62 g carbohydrates, 6 g fat, 2 g saturated fat, 6 mg cholesterol, 15 g dietary fiber, 1470 mg sodium

tortilla soup with lime

4	corn tortillas (6" diameter), halved and cut into ¼"-wide strips
2¼	cups chicken broth
1¼	cups water
12	ounces thinly sliced turkey breast cutlets, cut into ½"-thick strips
2	large onions, halved and thinly sliced
2	large red bell peppers, cut into thin strips
1	large jalapeño chile pepper, seeded and minced
2	teaspoons ground cumin
¼	teaspoon dried oregano, crushed
½	cup frozen corn kernels
½	cup cherry tomatoes, quartered
¼	cup chopped fresh cilantro
2	tablespoons lime juice
½	ripe avocado, diced

Preheat the oven to 400°F. Coat 1 or 2 large baking sheets with cooking spray.

Arrange the tortilla strips on the prepared baking sheets and bake for 2 minutes, or until crisped and lightly browned on the edges.

In a large saucepan, combine the broth, water, turkey, onions, bell peppers, chile pepper, cumin, and oregano. Bring to a boil over high heat. Reduce the heat to medium-low, cover, and simmer for 10 minutes.

Add the corn and simmer for 5 minutes. Stir in the tomatoes, cilantro, and lime juice. Ladle the soup into bowls and top each portion with avocado and tortilla crisps.

Makes 6 servings
Per serving: 232 calories, 16 g protein, 25 g carbohydrates, 8 g fat, 2 g saturated fat, 39 mg cholesterol, 6 g dietary fiber, 444 mg sodium

manhattan clam chowder

2	teaspoons olive oil
2	ribs celery with leaves, chopped
2	carrots, chopped
1	onion, finely chopped
1	small clove garlic, minced
1	large potato, peeled and diced
1	green bell pepper, chopped
1	red bell pepper, chopped
¾	cup bottled clam juice
2	cans (6½ ounces each) chopped clams, drained, with juice reserved
2½	cups reduced-sodium stewed tomatoes
1	teaspoon dried thyme, crushed
¼	teaspoon freshly ground black pepper
2–3	drops hot-pepper sauce

Heat the oil in a large saucepan or Dutch oven over medium heat. Add the celery, carrots, onion, and garlic, and cook, stirring, for 5 minutes, or until the onion is tender.

Add the potato, bell peppers, bottled clam juice, and the reserved clam juice. Bring to a boil. Reduce the heat to low, cover, and simmer, stirring, for 10 minutes, or until the potato is tender.

Add the tomatoes (with juice), thyme, black pepper, hot-pepper sauce, and the reserved clams. Bring to a simmer. Cover and simmer for 8 minutes, or until the flavors are blended.

Makes 4 servings
Per serving: 138 calories, 10 g protein, 20 g carbohydrates, 3 g fat,
1 g saturated fat, 17 mg cholesterol, 4 g dietary fiber, 754 mg sodium

plate power

pair with . . .

an open faced sandwich of braised italian peppers with onions, page 297, on top of a slice of grilled italian bread

or

baked stuffed potatoes with spinach and beans, page 283

plate power

pair with . . .

baby spinach salad with mushrooms, red onions, and mustard vinaigrette on page 133

or

mediterranean chickpea salad, page 129

neptune's bounty bouillabaisse

1	teaspoon olive oil
2	cloves garlic, minced
1	medium bulb fennel, white part only, cut into ¼"-thick slices
1	large onion, chopped
12	ounces small red potatoes, cut into ½" cubes
2	cups crushed tomatoes
1	jar (6½ ounces) clam juice
1	cup water
1	cup canned light coconut milk
½	teaspoon crushed saffron threads (optional)
¼	teaspoon salt
¼	teaspoon freshly ground black pepper
8	ounces halibut fillets, cut into 2" cubes
8	ounces sea scallops
8	ounces large shrimp, peeled and deveined
12	mussels, scrubbed and beards removed
½	teaspoon hot-pepper sauce (optional)

Heat the oil in a large saucepot or Dutch oven over medium heat. Add the garlic, fennel, and onion and cook, stirring often, for 7 minutes, or until the fennel is soft and tender. Add the potatoes, tomatoes, clam juice, water, coconut milk, saffron (if using), salt, and pepper. Cook for 15 minutes, or until the potatoes are just tender.

Add the halibut, scallops, shrimp, mussels, and hot-pepper sauce, if using. Reduce the heat to low, cover, and simmer for 5 minutes, or until the mussels have opened and the halibut and shrimp are opaque. (Discard any mussels that remain closed after 5 minutes of cooking time.)

Makes 4 servings

Per serving: 372 calories, 41 g protein, 33 g carbohydrates, 8 g fat, 1 g saturated fat, 6 g dietary fiber, 135 mg cholesterol, 883 mg sodium

COOKING TIPS

Shrimp, scallops, halibut, and mussels provide a healthy dose of omega-3 fatty acids in this elegant, yet easy seafood soup. Mussels need to be cleaned thoroughly before cooking. Soak for about an hour in a mixture of salted water and cornmeal to rid them of any excess sand. Before soaking, throw out any that are open.

The tomato-based broth is accented with tropical-tasting reduced-fat coconut milk. Canned light coconut milk can be found in the international aisle of most supermarkets and at Asian grocery stores. It's lower in fat than regular coconut milk and coconut cream.

pair
with . . .

½ cup cherries

or

*a side of roasted
asparagus tossed
with orange
vinaigrette,*
page 133

creamy white bean soup with cabbage and salmon

1	cup navy beans, picked over, rinsed, and soaked overnight
2½	cups water
2	cups chicken broth
6	cloves garlic, minced
1	bay leaf
2	tablespoons extra-virgin olive oil
½	head cabbage, coarsely chopped
1	large onion, chopped
½	pound skinned salmon fillet, cut into 1″ chunks
2	ounces (2 thick slices) Canadian bacon, coarsely chopped
1	tablespoon chopped fresh thyme

In a large saucepan or Dutch oven, combine the beans, water, broth, garlic, and bay leaf. Bring to a boil over high heat. Reduce the heat to low, cover, and simmer, stirring occasionally, for 50 minutes, or until the beans are very tender. Remove and discard the bay leaf.

In a food processor or blender, puree the soup in batches until smooth. Return the soup to the pot and bring to a boil over medium heat. Cover to keep warm.

Meanwhile, heat 1 tablespoon of the oil in a large nonstick skillet over high heat. Add the cabbage and onion. Cook, stirring frequently, for 6 minutes, or until lightly browned and tender. Add to the soup.

In the same skillet, heat the remaining 1 tablespoon oil over medium heat. Add the salmon and bacon. Sprinkle with the thyme. Cook, stirring gently, for 3 minutes, or until the salmon is lightly browned and just opaque.

Gently stir the salmon mixture into the soup.

Makes 4 servings
Per serving: 340 calories, 27 g protein, 37 g carbohydrates, 10 g fat, 2 g saturated fat, 37 mg cholesterol, 14 g dietary fiber, 536 mg sodium

country-style potato and green bean soup with ham

3	cloves garlic, minced
2	very large or 3 medium russet potatoes, quartered lengthwise and sliced ¼" thick
1	large onion, chopped
4	ounces coarsely cubed ham
1½	cups chicken broth
1½	cups water
1	teaspoon dried marjoram, crushed
¼	teaspoon freshly ground black pepper
12	ounces green beans, halved
3	carrots, sliced
½	cup (4 ounces) reduced-fat sour cream

In a large saucepot or Dutch oven, combine the garlic, potatoes, onion, ham, broth, water, marjoram, and pepper. Bring to a boil over high heat. Reduce the heat to low, cover, and simmer, stirring occasionally, for 15 minutes, or until the potatoes are very tender.

Using a potato masher, mash the potatoes slightly, breaking them up to give the soup a chunky (not smooth) texture.

Add the green beans and carrots, cover, and cook, stirring occasionally, for 10 minutes, or untikl tender. Add the sour cream and bring to a simmer, stirring constantly, until the soup is slightly thickened and creamy.

Makes 4 servings
Per serving: 288 calories, 13 g protein, 41 g carbohydrates, 9 g fat, 4 g saturated fat, 26 mg cholesterol, 8 g dietary fiber, 645 mg sodium

COOKING TIPS
Cut the ham from a well-trimmed ham steak instead of a deli slice. It will be more moist and flavorful, and you can freeze any remainder for another meal.

You can also make this soup without the ham, or substitute smoked turkey or chunks of smoked salmon, but add the salmon at the end of the cooking time.

plate power

split pea soup with ham and winter squash

1	smoked ham hock (12 ounces)
11	cups water
4	cloves garlic, minced
1	teaspoon dried thyme, crushed
½	teaspoon dried sage, crushed
½	teaspoon freshly ground black pepper
1	pound green split peas, picked over and rinsed
1	medium butternut squash (2 pounds), peeled and cut into ½" chunks
1	pound white potatoes, scrubbed and cut into ½" chunks
3	large carrots, cut into ½" chunks
3	ribs celery, sliced
2	large onions, coarsely chopped
¾	teaspoon salt

In a large saucepot or Dutch oven, combine the ham hock, water, garlic, thyme, sage, and pepper. Bring to a boil over high heat. Reduce the heat to low, cover, and simmer, turning the ham hock once, for 1 hour. Cool. Refrigerate for at least 4 hours or overnight.

After the broth has chilled, skim and discard the fat from the surface. Remove the ham hock and cut the meat off the bone; set aside. Discard the bone and any fat.

Add the split peas to the broth and bring to a boil over high heat. Skim off any foam that rises to the surface. Reduce the heat to low, cover, and simmer, stirring occasionally, for 1 hour, or until the peas are soft and tender.

Add the squash, potatoes, carrots, celery, onions, salt, and ham. Return to a boil. Cover and simmer, stirring occasionally, for 20 to 25 minutes, or until the vegetables are tender.

Makes 8 servings
Per serving: 350 calories, 20 g protein, 64 g carbohydrates, 3 g fat, 1 g saturated fat, 7 mg cholesterol, 19 g dietary fiber, 464 mg sodium

plate ↻ power

pair
with . . .

*terayaki tuna
burgers, page 221*

or

*baked scallops
newburg, page 242,
with a ½ cup
serving of long
grain and wild rice*

broccoli soup

1	tablespoon butter or margarine
1	onion, chopped
1	small bunch broccoli, coarsely chopped
1	can (14½ oz) chicken or vegetable broth
1	bay leaf
¼	cup low-fat milk
1	tablespoon unbleached or all-purpose flour
¾	cup fat-free evaporated milk
⅛	teaspoon ground nutmeg
¼	cup grated Parmesan cheese (optional)

Warm butter or margarine in a large saucepan over medium heat. Add the onion and cook for 5 minutes, or until tender. Set aside 6–8 broccoli florets. Add the broth, bay leaf, and remaining broccoli to the saucepan. Heat to boiling. Cover, reduce the heat to low, and simmer for 10 minutes.

Remove from the heat. Cool slightly and remove and discard the bay leaf. Puree the soup in a blender or food processor. Return the soup to the pan.

In a small bowl, combine the low-fat milk and the flour. Stir into the soup along with the evaporated milk and the nutmeg. Cook over medium heat, stirring, until the soup simmers and thickens. Add the reserved broccoli florets. Cook for 2 minutes.

Serve, sprinkled with the cheese, if using.

Makes 4 servings
Per serving: 117 calories, 7 g protein, 14 g carbohydrates, 4 g fat, 10 mg cholesterol, 2 g fiber, 534 sodium

sweet potato and leek soup

3	leeks
2	tablespoons unsalted butter
1	tablespoon olive oil
1	large onion, chopped
1-½	pounds sweet potatoes or yams, peeled and diced
3	cans (14-¾ oz) reduced-sodium chicken broth
¼	teaspoon ground red pepper

Cut off and discard the dark green leaves and roots from the leeks. Cut each leek lengthwise, up to the core. Rinse under running water, fanning the leaves to remove any grit. Slice the leeks.

In a large soup pot, over medium heat, melt the butter with the oil. Add the onion and the leeks. Cover and cook, stirring occasionally, for 7 minutes, or until soft. Add the sweet potatoes or yams and the broth. Heat to boiling. Reduce the heat to low, cover, and simmer, stirring occasionally, for 20–25 minutes, or until the potatoes are fork-tender. Cool slightly.

Puree the soup in a blender or food processor. Blend in the pepper.

Makes 4 servings
Per serving: 170 calories, 3 g protein, 28 g carbohydrates, 6 g fat, 8 mg cholesterol, 1 g fiber, 26 mg sodium

plate power

pair with . . .

fruited turkey salad, page 131

or

baked chicken with prunes, page 202

salads and sandwiches

A bowl of leafy greens and crisp vegetables is one of life's finest and simplest pleasures. So are slices of meat, cheese, and vegetables nestled between two slabs of bread. Salads and sandwiches are most often eaten for lunch because they are fast and easy—but don't limit them to just the midday meal. Both are a good choice when vegetables are the main focus. Try the many lettuces and greens available and experiment with vegetable combinations. Creativity with ingredients at mealtime keeps your weight-loss plan exciting.

In this chapter . . .

plate ↲ power

pair with . . .

fritatta with red pepper sauce, page 78

or

five-alarm shrimp, page 237, *with ½ cup cooked brown rice*

cool greens and tomatoes with creamy dill dressing

(quick)

2	tablespoons reduced-fat mayonnaise
2	tablespoons buttermilk
2	tablespoons minced fresh dill
2	teaspoons lemon juice
2	teaspoons coarse Dijon mustard
⅛	teaspoon salt
⅛	teaspoon freshly ground black pepper
1	package (5 ounces) mesclun leaves or baby greens
2	cups mixed red and yellow cherry tomatoes, halved
1	medium cucumber, peeled, halved, seeded, and thinly sliced
½	ripe avocado, cut into ¼" chunks
½	small red onion, chopped

In a large serving bowl, combine the mayonnaise, buttermilk, dill, lemon juice, mustard, salt, and pepper.

Add the greens, tomatoes, cucumber, avocado, and onion and toss to coat well.

Makes 4 servings
Per serving: 103 calories, 3 g protein, 10 g carbohydrates, 7 g fat, 1 g saturated fat, 0 mg cholesterol, 3 g dietary fiber, 184 mg sodium

strawberry (quick) and red onion salad

3	tablespoons strawberry all-fruit spread
2	teaspoons balsamic vinegar
2	teaspoons olive oil
1/8	teaspoon salt
1/8	teaspoon crushed red-pepper flakes
1	pound fresh strawberries, hulled and sliced
1/4	cantaloupe, cut into 1/4" chunks
1/2	small red bell pepper, finely chopped
1/2	small red onion, finely chopped
1	medium head escarole, torn (about 3 cups)
1/2	ripe avocado, cut into 1/4" chunks
	Freshly ground black pepper

In a medium glass bowl, combine the all-fruit spread, vinegar, olive oil, salt, and red-pepper flakes until well-blended. Gently fold in the strawberries, cantaloupe, bell pepper, and onion. Cover and let stand for 15 minutes to allow the flavors to blend.

Place the escarole in a serving bowl. Add the avocado and strawberry mixture and toss to coat well. Season with black pepper to taste.

Makes 4 servings
Per serving: 163 calories, 2 g protein, 27 g carbohydrates, 7 g fat, 1 g saturated fat, 0 mg cholesterol, 6 g dietary fiber, 110 mg sodium

plate power

pair with . . .

beef stroganoff, page 165

or

pan-seared red snapper with olive crust, page 228, *and 1/2 cup orzo pasta*

asian slaw (quick)

¼	cup rice wine vinegar or white wine vinegar
2	tablespoons soy sauce
1	tablespoon grated fresh ginger
2	teaspoons toasted sesame oil
½	head napa or savoy cabbage, shredded
3	scallions, sliced
2	carrots, shredded
½	red bell pepper, cut into thin strips
2	tablespoons chopped fresh cilantro
2	teaspoons sesame seeds, toasted (optional)

In a large bowl, combine the vinegar, soy sauce, ginger, and oil. Add the cabbage, scallions, carrots, pepper, and cilantro. Toss to coat well. Sprinkle with the sesame seeds, if using. Let stand for at least 15 minutes to allow the flavors to blend.

Makes 4 servings
Per serving: 106 calories, 4 g protein, 14 g carbohydrates, 3 g fat, 0 g saturated fat, 0 mg cholesterol, 5 g dietary fiber, 561 mg sodium

plate power

pair with . . .

teriyaki tuna burgers, page 221

or

salmon over noodles, page 224

pair with . . .

whole grain caprese pasta, page 262

or

½ of a grilled chicken breast and a slice of french bread rubbed with garlic

chopped salad with millet

½	cup millet
1¼	cups water
⅛	teaspoon + ½ teaspoon salt
3	tablespoons white wine vinegar (see note)
3	tablespoons extra-virgin olive oil
¼	teaspoon freshly ground black pepper
2	scallions, thinly sliced
1	pound thin asparagus, tips left whole and stems cut into 1″ slices
1	small head napa cabbage, chopped
6	radishes, chopped
2	medium carrots, shredded
1	roasted red pepper, blotted dry and finely chopped
¼	cup chopped flat-leaf parsley

In a medium saucepan over medium-high heat, cook the millet, stirring frequently, for 3 to 4 minutes, or until lightly browned and the grains begin to crackle. Add the water and ⅛ teaspoon of the salt. Bring to a boil over high heat. Reduce the heat to low, cover, and simmer for 25 minutes, or until the millet is tender, some grains have burst, and the water has evaporated. Remove from the heat and let stand for 10 minutes.

Fluff the millet with a fork and place in a medium bowl. Cover and refrigerate for 30 minutes, or until cooled.

Meanwhile, in a large serving bowl, whisk together the vinegar, olive oil, black pepper, and the remaining ½ teaspoon salt. Stir in the scallions and let stand for at least 10 minutes to allow the flavors to blend.

Place a steamer basket in a saucepan with ½" of water. Place the asparagus in the steamer. Bring to a boil over high heat. Reduce the heat to medium, cover, and cook for 4 minutes, or until tender-crisp. Rinse briefly under cold running water and drain.

Add the millet, cabbage, radishes, carrots, roasted pepper, parsley, and asparagus to the dressing. Toss to coat well. Let stand for at least 15 minutes to allow the flavors to blend.

Makes 6 servings
Per serving: 160 calories, 5 g protein, 19 g carbohydrates, 8 g fat, 1 g saturated fat, 0 mg cholesterol, 5 g dietary fiber, 275 mg sodium

pair
with . . .

*orange roughy
vera cruz, page 226
and cilantro and
tomato rice,*
page 249

or

*mediterranean
baked beans,*
page 276

garden bounty salad

6	ears corn
8	ounces green beans, halved
2	tablespoons lime juice
2	tablespoons extra-virgin olive oil
½	teaspoon ground cumin
½	teaspoon salt
½	teaspoon freshly ground black pepper
2	large tomatoes, cut into ½" chunks
½	small red onion, chopped
3	tablespoons chopped fresh cilantro

Preheat the grill. Rinse the corn to moisten the husks. Pull back the husks, remove the silks, and pull the husks back over the kernels (some kernels will be exposed). Place the corn on the grill rack. Grill the corn, turning, for 15 minutes, or until the kernels are tender and charred in spots.

Meanwhile, place a steamer basket in a saucepan with ½" of water. Place the green beans in the steamer. Bring to a boil over high heat. Reduce the heat to medium, cover, and cook for 6 minutes, or until tender-crisp. Rinse briefly under cold running water and drain.

In a large bowl, combine the lime juice, olive oil, cumin, salt, and pepper. Add the tomatoes, onion, cilantro, and green beans. Cut the kernels off the corn cobs and add to the bowl. Toss to coat well.

Makes 6 servings
Per serving: 193 calories, 6 g protein, 34 g carbohydrates, 6 g fat, 1 g saturated fat, 0 mg cholesterol, 6 g dietary fiber, 222 mg sodium

barley vegetable salad

⅓	cup pearl barley
½	teaspoon salt
2	tablespoons lemon juice
2	tablespoons extra-virgin olive oil
1	tablespoon chopped fresh mint or 1 teaspoon dried, crushed
¼	teaspoon freshly ground black pepper
3	medium tomatoes, seeded and chopped
1	medium cucumber, peeled, halved, seeded, and chopped
1	small sweet white onion, chopped
¼	cup chopped fresh cilantro

Bring 1½ cups water to a boil in a medium saucepan over high heat. Add the barley and ¼ teaspoon of the salt. Reduce the heat to low, cover, and simmer for 35 minutes, or until the barley is tender but firm to the bite. Drain off any remaining liquid. Place the barley in a medium bowl, cover, and refrigerate for 30 minutes, or until cooled.

Meanwhile, in a large serving bowl, whisk together the lemon juice, olive oil, mint, pepper, and the remaining ¼ teaspoon salt. Add the barley, tomatoes, cucumber, onion, and cilantro; toss to coat well. Let stand for at least 15 minutes to allow the flavors to blend.

Makes 4 servings
Per serving: 160 calories, 3 g protein, 23 g carbohydrates, 7 g fat, 1 g saturated fat, 0 mg cholesterol, 5 g dietary fiber, 306 mg sodium

plate power

pair with . . .

rosemary roast chicken with pan gravy, page 210, and fluffy garlic mashed potatoes, page 289

or

4 ounces of grilled tuna drizzled with lemon and ½ of a whole wheat pita

mediterranean chickpea salad (quick)

1	can (15 ounces) chickpeas, rinsed and drained
3	plum tomatoes, chopped
2	roasted red peppers, chopped
½	small red onion, quartered and thinly sliced
½	cucumber, peeled, halved, seeded, and chopped
2	tablespoons chopped parsley
2	cloves garlic, chopped
3	tablespoons lemon juice
1	tablespoon extra-virgin olive oil
¼	teaspoon salt

In a large bowl, combine the chickpeas, tomatoes, peppers, onion, cucumber, parsley, garlic, lemon juice, olive oil, and salt. Toss to coat well. Let stand for at least 15 minutes to allow the flavors to blend.

Makes 8 servings
Per serving: 104 calories, 4 g protein, 18 g carbohydrates, 3 g fat, 0 g saturated fat, 0 mg cholesterol, 4 g dietary fiber, 158 mg sodium

plate power

pair with . . .

lamb kebabs,
page 188, *and ½ cup of whole wheat couscous*

or

herbed chicken sandwiches,
page 152

fruited turkey salad

½	cup (4 ounces) fat-free sour cream
¼	cup low-fat mayonnaise
2	teaspoons chopped fresh thyme or 1 teaspoon dried, crushed
2	teaspoons lemon juice
½	teaspoon grated lemon peel
1	pound cooked skinless turkey breasts, cut into ½" cubes
2	ribs celery, chopped
1	apple, cut into ½" cubes
⅓	cup dried apricots, sliced
¼	cup toasted coarsely chopped walnuts

In a large bowl, combine the sour cream, mayonnaise, thyme, lemon juice, and lemon peel. Add the turkey, celery, apple, and apricots. Toss gently to coat. Sprinkle with the walnuts.

Makes 4 servings
Per serving: 322 calories, 38 g protein, 19 g carbohydrates, 10 g fat, 1 g saturated fat, 94 mg cholesterol, 2 g dietary fiber, 201 mg sodium

plate power

pair with . . .

cold tomato and cucumber soup, *page 86, and a slice of whole wheat bread*

or

toasted English muffin and ½ cup sliced strawberries

thai rice
and turkey salad

1	cup brown basmati rice
½	cup water
½	cup chicken broth
1	tablespoon grated fresh ginger
2	cloves garlic, minced
12	ounces boneless, skinless turkey breast, cut crosswise into strips
3	tablespoons smooth natural peanut butter
3	tablespoons lime juice
1	teaspoon honey
¼	teaspoon salt
2	cups shredded napa cabbage
1	large red bell pepper, finely chopped
1	small red onion, finely chopped
3	tablespoons coarsely chopped fresh mint
3	cups small tender spinach or kale leaves
2	tablespoons coarsely chopped roasted unsalted peanuts

Prepare the rice according to package directions. Spread the rice in a shallow baking pan and place it in the freezer for 10 minutes to chill slightly.

Meanwhile, place the water, broth, ginger, and garlic in a medium skillet. Bring to a boil over high heat. Reduce the heat to low, cover, and simmer for 5 minutes. Add the turkey, cover, and cook, stirring frequently, for 4 minutes, or until the turkey is no longer pink. Using a slotted spoon, remove the turkey to a plate; cover loosely with waxed paper to keep it moist.

Increase the heat to high and return the broth to a boil. Boil for 6 minutes, or until the broth is thickened and reduced to about ¼ cup.

In a large bowl, whisk together the peanut butter, lime juice, honey, and salt. Whisk in the reduced broth and continue whisking until smooth (add a few drops of hot water if the mixture becomes too thick). Add the rice, turkey and any accumulated juices, cabbage, pepper, onion, and mint. Toss to coat well.

Arrange the spinach or kale on a platter. Mound the salad in the center and sprinkle with the peanuts.

Makes 4 servings
Per serving: 408 calories, 30 g protein, 49 g carbohydrates, 9 g fat, 2 g saturated fat, 53 mg cholesterol, 7 g dietary fiber, 295 mg sodium

good-for-you salad dressing

Rich, creamy, and loaded with calories is how we often think of salad dressings. No more. These tasty dressings have just enough good oil to make them healthy, and plenty of great flavor to make them delicious. Each has less than 20 calories and 2 grams of fat per tablespoon. Always shake the dressings well before using.

Tomato Vinaigrette. In a small jar, combine ½ cup low-sodium tomato-vegetable juice; ¼ cup white balsamic vinegar; 2 tablespoons extra-virgin olive oil; 2 tablespoons chopped fresh herbs, such as basil, oregano, cilantro, or thyme; 1 small clove garlic, minced; and ⅛ teaspoon black pepper.

Orange Vinaigrette. In a small jar, combine ⅔ cup orange juice; 3 tablespoons white balsamic vinegar; 2 tablespoons extra-virgin olive oil; 2 tablespoons chopped fresh herbs, such as tarragon, basil, cilantro, or thyme; 1 small shallot, minced; 1 teaspoon sugar; ⅛ teaspoon salt; and ⅛ teaspoon black pepper.

Mustard Vinaigrette. In a small jar, combine ⅓ cup lemon juice; 3 tablespoons water; 2 tablespoons extra-virgin olive oil; 1 tablespoon Dijon mustard; 2 tablespoons chopped fresh herbs, such as tarragon, basil, cilantro, or thyme; 1 tablespoon minced chives; 1 teaspoon sugar; and ⅛ teaspoon black pepper.

moroccan carrot salad with toasted cumin

¾	teaspoon ground cumin
¼	teaspoon ground coriander
½	cup (4 ounces) reduced-fat sour cream
4	teaspoons lemon juice
1	tablespoon extra-virgin olive oil
¼	teaspoon freshly grated orange peel
¼	teaspoon salt
7	medium carrots, shredded
½	cup currants
2	tablespoons chopped red onion

In a small skillet over medium heat, cook the cumin and coriander, stirring often, for 2 minutes, or until fragrant and slightly darker in color. Place in a medium bowl and let cool. Stir in the sour cream, lemon juice, olive oil, orange peel, and salt.

Add the carrots, currants, and onion and toss to coat well. Let stand for 15 minutes to allow the flavors to blend.

Makes 4 servings
Per serving: 185 calories, 3 g protein, 29 g carbohydrates, 7 g fat, 3 g saturated fat, 12 mg cholesterol, 5 g dietary fiber, 201 mg sodium

plate power

pair with . . .

fish stew with couscous, page 233

or

jerk chicken with mango, page 206 and ½ cup of cooked brown rice

potato salad with warm onion dressing

2	pounds red potatoes, cut into large chunks
1	tablespoon canola oil
1	large red onion, chopped
1	clove garlic, chopped
3	tablespoons cider vinegar
3	tablespoons apple juice
1	tablespoon stone-ground mustard
1/4	cup chopped parsley
1/8	teaspoon salt

Place a steamer basket in a saucepan with 1/2" of water. Place the potatoes in the steamer. Bring to a boil over high heat. Reduce the heat to medium, cover, and cook for 20 minutes, or until tender. Rinse briefly under cold running water and drain. Place in a large serving bowl.

Meanwhile, heat the oil in a medium nonstick skillet over medium heat. Add the onion and garlic and cook, stirring, for 8 minutes, or until the onion is very soft.

Add the vinegar, apple juice, mustard, parsley, and salt. Cook for 2 minutes, or until heated through. Pour over the potatoes. Toss to coat well. Let stand for at least 15 minutes to allow the flavors to blend.

Makes 6 servings
Per serving: 145 calories, 4 g protein, 27 g carbohydrates, 3 g fat, 0 g saturated fat, 0 mg cholesterol, 3 g dietary fiber, 103 mg sodium

plate
power

pair
with . . .

spicy pork strips with garlic greens, page 180, *and 1/2 cup melon of your choice*

or

oven-fried chicken with red pepper-sweet onion relish, page 198, *and 1 ear of fresh corn on the cob*

pair
with . . .

cold beet borscht,
page 87

or

*small bunch of
chilled grapes*

grilled steak and potato salad

Steak and Vegetables

1	pound well-trimmed boneless beef top sirloin or top round steak, about 1" thick
4	cloves garlic, minced
½	teaspoon coarsely ground black pepper
¼	teaspoon salt
1	large red onion, cut into ½"-thick slices, rings separated
1	teaspoon extra-virgin olive oil
1	teaspoon red wine vinegar
8	small red or white new potatoes, scrubbed and halved

Salad

2½	teaspoons red wine vinegar
4	teaspoons extra-virgin olive oil
1½	teaspoons coarse Dijon mustard
1	teaspoon water
1	small clove garlic, minced
¼	teaspoon freshly ground black pepper
⅛	teaspoon salt
1	package (5 ounces) mesclun leaves or baby greens

To make the steak and vegetables: Coat a grill rack or broiler-pan rack with cooking spray. Preheat the grill or broiler.

Rub the steak on both sides with the garlic, pepper, and salt, pressing them into the surface. Place on one side of the prepared rack. On a plate, toss the onion with the oil and vinegar and place on the other side of the rack. Let stand for 5 minutes.

Meanwhile, place a steamer basket in a saucepan with ½" of water. Place the potatoes in the steamer. Bring to a boil over high heat. Reduce the heat to medium, cover, and cook for 7 minutes, or until fork-tender.

Grill or broil the steak and onion for 6 minutes, turning once, or until a thermometer inserted in the center of the steak registers 145°F for medium-rare. Place on a plate. Let stand for 10 minutes, then slice. Grill or broil the onion rings, turning frequently, for 4 minutes longer, or until tender and lightly charred.

To make the salad: In a large bowl, whisk together the vinegar, olive oil, mustard, water, garlic, pepper, and salt until well-blended. Add the greens, potatoes, onion, steak, and any accumulated meat juices; toss to coat well.

Makes 4 servings
Per serving: 273 calories, 30 g protein, 18 g carbohydrates, 9 g fat, 2 g saturated fat, 49 mg cholesterol, 3 g dietary fiber, 326 mg sodium

roasted sweet potato salad

2	tablespoons extra-virgin olive oil
¼	teaspoon salt
¼	teaspoon freshly ground black pepper
2	pounds sweet potatoes, scrubbed and cut into 1" chunks
2	large red bell peppers, cut into 1" pieces
2	tablespoons white balsamic or white wine vinegar
1	pound spinach or arugula, torn into bite-size pieces

Preheat the oven to 425°F.

In a large roasting pan, combine the oil, salt, and black pepper. Add the sweet potatoes and bell peppers and toss to coat well. Roast, stirring occasionally, for 40 minutes, or until the potatoes are tender. Remove from the oven and stir in the vinegar.

Place the spinach or arugula in a large serving bowl. Add the potato mixture and toss to coat well. Serve immediately.

Makes 4 servings
Per serving: 336 calories, 7 g protein, 61 g carbohydrates, 8 g fat, 1 g saturated fat, 0 mg cholesterol, 18 g dietary fiber, 312 mg sodium

plate power

pair with . . .

jerk chicken with mango, page 206

or

turkey-sage cutlets with mushrooms, page 218

balsamic tomato and roasted red pepper salad

1 ½	teaspoons balsamic vinegar
2	teaspoons extra-virgin olive oil
1	small clove garlic, minced
¼	teaspoon salt
⅛	teaspoon freshly ground black pepper
2	large red bell peppers, halved and seeded
2	large tomatoes, cut into ½"-thick slices
⅓	cup julienne-cut fresh basil leaves

Preheat the broiler. Coat a broiler-pan rack with cooking spray.

In a cup, whisk together the vinegar, olive oil, garlic, salt, and pepper; set aside.

Place the bell peppers, skin side up, on the prepared rack. Broil, without turning, for 8 to 12 minutes, or until the skins are blackened and blistered in spots.

Place the peppers in a bowl and cover with a kitchen towel. Let stand for 10 minutes, or until cool enough to handle. Peel the skin from the peppers and discard. Cut the peppers into ½"-wide strips.

Arrange the tomato slices on a platter. Scatter the pepper strips on top and sprinkle with the basil. Drizzle the dressing over the salad. Let stand for at least 15 minutes to allow the flavors to blend.

Makes 4 servings
Per serving: 53 calories, 1 g protein, 8 g carbohydrates, 3 g fat, 0 g saturated fat, 0 mg cholesterol, 2 g dietary fiber, 153 mg sodium

plate power

pair with . . .

greek-style lentil soup, page 99

or

chicken picatta with escarole, page 204, and 2 ounces of cooked penne pasta

plate ͮ
power

pair
with . . .

spiced brown rice
with cashews, page
248

or

make a tropical
wrap sandwich by
folding the salad
into a whole-wheat
tortilla

tropical pork salad

2	tablespoons sliced natural almonds
2	teaspoons ground cumin
1	cup chicken broth
12	ounces pork tenderloin, cut into 1" strips
1	tablespoon cornstarch
1	tablespoon cold water
¼	cup apricot nectar
2	tablespoons chopped fresh cilantro
1	tablespoon lime juice
1	tablespoon honey
¼	teaspoon freshly ground black pepper
⅛	teaspoon crushed red-pepper flakes
2	cups fresh pineapple chunks or juice-packed canned pineapple, drained
½	ripe papaya, peeled, seeded, and cut into chunks
1	ripe mango, peeled, seeded, and cut into chunks
4	cups (about 1 large bunch) torn watercress or spinach

In a medium nonstick skillet over medium-high heat, toast the almonds, tossing frequently, for 4 minutes, or until lightly browned. Place on a plate; set aside.

Reduce the heat to medium. Add the cumin to the skillet and cook, stirring frequently, for 4 minutes, or until the cumin is toasted and fragrant. Place half of the cumin in a large bowl. Pour the broth into the skillet and bring to a boil over high heat.

Add the pork to the skillet. Reduce the heat to medium, cover, and cook, stirring frequently, for 4 minutes, or until the pork is no longer pink. With a slotted spoon, remove the pork to the bowl with the cumin; toss to coat well.

Increase the heat to high and bring the cooking liquid to a boil. Boil for 3 minutes, or until the liquid is reduced to about ¼ cup.

In a cup, combine the cornstarch and water. Stir into the skillet and return to a boil, whisking constantly (the mixture will be extremely thick). Remove from the heat.

Place the thickened liquid in another bowl and whisk in the apricot nectar, cilantro, lime juice, honey, black pepper, and red-pepper flakes; continue whisking until smooth.

Add to the bowl with the pork, along with the pineapple, papaya, and mango. Toss to coat well.

Place the watercress or spinach on a large platter. Top with the pork salad and sprinkle with the toasted almonds.

Makes 4 servings
Per serving: 262 calories, 21 g protein, 33 g carbohydrates, 6 g fat, 1 g saturated fat, 55 mg cholesterol, 4 g dietary fiber, 207 mg sodium

roasted beet salad

4	medium beets (about 1 pound), stems trimmed to 1"
2	tablespoons apricot all-fruit spread
1	tablespoon white balsamic vinegar
1	tablespoon olive oil
2	tablespoons snipped fresh chives or thinly sliced scallion greens
½	teaspoon salt
¼	teaspoon freshly ground black pepper
2	medium navel oranges
4	cups mixed bitter salad greens, such as arugula, watercress, endive, and escarole

Preheat the oven to 400°F. Coat a 9" baking pan with cooking spray.

Place the beets in the prepared baking pan and cover tightly with foil. Roast for 1 hour, or until very tender. Uncover and let the beets stand until cool enough to handle.

Meanwhile, in a large bowl, whisk the all-fruit spread, vinegar, olive oil, chives or scallions, salt, and pepper.

Slip the skins off the beets and discard the skins. Chop the beets. Cut off the peel and white pith from the oranges. Section the oranges into the bowl with the dressing. Add the beets and toss to coat well. Let stand for at least 15 minutes to allow the flavors to blend.

Just before serving, arrange the greens on a serving plate. Top with the beet mixture.

Makes 4 servings
Per serving: 144 calories, 3 g protein, 27 g carbohydrates, 4 g fat, 0 g saturated fat, 0 mg cholesterol, 5 g dietary fiber, 390 mg sodium

plate power

pair with . . .

beef stroganoff, page 165

or

turkey-sage cutlets with mushrooms, page 218, *and rosemary roasted potatoes,* page 280

pasta salad with shrimp and broccoli

8	ounces small pasta shells
1½	cups broccoli florets
1	medium carrot, sliced
1	red bell pepper, sliced
2	tablespoons olive oil, divided
2	cloves garlic, minced
1	scallion, minced
12	ounces shrimp, peeled, deveined, and sliced lengthwise in half
1	large tomato, chopped
½	cup buttermilk
2	tablespoons red wine vinegar
1	tablespoon Dijon mustard
1	teaspoon freshly ground black pepper
½	teaspoon salt

Prepare the pasta according to package directions, adding the broccoli, carrot, and bell pepper during the last 5 minutes of cooking.

Meanwhile, heat 1 tablespoon of the olive oil in a large skillet over medium heat. Add the garlic and scallion and cook for 1 minute. Add the shrimp and cook, stirring frequently, for 3 minutes, or until the shrimp are opaque. Add the tomato and cook for 1 minute. Remove from the heat.

Meanwhile, in a large bowl, combine the buttermilk, vinegar, mustard, black pepper, and salt. Add the shrimp mixture and pasta mixture and toss to coat well.

Makes 4 servings
Per serving: 412 calories, 28 g protein, 53 g carbohydrates, 10 g fat, 2 g saturated fat, 135 mg cholesterol, 5 g dietary fiber, 570 mg sodium

the power of
BROCCOLI
Broccoli is your best bet in green vegetables. In addition to providing maximum nutrition per calorie, broccoli is high in fiber. When you include fiber rich foods on your plate, you feel full while eating less.

When purchasing, look for dark—almost purple—heads. Lightly steam broccoli and serve it tender-crisp to reap the most benefits.

asian noodle salad

1	pound sea scallops or peeled and deveined large shrimp, either halved crosswise
¼	teaspoon ground red pepper
8	ounces whole wheat spaghetti
2	medium carrots, cut into julienne strips
1	teaspoon toasted sesame oil
¼	cup smooth natural peanut butter
2	tablespoons low-sodium soy sauce
2	tablespoons grated fresh ginger
1	clove garlic, minced
2	cucumbers, peeled, halved, seeded, and cut into strips

Preheat the broiler. Coat a baking sheet with cooking spray.

Place the scallops or shrimp on the prepared sheet and coat with the pepper. Let stand for 5 minutes.

Prepare the spaghetti according to package directions, adding the carrots during the last 2 minutes of cooking. Reserve ½ cup of the cooking liquid. Drain the spaghetti and carrots. Rinse briefly under cold running water and toss with the oil.

Meanwhile, broil the scallops or shrimp, turning often, for 4 minutes, or until the scallops or shrimp are opaque.

In a large bowl, combine the peanut butter, soy sauce, ginger, garlic, and 2 to 3 tablespoons of the pasta cooking liquid. Add the scallops or shrimp, spaghetti mixture, and cucumbers. Toss to coat well.

Makes 4 servings
Per serving: 466 calories, 33 g protein, 58 g carbohydrates, 14 g fat, 2 g saturated fat, 36 mg cholesterol, 8 g dietary fiber, 812 mg sodium

smoked turkey salad

2	eggs
2	tablespoons frozen apple juice concentrate
4	teaspoons extra-virgin olive oil
2	teaspoons red wine vinegar
¼	teaspoon salt
¼	teaspoon freshly ground black pepper
	Pinch of ground cinnamon
6	cups loosely packed fresh spinach
2	large nectarines, cut into thin wedges
3	ounces smoked turkey, cut into small pieces
½	small red onion, thinly sliced
⅓	cup sliced natural almonds, toasted

Place the eggs in their shells in a small saucepan and cover with cold water. Bring to a boil over high heat. Boil for 1 minute. Remove from the heat, cover, and let stand for 10 minutes. Drain and run cold water into the pan. Let the eggs cool, then shell and slice.

In a large serving bowl, whisk together the apple juice concentrate, olive oil, vinegar, salt, pepper, and cinnamon. Add the spinach, nectarines, turkey, and onion and toss to coat well. Top with the eggs and almonds.

Makes 4 servings
Per serving: 230 calories, 14 g protein, 15 g carbohydrates, 13 g fat, 2 g saturated fat, 121 mg cholesterol, 7 g dietary fiber, 250 mg sodium

plate power

pair with . . .

2 small breadsticks

or

a slice of toasted garlic bread

plate ↄ power

pair
with . . .

*mediterranean
chickpea salad,*
page 129

or

*cold tomato and
cucumber soup,*
page 86

herbed chicken sandwiches

quick

Lemon-Dill Mayonnaise

½	cup low-fat mayonnaise
1	teaspoon lemon juice
2	teaspoons chopped fresh basil or ½ teaspoon dried, crushed
2	teaspoons chopped fresh dill or ½ teaspoon dried, crushed

Sandwiches

12	thin slices multigrain bread, toasted
½	pound cooked skinless chicken breast, sliced
⅓	English cucumber, thinly sliced
1	large tomato, cut into 8 slices
1	cup mesclun or spring mix salad greens

To make the lemon-dill mayonnaise: In a small bowl, combine the mayonnaise, lemon juice, basil, and dill.

To make the sandwiches: Place 4 of the bread slices on a work surface. Spread 2 teaspoons of the lemon-dill mayonnaise on each slice. Top with layers of chicken and cucumber.

Spread 4 of the remaining bread slices each with 2 teaspoons of the lemon-dill mayonnaise. Place the bread, mayonnaise side up, on the 4 sandwiches. Top with layers of tomato and greens.

Spread the remaining 4 bread slices with the remaining lemon-dill mayonnaise. Place, mayonnaise side down, on top of the sandwiches. Cut in half diagonally and secure with wooden picks.

Makes 4 servings
Per serving: 375 calories, 26 g protein, 44 g carbohydrates, 11 g fat, 2 g saturated fat, 56 mg cholesterol, 5 g dietary fiber, 587 mg sodium

roast beef (quick) and charred vegetable sandwiches

¼	cup buttermilk or fat-free plain yogurt
2	tablespoons low-fat mayonnaise
¼	cup (1 ounce) crumbled blue cheese
2	tablespoons chopped fresh chives or scallion greens
4	plum tomatoes, halved lengthwise
1	small red onion, cut into 4 slices
¾	pound thinly sliced cooked lean roast beef
4	leaves lettuce
4	onion sandwich buns, toasted

In a small bowl, combine the buttermilk or yogurt, mayonnaise, cheese, and chives or scallion greens.

Heat a large nonstick skillet coated with cooking spray over medium-high heat. Add the tomatoes and onion and cook for 3 minutes per side, or until lightly charred.

Layer the roast beef, onion, tomatoes, and lettuce on the bottoms of the buns. Drizzle with the blue cheese dressing. Cover with the bun tops.

Makes 4 servings
Per serving: 428 calories, 35 g protein, 40 g carbohydrates, 14 g fat, 4 g saturated fat, 69 mg cholesterol, 3 g dietary fiber, 544 mg sodium

plate power

pair with . . .

1 medium pear, sliced

or

turnip and carrot soup with parmesan, page 90

grilled tomato and cheese sandwiches

8	slices multigrain bread
8	slices low-fat Jarlsberg or Cheddar cheese
1	large tomato, cut into 8 slices
2	roasted red peppers, halved
12	large fresh basil leaves

Coat both sides of the bread with olive oil–flavored cooking spray. In a large nonstick skillet over medium heat, cook the bread on 1 side for 2 minutes, or until lightly toasted. Do this in batches, if necessary. Remove from the pan.

Arrange 4 of the slices, toasted side up, on a work surface. Top with the cheese, tomato, peppers, and basil. Top with the remaining bread slices, toasted sided down.

Carefully place the sandwiches in the skillet. Cook for 2 minutes per side, or until toasted and the cheese melts.

Makes 4 servings
Per serving: 264 calories, 22 g protein, 33 g carbohydrates, 6 g fat, 2 g saturated fat, 20 mg cholesterol, 6 g dietary fiber, 451 mg sodium

plate power

pair with . . .

curried sweet potato and apple soup, page 89 *(you may want to omit the basil from your sandwich)*

or

spicy oven fries, page 281

plate ∼ power

grilled vegetable melts

quick

Basil Spread

1	cup packed fresh basil leaves
2	tablespoons grated Parmesan cheese
1	tablespoon walnuts, toasted
1	clove garlic
¼	cup (2 ounces) fat-free cream cheese or sour cream

Sandwiches

2	zucchini, cut lengthwise into ¼"-thick slices
2	yellow and/or red bell peppers, quartered
1	red onion, cut crosswise into ¼"-thick slices
¼	teaspoon salt
1½	tablespoons balsamic vinegar
8	slices Italian bread, lightly toasted
4	slices low-fat Jarlsberg cheese

To make the basil spread: In a food processor, combine the basil, Parmesan, walnuts, and garlic. Process to puree. Add the cream cheese or sour cream. Process to mix. Set aside.

To make the sandwiches: Preheat the grill or broiler. Coat a grill rack or broiler-pan rack with cooking spray.

Arrange the zucchini, peppers, and onion in a single layer on the prepared rack. Coat lightly with cooking spray. Sprinkle with the salt. Grill or broil for 10 minutes, turning once, or until lightly browned. Place on a plate and drizzle with the vinegar.

Arrange 4 of the bread slices on the rack. Spread with the basil mixture. Top with layers of zucchini, bell pepper, onion, and cheese. Grill or broil for 1 minute, or until the cheese melts. Top with the remaining bread slices.

Makes 4 servings
Per serving: 311 calories, 20 g protein, 46 g carbohydrates, 6 g fat, 2 g saturated fat, 13 mg cholesterol, 5 g dietary fiber, 705 mg sodium

mediterranean muffuletta

2	tablespoons chopped dry-packed sun-dried tomatoes
1	large eggplant (1 pound), cut lengthwise into ¼"-thick slices
1	large yellow squash, cut lengthwise into ¼"-thick slices
1	red onion, sliced crosswise
2	red bell peppers, cut into strips
2	ounces fat-free cream cheese, at room temperature
2	ounces goat cheese, crumbled
2	tablespoons fat-free sour cream
2	teaspoons chopped fresh thyme
1	tablespoon chopped pistachios (optional)
1	loaf crusty multigrain French bread, halved lengthwise through the side

Coat a grill rack with cooking spray. Preheat the grill.

Place the tomatoes in a small bowl. Cover with boiling water and let soak for 10 minutes, or until soft. Drain and discard the liquid.

Meanwhile, place the eggplant, squash, onion, and peppers on the prepared grill rack and cook for 6 minutes, turning once, or until lightly browned and softened; remove from the grill and set aside.

In another small bowl, combine the cream cheese, goat cheese, sour cream, thyme, pistachios (if using), and tomatoes.

Remove the soft insides from the crust of each half of the bread. Reserve for another use. Spread the tomato mixture over both halves of the bread. Layer the grilled vegetables on the bottom half, then cover with the top half of the bread. Cut into 4 sandwiches.

Makes 4 servings
Per serving: 290 calories, 13 g protein, 47 g carbohydrates, 7 g fat, 4 g saturated fat, 13 mg cholesterol, 8 g dietary fiber, 508 mg sodium

the power of
NUTS
Take nuts off your taboo list! Just a few nuts deliver a jolt of heart-healthy monounsaturated or omega-3 fats, while satisfying your hunger.

But here's a nutty problem: How do you eat "just a few"? Nuts are high in calories and fat, so you need to stay in control. One ounce is the perfect serving (about ¼ cup whole) and can be easily added to many dishes. Here are some suggestions.

- Toss on salads, soups, and stews.
- Use as a topping for casseroles.
- Add finely chopped nuts into bread coating for fish or chicken.
- Add to batter for baked goods such as scones, muffins, and quick breads.
- Sprinkle on cereal, yogurt, or canned fruit.
- Grind and add to sauces to thicken.

niçoise salad pockets

quick

Dressing

½	cup balsamic or cider vinegar
2	tablespoons extra-virgin olive oil
1	teaspoon Dijon mustard
1	teaspoon dried Italian seasoning, crushed
1	clove garlic, minced

Sandwiches

¾	pound red potatoes, cut into ¼"-thick slices
¼	pound small green beans
1	can (6 ounces) water-packed white tuna, drained and flaked
¼	red onion, thinly sliced
2	hard-cooked egg whites, coarsely chopped
¼	cup coarsely chopped niçoise olives
2	cups baby spinach leaves
4	whole wheat pitas, halved crosswise

To make the dressing: In a large bowl, combine the vinegar, olive oil, mustard, Italian seasoning, and garlic.

To make the sandwiches: Place a steamer basket in a saucepan with ½" of water. Place the potatoes and beans in the steamer. Bring to a boil over high heat. Reduce the heat to medium, cover, and cook for 7 minutes, or until tender-crisp. Rinse briefly under cold running water and drain.

To the bowl with the dressing, add the potatoes, beans, tuna, onion, egg whites, olives, and spinach. Toss to coat well.

Spoon the tuna mixture into each pita pocket. Drizzle lightly with any dressing left in the bowl.

Makes 4 servings
Per serving: 406 calories, 21 g protein, 56 g carbohydrates, 12 g fat, 1 g saturated fat, 18 mg cholesterol, 9 g dietary fiber, 633 mg sodium

beef, pork, and lamb

Although meat has gotten a lot of bad press, you don't have to give it up entirely in order to lose weight. Meats are wonderful sources of vitamins, minerals, and protein. They also deliver satisfying tastes and textures, whether you're preparing a burger, grilled steak, or lamb stew. Choosing the leanest cuts and the healthiest cooking methods allows meat to be a perfect part of a healthy weight-loss plan.

In this chapter . . .

plate ᴠ power

pair
with . . .

broccoli soup,
page 116

or

*strawberry and
red onion salad,*
page 121

mile-high burgers

1½	ounces dry-packed sun-dried tomatoes
2	tablespoons low-fat mayonnaise
⅓	cup packed fresh basil leaves
1	clove garlic
1¼	pounds extra-lean ground beef
2	roasted red peppers, cut into thirds
3	slices (3 ounces) low-fat mozzarella cheese, halved
6	large leaves lettuce
6	Italian-style sandwich buns

Coat a grill rack or broiler-pan rack with cooking spray. Preheat the grill or broiler.

Place the sun-dried tomatoes in a medium bowl. Cover with boiling water and soak for 10 minutes, or until very soft. Drain and discard the liquid. In a food processor, combine the tomatoes, mayonnaise, basil, and garlic. Process until smooth.

Combine the beef and tomato mixture in the same bowl. Mix just until blended. Shape into 4 burgers.

Place the burgers on the prepared rack. Cook 4" from the heat for 4 minutes per side, or until a thermometer inserted in the center registers 160°F and the meat is no longer pink. Top each burger with a slice of pepper and cheese. Cook for 30 seconds longer, or until the cheese melts.

Divide the lettuce among the buns. Top each with a burger.

Makes 6 servings
Per serving: 405 calories, 30 g protein, 36 g carbohydrates, 15 g fat, 6 g saturated fat, 43 mg cholesterol, 2 g dietary fiber, 495 mg sodium

beef stroganoff quick

12	ounces medium no-yolk egg noodles
1	teaspoon vegetable oil
¾	pound beef tenderloin or top round, cut into thin strips
¼	teaspoon salt
1	onion, cut into thin wedges
8	ounces shiitake mushrooms, stems removed and caps sliced
1½	tablespoons whole wheat flour
2	cups vegetable or beef broth
1	teaspoon Worcestershire sauce
¼	cup (2 ounces) reduced-fat sour cream
2	tablespoons chopped parsley

Prepare the noodles according to package directions. Drain and place in a serving bowl.

Meanwhile, heat the oil in a large nonstick skillet over medium-high heat. Sprinkle the beef with the salt. Place in the skillet and cook, turning occasionally, for 3 minutes, or until browned. Remove to a plate and keep warm.

Coat the skillet with cooking spray and reduce the heat to medium. Add the onion and cook, stirring occasionally, for 3 minutes. Add the mushrooms and cook, stirring occasionally, for 3 minutes, or until they begin to release liquid. Sprinkle with the flour and cook, stirring constantly, for 1 minute. Add the broth and Worcestershire sauce and cook, stirring, for 3 minutes, or until slightly thickened. Remove from the heat. Stir in the beef, sour cream, and parsley. Serve over the noodles.

Makes 6 servings
Per serving: 427 calories, 23 g protein, 54 g carbohydrates, 14 g fat, 5 g saturated fat, 41 mg cholesterol, 5 g dietary fiber, 406 mg sodium

plate power

pair with . . .

roasted beet salad,
page 147

or

artichoke gratin,
page 303

italian chili

¾	pound lean ground beef
1	tablespoon extra-virgin olive oil
2	large onions, chopped
2	large red bell peppers, chopped
1	large green bell pepper, chopped
5	cloves garlic, minced
2	tablespoons chili powder
1	teaspoon dried Italian herb seasoning, crushed
1	teaspoon salt
¼	cup dry red wine
3	small zucchini, chopped
1	can (14½ ounces) diced tomatoes with mild green chile peppers
1	can (14½ ounces) crushed tomatoes
2	tablespoons tomato paste
1	can (14–19 ounces) cannellini beans, rinsed and drained

In a large saucepot or Dutch oven over high heat, cook the beef, stirring occasionally, for 5 minutes, or until no longer pink. Drain and set aside. Wipe the pot with a paper towel.

Heat the oil in the same pot over medium-high heat. Add the onions, bell peppers, and garlic and cook, stirring frequently, for 5 minutes, or until soft.

Add the chili powder, Italian seasoning, and salt and cook, stirring constantly, for 1 minute. Add the wine and bring to a boil.

Add the zucchini, diced tomatoes (with juice), crushed tomatoes, tomato paste, and beef. Bring to a boil. Reduce the heat to low, cover, and simmer, stirring occasionally, for 30 minutes.

Add the beans and return to a simmer. Cover and cook, stirring occasionally, for 15 minutes, or until the zucchini is tender.

Makes 8 servings
Per serving: 257 calories, 15 g protein, 25 g carbohydrates, 11 g fat, 4 g saturated fat, 32 mg cholesterol, 7 g dietary fiber, 670 mg sodium

the power of
ONIONS
Many recipes begin by cooking onions prior to adding other ingredients in the dish. Not only does this flavor the dish beautifully, but ½ cup adds a scant 22 calories to your meal. Choose red and yellow onions, which have the highest nutrient content; white onions have the least.

plate ∿ power

orange beef and broccoli

¹/₄	cup chicken broth
3	tablespoons dry sherry or chicken broth
¹/₂	cup orange juice
2	tablespoons soy sauce
1	tablespoon grated fresh ginger
2	teaspoons cornstarch
1	teaspoon toasted sesame oil
¹/₂	teaspoon crushed red-pepper flakes
³/₄	pound beef sirloin, trimmed of visible fa, cut into ¹/₄"-thick strips
2	teaspoons vegetable oil
1	large bunch broccoli, cut into florets
1	bunch scallions, cut into ¹/₄"-thick diagonal slices
3	cloves garlic, minced
2	cups cooked basmati rice

In a medium bowl, combine the broth, sherry or broth, orange juice, soy sauce, ginger, cornstarch, sesame oil, and red-pepper flakes. Add the beef, tossing to coat. Let stand for 10 minutes.

Heat 1 teaspoon of the vegetable oil in a large skillet over medium-high heat. Add the beef to the skillet; reserve the marinade. Cook the beef, stirring, for 3 minutes, or until browned. Remove to a plate.

Add the remaining 1 teaspoon vegetable oil to the skillet. Add the broccoli, scallions, and garlic; cook, stirring, for 2 minutes. Add 2 tablespoons water. Cover and cook for 2 minutes, or until the broccoli is tender-crisp. Add the reserved marinade and cook, stirring, for 3 minutes, or until the mixture boils and thickens slightly. Return the beef to the pan and cook, stirring, for 2 minutes, or until heated through. Serve over the rice.

Makes 4 servings
Per serving: 395 calories, 25 g protein, 40 g carbohydrates, 15 g fat, 5 g saturated fat, 56 mg cholesterol, 7 g dietary fiber, 432 mg sodium.

plate ~
power

pair
with . . .

**garlic and red
pepper grits,**
page 256

or

**baked stuffed
potatoes with
spinach and beans,**
page 283

grilled flank steak with chile-tomato salsa

2	tablespoons ground cumin
3	cloves garlic, minced
3	tablespoons lime juice
1	teaspoon coarsely ground black pepper
¾	teaspoon salt
1	beef flank steak or top round steak (1¼ pounds), trimmed of all visible fat
1	large tomato, finely chopped
1	can (4½ ounces) chopped mild green chiles, drained
3	scallions, thinly sliced

Lightly oil a grill rack or broiler-pan rack. Preheat the grill or broiler.

Place the cumin in a small skillet over medium heat and cook, stirring, for 3 minutes, or until fragrant and darker in color. Place in a small bowl and let cool.

Remove 1 teaspoon toasted cumin and place in a medium bowl. To the small bowl, add the garlic, 2 tablespoons of the lime juice, the black pepper, and ½ teaspoon of the salt and mix well. Place the steak on the prepared rack and rub the cumin mixture over both sides of the steak. Let stand at room temperature.

Meanwhile, in the medium bowl with the reserved cumin, combine the tomato, chiles, scallions, the remaining 1 tablespoon lime juice, and the remaining ¼ teaspoon salt. Let stand at room temperature.

Grill or broil the steak for 4 minutes per side, or until a thermometer inserted in the center registers 145°F for medium-rare.

Place the steak on a cutting board and let stand for 5 minutes. Cut the steak into thin slices and serve with the salsa.

Makes 4 servings
Per serving: 269 calories, 33 g protein, 7 g carbohydrates, 11 g fat, 5 g saturated fat, 58 mg cholesterol, 2 g dietary fiber, 605 mg sodium

COOKING TIP
The steak may be rubbed with the spice mixture and refrigerated for up to 1 day ahead.

plate ⌒ power

pair with . . .

baked barley with mushrooms and carrots, *page 266*

or

fluffy garlic mashed potatoes, *page 289, and ½ cup steamed green beans*

pot roast with dried fruit and red wine

1	well-trimmed boneless beef rump roast (2 pounds), tied
¾	teaspoon salt
½	teaspoon freshly ground black pepper
1	cup beef broth
1	cup dry red wine
½	cup orange juice
½	teaspoon ground allspice
2	large red onions, cut into wedges
2	cups pitted prunes
2	cups dried apricot halves

Preheat the oven to 325°F. Rub the roast with the salt and pepper.

In an ovenproof Dutch oven, bring the broth, wine, orange juice, and allspice to a boil over high heat. Place the roast in the pot and return to a boil.

Cover the pot and place in the oven. Bake, turning the roast several times, for 2 hours. Add the onions, prunes, and apricots and cook for 1 hour, or until the roast is very tender. Place on a cutting board, cover, and let stand for 15 minutes.

Remove the strings from the roast and cut into thin slices. Arrange the meat on a platter and spoon the pan juices and fruit over top.

Makes 8 servings
Per serving: 415 calories, 28 g protein, 59 g carbohydrates, 6 g fat, 2 g saturated fat, 66 mg cholesterol, 6 g dietary fiber, 405 mg sodium

chinese barbecued pork chops

⅓	cup tomato sauce
¼	cup hoisin sauce
3	tablespoons rice wine vinegar or white wine vinegar
2	tablespoons dry sherry or chicken broth
3	cloves garlic, minced
1	tablespoon grated fresh ginger
4	boneless center-cut pork chops (4 ounces each), trimmed of all visible fat

Coat a grill rack or broiler-pan rack with cooking spray. Preheat the grill or broiler.

In a small saucepan, combine the tomato sauce, hoisin sauce, vinegar, sherry or broth, garlic, and ginger. Bring to a boil over medium-high heat. Cook, stirring often, for 3 minutes, or until reduced to a syrupy consistency. Set aside.

Meanwhile, grill or broil the chops 4" from the heat for 8 minutes, turning once. Cook, brushing with the reserved sauce and turning occasionally, for 3 minutes longer, or until a thermometer inserted in the center of a chop registers 160°F and the juices run clear.

Makes 4 servings
Per serving: 239 calories, 23 g protein, 10 g carbohydrates, 10 g fat, 3 g saturated fat, 73 mg cholesterol, 1 g dietary fiber, 457 mg sodium

plate power

pair with . . .

asian slaw, page 123, *and ½ cup cooked brown rice*

or

stir-fried asparagus with ginger, sesame, and soy, page 299, *tossed with ½ cup cooked linguine*

plate ~
power

pair
with . . .

*a southwestern
double-corn
muffin,* page 65

or

*a buttermilk
biscuit*

beef and vegetable stew

¾	teaspoon dried thyme, crushed
½	teaspoon dried sage, crushed
½	teaspoon salt
½	teaspoon freshly ground black pepper
1¼	pounds top round steak or sirloin steak, trimmed of all visible fat and cut into 2" cubes
1	tablespoon canola oil
4	cloves garlic, minced
2	tablespoons minced fresh ginger
1¾	cups fat-free beef broth
1	cup water
2	medium tomatoes, chopped, or 1 can (14½ ounces) diced tomatoes, drained
2	large sweet potatoes, peeled and cut into ¾" chunks
8	ounces small cremini or white button mushrooms, quartered
4	small onions, quartered
3	large carrots, cut into 1" pieces
¾	pound spinach, mustard greens, or kale, chopped

In a large bowl, combine the thyme, sage, salt, and pepper. Add the beef and toss to coat well.

Heat the oil in a large saucepot or Dutch oven over high heat. Add half of the beef and cook, stirring, for 4 minutes, or until browned. Place the browned beef in a bowl. Repeat with the remaining beef.

Return all the browned beef to the pot. Add the garlic and ginger and cook, stirring, for 1 minute. Stir in the broth and water and bring to a boil. Reduce the heat to low, cover, and simmer, stirring occasionally, for 1½ hours, or until the beef is tender.

Add the tomatoes, sweet potatoes, mushrooms, onions, and carrots. Bring to a boil over high heat. Reduce the heat to low, cover, and simmer, stirring occasionally, for 40 minutes, or until the vegetables are tender. Add the spinach, mustard greens, or kale, cover, and cook for 2 minutes, or until wilted.

Makes 6 servings
Per serving: 310 calories, 28 g protein, 27 g carbohydrates, 10 g fat, 3 g saturated fat, 57 mg cholesterol, 11 g dietary fiber, 404 mg sodium

plate ⌁ power

pair with . . .

indian-spiced potatoes and spinach, page 286

or

spiced brown rice with cashews, page 248, *and cinnamon carrot coins,* page 304

spiced pork scallops with fruit chutney

1	teaspoon ground cumin
¾	teaspoon ground coriander
¼	teaspoon ground cinnamon
¼	teaspoon salt
¼	teaspoon freshly ground black pepper
4	well-trimmed boneless pork chops (1 pound)
2	tablespoons butter
1	small onion, coarsely chopped
2–3	small tart apples, cored and cut into ¾" chunks
⅓	cup dried apricots, halved
¼	cup pitted prunes, halved
¼	cup water
3	tablespoons frozen apple juice concentrate

In a cup, combine the cumin, coriander, and cinnamon. Reserve ½ teaspoon for the chutney. Stir the salt and pepper into the spice mixture in the cup. Rub over both sides of the chops. Place the chops on a plate, cover, and let stand at room temperature.

Meanwhile, melt 1 tablespoon of the butter in a medium saucepan over medium-high heat. Add the onion and cook, stirring frequently, for 3 minutes, or until soft.

Add the apples, apricots, prunes, water, apple juice concentrate, and the reserved ½ teaspoon spice mixture. Bring to a boil over high heat. Reduce the heat to low, cover, and simmer, stirring occasionally, for 20 minutes, or until the fruit is very tender and the juices have thickened into a glaze. Remove from the heat and cover to keep warm.

Melt the remaining 1 tablespoon butter in a large nonstick skillet over medium-high heat. Add the chops and cook for 6 minutes, turning once, or until a thermometer inserted in the center of a chop registers 160°F and the juices run clear.

Serve the pork with the chutney.

Makes 4 servings
Per serving: 320 calories, 25 g protein, 33 g carbohydrates, 11 g fat, 5 g saturated fat, 90 mg cholesterol, 4 g dietary fiber, 271 mg sodium

simple ways to eat more fruit

Eating enough fruit may often seem like a chore, but it really can be easy, and fun. Try these tips to easily increase your fruit intake—and add new life to old favorites.

- Add orange sections to your favorite Chinese stir-fry.
- Stir diced apple into curry dishes.
- Toss some raisins or chopped prunes into salads.
- Spread natural peanut butter on half a banana for an energy-boosting snack.
- Halve grapes and add to light chicken dishes.

- Layer thinly sliced pears on meat sandwiches—great with honey-mustard.
- Top ice cream with mashed fresh berries tossed with a bit of sugar.
- Top spicy chicken dishes with chopped mango.
- Use fruit juices instead of wine in savory sauces.
- Fold pineapple chunks into chicken or tuna salad.
- Stir chopped berries into cream cheese before spreading on toast or bagels.
- Stir chopped fruit into yogurt.

plate ʎ
power

pair
with . . .

½ cup steamed brown rice or whole wheat linguine

and

1 medium orange or a small bunch of grapes

pork and pepper stir-fry

2	tablespoons apricot all-fruit spread
2	tablespoons soy sauce
½	teaspoon crushed red-pepper flakes
1	pound pork tenderloin, cut into ½" strips
4	teaspoons canola oil
½	cup chicken or vegetable broth
1	tablespoon cornstarch
6	cloves garlic, thinly sliced
1	tablespoon grated fresh ginger
2	large red bell peppers, cut into thin strips
2	large green bell peppers, cut into thin strips
1	large onion, cut into wedges

In a medium bowl, combine the all-fruit spread, 1 tablespoon of the soy sauce, and ¼ teaspoon of the red-pepper flakes. Add the pork and toss to coat well. Cover and marinate for 20 minutes at room temperature.

Heat 2 teaspoons of the oil in a large nonstick skillet over high heat. Add the pork mixture and cook, stirring frequently, for 3 minutes, or until the pork is slightly pink in the center. Place in a bowl and keep warm. Wipe the skillet with a paper towel.

In a cup, whisk together the broth and cornstarch and set aside.

Add the remaining 2 teaspoons oil to the same skillet and place over medium-high heat. Add the garlic, ginger, and the remaining ¼ teaspoon red-pepper flakes and cook, stirring constantly, for 2 minutes, or until the garlic is golden.

Add the bell peppers, onion, and the remaining 1 tablespoon soy sauce and cook, stirring, for 6 minutes, or until tender.

Add the pork and any accumulated juices to the pepper mixture. Stir the cornstarch mixture and add to the skillet. Cook, stirring constantly, for 1 minute, or until thickened.

Makes 4 servings
Per serving: 285 calories, 27 g protein, 25 g carbohydrates, 9 g fat, 2 g saturated fat, 74 mg cholesterol, 4 g dietary fiber, 665 mg sodium

plate ⌢ power

pair with . . .

potato salad with warm onion dressing, page 137, and ½ cup melon chunks of your choice

or

garlic and red pepper grits, page 256

spicy pork strips with garlic greens

Greens

1	tablespoon olive oil
1	large red bell pepper, chopped
6	large cloves garlic, minced
2	packages (10 ounces each) frozen chopped collard greens, thawed, with juices reserved
½	cup water
2	tablespoons cider vinegar
¼	teaspoon salt

Pork

1	pound pork tenderloin, cut into ½" strips
1–2	serrano chile peppers, most seeds removed, finely chopped (wear plastic gloves when handling)
½	teaspoon coarsely ground black pepper
¼	teaspoon salt
1	tablespoon olive oil

To make the greens: Heat the oil in a large nonstick skillet over medium heat. Add the pepper and garlic and cook, stirring often, for 2 minutes, or until lightly browned.

Add the greens and water and bring to a boil. Reduce the heat to low, cover, and simmer, stirring occasionally, adding additional water if needed, for 20 minutes, or until tender. Stir in the vinegar and salt.

Place the greens in a serving dish and keep warm. Wipe the skillet with a paper towel.

To make the pork: While the greens are cooking, in a medium bowl, combine the pork, chile peppers, black pepper, and salt.

Heat the oil in the same skillet over high heat. Add the pork mixture and cook, stirring constantly, for 3 minutes, or until slightly pink in the center.

Spoon the pork strips on top of the greens and serve.

Makes 4 servings
Per serving: 271 calories, 32 g protein, 15 g carbohydrates, 10 g fat, 2 g saturated fat, 67 mg cholesterol, 5 g dietary fiber, 421 mg sodium

mexican pork stew

2	tablespoons olive oil
1	pound pork tenderloin, cut into 1½" cubes
1	large onion, chopped
2	cloves garlic, minced
½	teaspoon ground cumin
¼	teaspoon ground cinnamon
2	cups low-sodium vegetable broth
1	can (15 ounces) diced tomatoes
1	can (4½ ounces) chopped green chiles, drained
¼	teaspoon freshly ground black pepper
1	small butternut squash or pumpkin (2 pounds), peeled, halved, seeded, and cut into ¾" chunks
1	medium zucchini, halved lengthwise and cut into ½"-thick slices
1	large red bell pepper, cut into thin strips
¼	cup whole blanched almonds, ground

Heat the oil in a large saucepot or Dutch oven over high heat. Add the pork, onion, garlic, cumin, and cinnamon. Cook, stirring, for 5 minutes, or until the pork is lightly browned.

Add the broth, tomatoes (with juice), chiles, and black pepper and bring to a boil. Reduce the heat to low, cover, and simmer, stirring occasionally, for 25 minutes.

Stir in the butternut squash or pumpkin, zucchini, and bell pepper. Cover and simmer, stirring occasionally, for 1 hour, or until the pork and squash are tender. Stir in the almonds. Cover and simmer for 5 minutes longer, or until slightly thickened.

Makes 4 servings
Per serving: 244 calories, 24 g protein, 18 g carbohydrates, 10 g fat, 2 g saturated fat, 45 mg cholesterol, 4 g dietary fiber, 594 mg sodium

plate power

pair with . . .

southwestern double-corn muffin, page 65

or

1 whole wheat tortilla

plate ∿ power

pair with . . .

cold beet borscht, page 87

or

sweet and sour red cabbage and apples, page 305

pork tenderloin with vegetables

1	pound small red potatoes, cut into 1"-thick wedges
3	large carrots, cut into 1" chunks
1	tablespoon grated lemon peel
2	teaspoons dried rosemary, crushed, + rosemary sprigs for garnish
1	teaspoon fennel seeds, crushed
¾	teaspoon cracked black pepper
½	teaspoon salt
1	pound pork tenderloin
1	teaspoon +1 tablespoon extra-virgin olive oil
4	medium plum tomatoes, each cut into 4 wedges
1	onion, cut into ½"-thick wedges
⅓	cup chicken broth

Preheat the oven to 450°F. Coat a roasting pan with cooking spray.

Place a steamer basket in a large saucepan with ½" of water. Place the potatoes and carrots in the steamer. Bring to a boil over high heat. Reduce the heat to medium, cover, and cook for 5 minutes, or until the potatoes are just tender. Remove from the heat.

Meanwhile, in a large bowl, combine the lemon peel, dried rosemary, fennel, pepper, and salt. Rub the pork with 2 teaspoons of the herb mixture. Place the pork in the center of the prepared roasting pan and drizzle with 1 teaspoon of the oil.

Add the potatoes, carrots, tomatoes, and onion to the herb mixture remaining in the bowl. Add the remaining 1 tablespoon oil and toss to coat well. Arrange the vegetables around the roast. Drizzle the vegetables with the broth.

Roast for 30 minutes, or until a thermometer inserted in the center reaches 155°F, the juices run clear, and the vegetables are tender and lightly browned on the edges. Place the pork on a cutting board and let stand for 5 minutes.

Slice the pork on the diagonal and place on a platter with the vegetables. Drizzle with the pan juices and garnish with rosemary sprigs.

Makes 4 servings
Per serving: 320 calories, 29 g protein, 31 g carbohydrates, 9 g fat, 2 g saturated fat, 74 mg cholesterol, 6 g dietary fiber, 427 mg sodium

barbecued butterflied leg of lamb

¼	cup extra-virgin olive oil
⅓	cup lemon juice
10	cloves garlic, minced
2	tablespoons chopped fresh rosemary or 2 teaspoons dried, crushed
1	tablespoon grated lemon peel
1¼	teaspoons salt
1¼	teaspoons freshly ground black pepper
1	butterflied, well-trimmed leg of lamb (4 pounds)

In a large shallow baking dish or a large bowl, combine the oil, lemon juice, garlic, rosemary, lemon peel, salt, and pepper.

Add the lamb, and turn to coat well. Cover and refrigerate, turning the lamb several times, overnight or for at least 2 hours.

Preheat a grill. Place the lamb on the grill rack and drizzle with any remaining marinade. Grill, turning 2 or 3 times, for 25 to 35 minutes, or until a thermometer inserted in the thickest part registers 145°F for medium-rare. (Thinner parts will be more well-done.)

Place the lamb on a cutting board and let stand for 10 minutes. Cut into thin slices.

Makes 16 servings
Per serving: 180 calories, 23 g protein, 1 g carbohydrates, 9 g fat, 2 g saturated fat, 73 mg cholesterol, 0 g dietary fiber, 253 mg sodium

plate power

pair with . . .

minestrone verde, page 94, **and** **polenta with fresh tomato sauce,** page 254

or

kasha with onions, page 251, **and** **roasted beet salad,** page 147

plate ᒪ power

pair with . . .

mediterranean chickpea salad, page 129, and ½ cup whole wheat couscous

or

kamut, orange, and fennel salad, page 252

lamb kebabs

2	tablespoons lemon juice
1	tablespoon extra-virgin olive oil
2	tablespoons chopped fresh oregano
1	pound leg of lamb, trimmed of all visible fat and cut into 1" cubes
16	cherry tomatoes
2	yellow bell peppers, each cut into 8 pieces
2	zucchini, each cut into 8 pieces
1	large red onion, cut into 16 chunks
½	teaspoon salt
¼	teaspoon freshly ground black pepper

In a medium bowl, combine the lemon juice, oil, and oregano. Add the lamb and toss to coat well. Cover and refrigerate for at least 2 hours or up to 8 hours.

Coat a grill rack or broiler-pan rack with cooking spray. Preheat the grill or broiler.

Evenly divide the lamb onto 4 metal skewers, leaving ¼" space between the pieces of meat. Discard the marinade.

Evenly divide the tomatoes, bell peppers, zucchini, and onion onto 8 metal skewers, alternating the vegetables. Sprinkle the meat and vegetables with the salt and black pepper.

Cook the skewers 4" from the heat for 8 minutes, turning occasionally, or until the lamb is pink inside and the vegetables are tender.

Makes 4 servings
Per serving: 284 calories, 31 g protein, 15 g carbohydrates, 11 g fat, 3 g saturated fat, 90 mg cholesterol, 3 g dietary fiber, 368 mg sodium

lamb and barley stew

1	tablespoon olive oil
1	pound cubed lamb
1	large onion, chopped
2	cloves garlic, minced
2	cups low-sodium beef broth
3	cups water
1	cup pearl barley
1	teaspoon dried thyme, crushed
1/4	teaspoon salt
1/4	teaspoon freshly ground black pepper
3	large carrots, sliced
6	ounces shiitake mushrooms, sliced
2	medium tomatoes, chopped
1	cup frozen petite peas

Preheat the oven to 350°F.

Heat the oil in a large saucepot or Dutch oven over medium-high heat. Add the lamb and onion and cook, stirring occasionally, for 5 minutes, or until browned. Add the garlic and cook for 1 minute. Add the broth, water, barley, thyme, salt, and pepper. Bring to a boil over high heat. Reduce the heat to low, cover, and simmer for 1 hour.

Add the carrots, mushrooms, and tomatoes and cook, stirring occasionally, for 45 minutes, or until the barley is tender. Add the peas during the last 5 minutes.

Makes 4 servings
Per serving: 471 calories, 34 g protein, 60 g carbohydrates, 11 g fat, 3 g saturated fat, 74 mg cholesterol, 13 g dietary fiber, 329 mg sodium

plate ᔐ power

pair with . . .

small spinach salad with mustard vinaigrette,
page 133

or

cold tomato and cucumber soup,
page 86

minted lamb chops with white beans

3	anchovy fillets, rinsed and patted dry
1	teaspoon extra-virgin olive oil
3	tablespoons chopped fresh mint or 3 teaspoons dried, crushed
½	teaspoon freshly ground black pepper
4	lamb loin chops (about 1¼ pounds), well-trimmed
4	plum tomatoes, coarsely chopped
1	clove garlic, crushed
3	cups rinsed and drained canned cannellini beans
2	tablespoons beef broth
¼	teaspoon salt
	Mint sprigs + additional chopped mint for garnish (optional)

Coat a broiler-pan rack with cooking spray. Preheat the broiler.

On a cutting board, finely chop the anchovies. Sprinkle with the oil, 1 tablespoon of the fresh mint or 1 teaspoon dried, and ¼ teaspoon of the pepper, then mash to a paste with the flat side of a chef's knife or a fork. Place the chops on the prepared rack and rub the anchovy paste over both sides of the chops. Let stand at room temperature

Meanwhile, in a medium nonstick skillet, combine the tomatoes and garlic and cook, stirring frequently, over medium-high heat for 2 minutes, or until the tomatoes begin to give up their juices. Reduce the heat to medium, cover, and cook for 3 minutes, or until the tomatoes are very soft.

Stir in the beans, broth, salt, 2 tablespoons of the remaining fresh mint or 2 teaspoons dried, and the remaining ¼ teaspoon pepper. Bring to a boil over high heat. Reduce the heat to low, cover, and simmer, stirring occasionally, for 10 minutes to blend the flavors.

While the beans are simmering, broil the lamb chops 4" from the heat for 8 minutes per side, or until a thermometer inserted in the center registers 145°F for medium-rare.

To serve, evenly divide the bean mixture among 4 plates and top each with a lamb chop. Garnish with the mint, if using.

Makes 4 servings
Per serving: 476 calories, 47 g protein, 45 g carbohydrates, 13 g fat, 4 g saturated fat, 98 mg cholesterol, 12 g dietary fiber, 667 mg sodium

poultry
and seafood

Poultry, fish, and shellfish are great sources of low-fat protein. Chicken and turkey are inexpensive, versatile, and simple to prepare, making them a favorite for most cooks. Look for quick-cooking cuts including strips for cutlets, stir-frying, and boneless thighs and drumsticks. (Remember to skin the chicken before cooking.)

When prepared properly, fish and shellfish are among the healthiest foods that you can eat, and are available in many types–so experiment! Ask your fishmonger to suggest varieties that would be appropriate for your weight-loss meal plans.

In this chapter . . .

roasted red pepper chicken

4	boneless, skinless chicken breast halves
1	bottle (8 ounces) fat-free Italian dressing
4	large red bell peppers
4	thin slices fresh mozzarella cheese
	Fresh basil leaves, for garnish

Place the chicken in a 13" × 9" baking dish and pierce in several places with a fork. Pour the dressing over the chicken and turn to coat both sides. Cover and refrigerate for 1 hour.

Preheat the broiler.

Cut the tops off the peppers and cut the peppers in half. Remove the cores and seeds. Place the peppers, cut sides down, on a baking sheet. Broil for 10 minutes, or until the skins are charred. Place in a paper bag and allow to cool. When cool enough to handle, remove and discard the skins. Cut the pepper halves into ½" strips.

Change the oven temperature to 350°F.

Cut a pocket into the thick end of each chicken breast half. Stuff each piece with some of the sliced peppers. Place a slice of cheese on top of each piece. Top with the remaining pepper strips, covering the cheese.

Place the chicken in a clean 13" × 9" baking dish and bake for 40 minutes, or until a thermometer inserted in the thickest portion registers 160°F and the juices run clear. Let stand for 5 minutes before serving. Garnish with the basil leaves, if using.

Makes 4 servings
Per serving: 315 calories, 33 g protein, 27 g carbohydrate, 8 g fat, 88 mg cholesterol, 714 mg sodium, 4 g dietary fiber

plate power

pair with . . .

2 ounces cooked fettucine tossed with 1 teaspoon olive oil and a tablespoon of parmesan cheese, and ½ cup of green beans

or

pesto pasta, page 260 and small garden salad with tomato vinaigrette, page 133

one-pot chicken and rice

2	tablespoons olive oil
3	cloves garlic, minced
1	large onion, chopped
1¼	cups brown rice
4	chicken thighs, skin and visible fat removed
1	can (14½ ounces) diced tomatoes, drained
2	cups chicken broth
1	teaspoon dried thyme, crushed
½	teaspoon freshly ground black pepper

Preheat the oven to 325°F.

Heat the oil in an ovenproof Dutch oven over medium heat. Add the garlic and onion and cook, stirring frequently, for 4 minutes, or until softened.

Add the rice and cook, stirring, for 2 minutes, or until it starts to brown. Stir in the chicken, tomatoes, broth, thyme, and pepper. Bring to a boil over high heat.

Cover the pot and place in the oven. Bake for 1 hour and 15 minutes, or until the rice is tender and the liquid is absorbed.

Makes 6 servings
Per serving: 315 calories, 19 g protein, 37 g carbohydrates, 10 g fat, 2 g saturated fat, 64 mg cholesterol, 3 g dietary fiber, 474 mg sodium

chunky chicken chili

2	tablespoons olive oil
4	cloves garlic, minced
2	jalapeño or serrano chile peppers, partially seeded, and minced (wear plastic gloves when handling)
1	large onion, chopped
1	pound fresh tomatillos, husked, rinsed, and coarsely chopped
2	teaspoons ground cumin
1/2	teaspoon salt
1/4	teaspoon freshly ground black pepper
1 1/2	cups chicken broth
1	pound boneless, skinless chicken breasts, cut into 3/4" cubes
2	cups frozen cut leaf spinach (from a bag)
1	can (15 1/2 ounces) whole hominy, drained and rinsed
1/2	cup chopped fresh cilantro

Heat the oil in a large saucepot or Dutch oven over medium heat. Add the garlic, chile peppers, and onion and cook, stirring frequently, for 8 minutes, or until soft.

Stir in the tomatillos, cumin, salt, and pepper. Reduce the heat to low, cover, and cook, stirring frequently, for 5 minutes, or until the tomatillos are softened.

Stir in the broth, chicken, spinach, and hominy. Bring to a boil over high heat. Reduce the heat to low and cook, stirring occasionally, for 5 minutes, or until the chicken is no longer pink.

Stir in the cilantro.

Makes 6 servings
Per serving: 237 calories, 22 g protein, 20 g carbohydrates, 7 g fat, 1 g saturated fat, 44 mg cholesterol, 6 g dietary fiber, 662 mg sodium

plate power

pair with . . .

southwestern double-corn muffin, *page 65*

or

cilantro and tomato rice, *page 249*

COOKING TIP
Tomatillos are Mexican green tomatoes. Smaller than their red tomato cousins, they are often sold with a papery husk. Remove and discard the husk before using.

plate power

pair with . . .

roasted sweet potato salad, page 141

or

vegetarian baked beans, an ear of corn, and a slice of melon

oven-fried chicken with red pepper– sweet onion relish

Chicken

⅔	cup buttermilk or fat-free plain yogurt
2	tablespoons lime juice
½	teaspoon salt
½	teaspoon freshly ground black pepper
1¼	cups yellow cornmeal
6	split chicken breasts, skin and visible fat removed

Relish

1	large red bell pepper, finely chopped
1	small red onion, finely chopped
½	cup chopped fresh cilantro
2	tablespoons lime juice
1	tablespoon extra-virgin olive oil
⅛	teaspoon salt

To make the chicken: Preheat the oven to 425°F. Coat a large baking sheet with sides with cooking spray.

In a large bowl, combine the buttermilk or yogurt, lime juice, salt, and pepper. Place the cornmeal in a pie plate.

Dip the chicken in the buttermilk mixture, turning to coat well. (The chicken may be marinated in the buttermilk mixture in the refrigerator for up to 1 day.)

One at a time, roll the chicken pieces in the cornmeal, pressing to coat thoroughly. Place the chicken, skinned side up, on the prepared baking sheet. Discard any remaining buttermilk mixture and cornmeal.

Coat the chicken well with cooking spray. Bake for 40 minutes, or until a thermometer inserted in the thickest portion registers 170°F and the juices run clear.

To make the relish: Meanwhile, in a medium bowl, combine the bell pepper, onion, cilantro, lime juice, oil, and salt. Cover and let stand at room temperature.

Serve the chicken with the relish.

Makes 6 servings
Per serving: 204 calories, 17 g protein, 25 g carbohydrates, 4 g fat, 1 g saturated fat, 35 mg cholesterol, 3 g dietary fiber, 334 mg sodium

plate & power

pair with . . .

barley risotto,
page 267

or

slice of sourdough bread

california chicken

1	tablespoon whole grain mustard
1	egg white
1	cup fresh whole wheat bread crumbs
⅓	cup (1½ ounces) freshly grated Parmesan cheese
1	teaspoon grated lemon peel
4	boneless, skinless chicken breast halves, pounded to ½" thickness
¼	cup chopped fresh basil
1	tablespoon balsamic vinegar
2	teaspoons extra-virgin olive oil
⅛	teaspoon salt
2	bunches watercress or arugula
3	large plum tomatoes, chopped
½	small red onion, finely chopped

Coat a broiler-pan rack with cooking spray. Preheat the broiler.

In a shallow bowl, combine the mustard and egg white. In another shallow bowl, combine the bread crumbs, cheese, and lemon peel. Dip the chicken into the mustard mixture, turning to coat, and then into the bread-crumb mixture, pressing to coat thoroughly with crumbs. Place the chicken on the prepared rack.

Broil 6" from the heat for 10 minutes, turning once, or until golden brown and a thermometer inserted in the thickest portion registers 160°F and the juices run clear. If the chicken browns too quickly, turn off the broiler and bake the chicken in a 350°F oven for 15 minutes, or until golden brown and a thermometer inserted in the thickest portion registers 160°F and the juices run clear.

Meanwhile, in a medium bowl, whisk together the basil, vinegar, oil, and salt. Add the watercress or arugula, tomatoes, and onion, and toss to coat well. Evenly divide the salad among 4 plates. Top each with a chicken breast.

Makes 4 servings
Per serving: 264 calories, 34 g protein, 15 g carbohydrates, 8 g fat, 3 g saturated fat, 72 mg cholesterol, 3 g dietary fiber, 483 mg sodium

plate  power

pair
with . . .

*kamut, orange,
and fennel salad,*
page 252

or

*baked barley with
mushrooms and
carrots,* page 266

baked chicken
with prunes

4	boneless, skinless chicken breast halves
1/4	cup red wine
16	pitted prunes
1	teaspoon finely chopped fresh rosemary
1/4	teaspoon salt
1/8	teaspoon freshly ground black pepper

Preheat the oven to 350°F. Coat a 13" × 9" baking dish with cooking spray.

Place the chicken in the prepared baking dish.

In a small microwaveable measuring cup, combine the wine and prunes. Microwave on high power for 1 minute, or until the wine boils. Pour over the chicken. Sprinkle with the rosemary, salt, and pepper.

Bake for 30 minutes, or until a thermometer inserted in the thickest portion registers 160°F and the juices run clear.

Makes 4 servings
Per serving: 228 calories, 25 g protein, 21 g carbohydrates, 4 g fat, 1 g saturated fat, 79 mg cholesterol, 2 g dietary fiber, 236 mg sodium

chicken breasts arrabbiata

1	tablespoon extra-virgin olive oil
1	large red bell pepper, chopped
1	large onion, chopped
¼	cup seeded, rinsed, and chopped pepperoncini
3	cloves garlic, crushed
1	teaspoon dried basil, crushed
½	teaspoon freshly ground black pepper
¼	teaspoon salt
3	cups coarsely chopped plum tomatoes
¼	cup chicken broth
1	tablespoon balsamic vinegar
1	tablespoon tomato paste
4	boneless, skinless chicken breast halves

Heat the oil in a large skillet over medium-high heat. Add the bell pepper, onion, pepperoncini, garlic, basil, black pepper, and salt; cook, stirring, for 4 minutes, or until the vegetables are tender. Add the tomatoes, broth, vinegar, and tomato paste. Increase the heat to medium-high and cook, stirring, for 3 minutes, or until the tomatoes start to release their juices.

Add the chicken, reduce the heat to medium-low, cover, and simmer for 15 minutes, or until a thermometer inserted in the thickest portion registers 160°F and the juices run clear.

Makes 4 servings
Per serving: 225 calories, 30 g protein, 14 g carbohydrates, 6 g fat, 1 g saturated fat, 66 mg cholesterol, 3 g dietary fiber, 491 mg sodium

plate power

pair with . . .

½ cup pasta of your choice and a small side salad with the tomato vinaigrette on page 133

or

fluffy garlic mashed potatoes, page 289, *and a side of broccoli rabe*

pair
with . . .

quinoa with peperonata, page 268

or

balsamic tomatoes with roasted pepper salad, page 143, *and* ½ *cup garlic-flavored rice*

chicken piccata with escarole (quick)

4	boneless, skinless chicken breast halves
½	teaspoon dried thyme, crushed
¼	teaspoon freshly ground black pepper
¼	teaspoon salt
2	cloves garlic, minced
5	cups loosely packed cut-up escarole
1	cup cherry tomatoes, halved
½	cup fat-free chicken broth
2	teaspoons cornstarch
½	teaspoon grated lemon peel
1	tablespoon lemon juice
1	tablespoon butter

Coat the broiler-pan rack with cooking spray. Preheat the broiler.

Season both sides of the chicken breasts with the thyme, pepper, and ⅛ teaspoon of the salt. Place the chicken on the broiler-pan rack and broil 2" to 3" from the heat for 5 minutes per side, or until a thermometer inserted in the thickest portion registers 160°F and the juices run clear. Place the chicken on a platter and keep warm.

Meanwhile, heat a large skillet coated with cooking spray over medium-high heat. Add the garlic and cook, stirring constantly, for 30 seconds, or until fragrant. Add the escarole and cook, stirring frequently, for 3 minutes, or until the greens begin to wilt. Add the tomatoes and the remaining ⅛ teaspoon salt and cook for 3 minutes, or until the tomatoes are soft and the escarole is completely wilted. Place the vegetables on the platter with the chicken.

In a cup, combine the broth and cornstarch and stir until dissolved. In the same skillet, whisk together the cornstarch mixture, lemon peel, and lemon juice and bring to a boil over high heat, stirring constantly. Cook, stirring, for 1 minute, or until the sauce is slightly thickened. Add the butter and any juices that have collected on the platter and return to a boil, stirring constantly. Cook just until the butter is melted and the sauce has thickened. Pour the sauce over the chicken and vegetables.

Makes 4 servings
Per serving: 151 calories, 21 g protein, 6 g carbohydrates, 4 g fat,
2 g saturated fat, 58 mg cholesterol, 3 g dietary fiber, 257 mg sodium

plate 〜 power

pair with . . .

tabbouleh with fruit, page 247

or

roasted sweet potato salad, page 141

jerk chicken with mango

2	jalapeño chile peppers, halved and seeded (wear plastic gloves when handling)
½	small onion, halved
2	cloves garlic, minced
1	slice (¼" thick) peeled fresh ginger
1	tablespoon olive oil
1	tablespoon white wine vinegar
1½	teaspoons dried thyme, crushed
1	teaspoon ground allspice
¼	teaspoon salt
4	skinless bone-in chicken breast halves
1	mango, peeled and diced
1	tablespoon chopped fresh mint

Preheat the oven to 450°F. Coat a 13" × 9" baking pan with cooking spray.

In a food processor, combine the peppers, onion, garlic, ginger, oil, vinegar, thyme, allspice, and salt. Process until very finely chopped, stopping the machine a few times to scrape down the sides of the container.

Spread the jalapeño mixture on both sides of the chicken breasts. Place them, skinned side up, in the prepared baking pan.

Bake for 30 minutes, or until a thermometer inserted in the thickest portion registers 170°F and the juices run clear.

Place the chicken on plates and scatter the mango on top. Sprinkle with the mint.

Makes 4 servings
Per serving: 199 calories, 26 g protein, 12 g carbohydrates, 5 g fat, 1 g saturated fat, 64 mg cholesterol, 2 g dietary fiber, 220 mg sodium

plate ⌇ power

pair with . . .

potato salad with warm onion dressing, page 137, and 1 ear of corn on the cob

or

baked potato and ½ cup steamed sugar snap peas with fresh mint

baked chicken barbecue

1	medium red bell pepper, cut into thin strips
1	medium green bell pepper, cut into thin strips
1	small onion, halved and sliced
2	cloves garlic, minced
2	tablespoons chicken broth
2	tablespoons water
2	cans (8 ounces each) tomato sauce
¼	cup raisins
3	tablespoons molasses
1	tablespoon cider vinegar
½–1	teaspoon hot-pepper sauce
1	teaspoon mustard powder
½	teaspoon freshly ground black pepper
¼	teaspoon salt
4	whole chicken legs, separated into thighs and drumsticks

Preheat the oven to 425°F. Coat a roasting pan with cooking spray.

In a medium saucepan, combine the bell peppers, onion, garlic, broth, and water. Bring to a boil over high heat. Reduce the heat to medium, cover, and simmer, stirring occasionally, for 5 minutes, or until the vegetables are tender-crisp.

Stir in the tomato sauce, raisins, molasses, vinegar, hot-pepper sauce, mustard powder, black pepper, and salt. Bring to a boil over high heat.

Place the chicken pieces in the prepared roasting pan. Spoon the sauce over the chicken, turning to coat.

Bake, turning the pieces and basting occasionally with the sauce, for 30 minutes, or until a thermometer inserted in the thickest portion registers 170°F and the juices run clear.

Makes 4 servings
Per serving: 380 calories, 44 g protein, 33 g carbohydrates, 8 g fat, 2 g saturated fat, 159 mg cholesterol, 4 g dietary fiber, 761 mg sodium

pair
with . . .

stuffed acorn squash, page 310

or

root vegetable mash, page 291, *and roasted beets with garlic and herbs,* page 292

rosemary roast chicken with pan gravy

1	broiler-fryer chicken (3 pounds)
3	teaspoons dried rosemary, crushed
1	lemon, sliced
¼	teaspoon salt
1	small onion, chopped
4	cups chicken broth
1	tablespoon cornstarch
⅓	cup Madeira wine

Preheat the oven to 450°F. Coat a roasting rack and roasting pan with cooking spray.

Season the cavity of the chicken with 1 teaspoon of the rosemary. Place the lemon inside the cavity. Place the chicken, breast side up, on the prepared rack. Rub 1 teaspoon of the remaining rosemary and the salt over the breast meat under the skin of the chicken. Scatter the onion around the bottom of the pan. Add 2 cups of the broth.

Roast the chicken for 20 minutes, basting with the pan juices occasionally. Reduce the heat to 350°F. Roast, basting every 15 minutes, for 55 minutes longer, or until a thermometer inserted in a breast registers 180°F and the juices run clear. Place the chicken on a cutting board and keep warm. Skim the fat from the pan juices.

In a small bowl, whisk together the cornstarch and ¼ cup of the remaining broth until smooth.

Place the roasting pan on the stove top over medium-high heat. Add the wine. Boil for 3 minutes, stirring to loosen browned bits from the pan, or until reduced to ¼ cup. Add the remaining 1¾ cups broth and bring to a boil. Add the reserved cornstarch mixture and the remaining 1 teaspoon rosemary. Cook, stirring constantly, for 2 minutes, or until slightly thickened.

Carve the chicken, removing and discarding the skin before eating. Serve with the gravy.

Makes 6 servings
Per serving: 166 calories, 25 g protein, 5 g carbohydrates, 4 g fat, 1 g saturated fat, 79 mg cholesterol, 1 g dietary fiber, 566 mg sodium

southwestern chicken sauté

1	tablespoon chili powder
1¼	teaspoons ground cumin
¼	teaspoon salt
⅛	teaspoon ground red pepper
2	teaspoons olive oil
4	boneless, skinless chicken breast halves
½	cup chicken broth
1	tablespoon cider vinegar
2	plum tomatoes, diced
1	cup frozen corn kernels
1	can (4 ounces) mild green chiles, drained
¼	cup chopped fresh cilantro

In a cup, combine the chili powder, cumin, salt, and red pepper. Rub both sides of the chicken breasts with 1 table-spoon of the spice mixture.

Heat the oil in a large nonstick skillet over medium-high heat. Add the chicken and cook, turning once, for 6 minutes, or until the spice coating is browned and the surface of the chicken is opaque. Place the chicken on a plate and keep warm.

Add the broth, vinegar, and the remaining spice mixture to the skillet. Bring to a boil over high heat, stirring to loosen the browned bits from the pan. Boil for 2 minutes, or until the liquid is slightly reduced.

Return the chicken to the skillet, adding any juices that have collected on the plate. Add the tomatoes, corn, and chiles and bring to a boil. Reduce the heat to medium, cover, and simmer for 5 minutes, or until a thermometer inserted in the thickest portion of the chicken registers 160°F and the juices run clear. Sprinkle with the cilantro.

Makes 4 servings
Per serving: 342 calories, 57 g protein, 14 g carbohydrates, 6 g fat, 1 g saturated fat, 137 mg cholesterol, 3 g dietary fiber, 460 mg sodium

simple ways to sneak vegetables into your favorite dishes

Getting the recommended amount of vegetables into your meals can often be a challenge. Here are some surefire ways to help you reach your healthy-plate weight-loss goals.

- Stir shredded carrots and zucchini into your favorite meat loaf.
- Spike your rice, mashed potatoes, or grains with a mixture of garlic, onions, carrots, and celery sautéed in olive oil. Splash with some balsamic vinegar before stirring into the dish.
- Stir thawed and squeezed-dry frozen chopped spinach into meatballs or burgers.

- Add frozen, thawed corn kernels into meat taco filling.
- Stir steamed cauliflower into macaroni and cheese before baking.
- Place carrot and celery sticks on the table with meals and watch them disappear.
- Sauté chopped onion and bell pepper and add to scrambled eggs.
- Cook diced potatoes with cream soups to thicken upon pureeing.
- Stir thawed frozen corn kernels and chopped roasted red peppers into cornbread or muffins.
- Add frozen mixed vegetables to tuna noodle casserole.

plate ⌒ power

pair
with . . .

indian spiced potatoes and spinach, page 286, **with sliced cucumbers**

or

potato salad with warm onion dressing, page 137, **and asian slaw,** page 123

spicy chicken with cool green dipping sauce

1	teaspoon oregano
1	teaspoon ground cumin
¼	teaspoon salt
⅛	teaspoon ground red pepper
8	bone-in chicken drumsticks, skin and visible fat removed
½	cup loosely packed fresh cilantro sprigs
¼	cup loosely packed parsley sprigs
¼	cup blanched slivered almonds
1	clove garlic
1	serrano chile pepper, seeded (or leave half the seeds in for a spicier sauce); wear plastic gloves when handling
⅛	teaspoon salt
2	tablespoons lime juice
2	tablespoons olive oil
2	tablespoons water

Preheat the grill or broiler. Coat a grill rack or broiler-pan rack with cooking spray.

In a cup, combine the oregano, cumin, salt, and red pepper. Cut two ½"-deep slashes in each side of the drumsticks. Rub the spice mixture over the drumsticks, pressing it into the slits. Place the drumsticks in a baking pan and coat completely with cooking spray. Let stand for 10 minutes.

In a food processor, combine the cilantro, parsley, almonds, garlic, chile pepper, and salt. Process until chopped. While the processor is running, add the lime juice and oil through the feed tube, stopping the machine once or twice to scrape down the sides of the container until the sauce is smooth. Pour the sauce into a bowl. Stir in the water, cover, and chill until ready to serve.

Place the drumsticks on the prepared rack and grill or broil 6" from the heat, turning several times, for 25 minutes, or until a thermometer inserted in the thickest portion registers 170°F and the juices run clear.

Serve with the sauce.

Makes 4 servings
Per serving: 268 calories, 29 g protein, 4 g carbohydrates, 15 g fat, 2 g saturated fat, 89 mg cholesterol, 2 g dietary fiber, 346 mg sodium

plate ↄ power

pair with . . .

stuffed acorn squash, page 310

or

root vegetable mash, page 291, *stuffed vidalia onion,* page 294, *and ½ cup brussels sprouts glazed with 1 teaspoon maple syrup*

orange and sage roast turkey breast with pan gravy

1½	tablespoons rubbed sage
1	teaspoon salt
1	teaspoon coarsely ground black pepper
1	bone-in turkey breast (6½–7 pounds)
½	cup orange juice
1	tablespoon extra-virgin olive oil
1	cup + 2 tablespoons water
1¾	cups chicken broth
2	tablespoons cornstarch
2	tablespoons butter, cut into small pieces
1	tablespoon balsamic vinegar
½	teaspoon freshly grated orange peel

Preheat the oven to 350°F. Place a rack in a roasting pan.

In a cup, combine the sage, salt, and pepper. Gently loosen the skin on the turkey breast, working your hand underneath it from the bottom of the breast. Rub some of the herb mixture under the turkey skin. Rub the remainder all over the turkey. Place the turkey breast on the rack in the roasting pan.

In a cup, combine the orange juice and the oil.

Roast the turkey breast, basting with the juice mixture and the pan juices every 15 minutes, for 2 to 2½ hours, or until a thermometer inserted in the thickest part (not touching the bone) registers 170°F.

Remove the turkey from the oven and place on a cutting board. Let stand for 15 minutes.

Add 1 cup of the water to the roasting pan and stir to loosen browned bits from the pan. Strain the pan juices into a measuring cup. Let settle for 10 minutes, then skim off the fat that rises to the surface.

Pour the pan juices and the broth into the roasting pan. Place on the stove top and bring to a boil over high heat. Reduce the heat to medium-low and simmer for 5 minutes.

In a cup, combine the cornstarch with the remaining 2 tablespoons water. Add the mixture to the pan and bring to a boil, stirring constantly, until the sauce is thickened.

Whisk in the butter until melted and smooth. Remove from the heat and stir in the vinegar and orange peel. Pour into a gravy boat. Slice the turkey and serve with the gravy.

Makes 12 servings
Per serving: 188 calories, 33 g protein, 3 g carbohydrates, 4 g fat, 2 g saturated fat, 88 mg cholesterol, 0 g dietary fiber, 364 mg sodium

plate ↄ
power

pair
with . . .

roasted sweet
potato salad,
page 141

or

roasted beet salad,
page 147, **and**
rosemary roasted
potatoes, page 280

turkey-sage cutlets with mushrooms

¼	ounce (⅓ cup) dried porcini mushrooms
1	cup boiling water
1	tablespoon all-purpose flour
1	tablespoon freshly grated Parmesan cheese
¼	teaspoon salt
¼	teaspoon freshly ground black pepper
4	thin-sliced turkey cutlets
4	teaspoons olive oil
12	ounces white button mushrooms, sliced
3	tablespoons dry Marsala wine or 3 tablespoons white grape juice
1	tablespoon chopped fresh sage or 1 teaspoon rubbed

Place the dried mushrooms and boiling water in a bowl and let stand for 15 minutes. Meanwhile, line a small strainer with cheesecloth and place over a small bowl.

Using a slotted spoon, remove the mushrooms from the soaking liquid to a cutting board and chop. Pour the soaking liquid through the strainer. Reserve about ¼ cup of the soaking liquid.

In a shallow bowl, combine the flour, cheese, salt, and pepper. Place the cutlets in the flour mixture, pressing to coat thoroughly.

Heat 2 teaspoons of the oil in a large nonstick skillet over medium-high heat. Add the cutlets and cook for 8 minutes, turning once, or until no longer pink and the juices run clear. Remove to a platter and keep warm.

Add the remaining 2 teaspoons oil to the skillet and heat over medium-high heat. Add the fresh mushrooms and softened dried mushrooms and cook, stirring frequently, for 2 minutes. Add the wine or grape juice and 2 tablespoons of the reserved soaking liquid and cook, stirring frequently, for 3 minutes, or until the mushrooms are tender and the liquid is absorbed. Add a little more soaking liquid if the pan gets too dry.

Pour any juices from the platter over the mushrooms, sprinkle with the sage, and simmer for 30 seconds. Top the cutlets with the sauce and mushrooms.

Makes 4 servings
Per serving: 233 calories, 29 g protein, 7 g carbohydrates, 10 g fat, 2 g saturated fat, 75 mg cholesterol, 1 g dietary fiber, 255 mg sodium

turkey and bean soft tacos

8	corn tortillas (6″ diameter)
8	ounces (2 cups) shredded cooked turkey breast
1	cup drained and rinsed canned kidney or pinto beans
1¼	cups mild or medium-spicy salsa + additional for topping
½	teaspoon ground cumin
1½	cups finely shredded cabbage
1	large carrot, shredded
¼	cup finely chopped sweet white onion
¼	cup reduced-fat cucumber ranch dressing

Preheat the oven to 350°F.

Stack the tortillas and wrap them in foil. Place the tortillas in the oven and heat for 10 minutes.

Meanwhile, heat a large skillet coated with cooking spray over high heat. Add the turkey, beans, 1¼ cups of the salsa, and cumin and bring to a boil. Reduce the heat to low, cover, and simmer, stirring, for 10 minutes, or until heated through.

In a medium bowl, combine the cabbage, carrot, onion, and ranch dressing.

Spoon about ⅓ cup of the turkey filling into a tortilla. Top with ¼ cup of the cabbage mixture and fold over. Repeat with the remaining tortillas, turkey filling, and cabbage mixture. Top with the remaining salsa.

Makes 4 servings
Per serving: 330 calories, 24 g protein, 44 g carbohydrates, 6 g fat, 1 g saturated fat, 47 mg cholesterol, 8 g dietary fiber, 676 mg sodium

teriyaki tuna burgers

1¼	pounds tuna steak, skin and dark edges trimmed
2	tablespoons lite teriyaki marinade and sauce
1	scallion, chopped
2	teaspoons grated fresh ginger
2	cloves garlic, minced
2	slices (2 ounces) low-fat mozzarella cheese, halved
4	sesame seed sandwich buns
4	leaves lettuce
1	can (6 ounces) unsweetened pineapple slices

Coat a grill rack or broiler-pan rack with cooking spray. Pre-heat the grill or broiler.

Finely chop the tuna to the consistency of ground meat. Place in a bowl. Add the teriyaki sauce, scallion, ginger, and garlic. Stir just until blended. Shape into 4 burgers. Coat lightly with cooking spray.

Grill or broil the burgers 6" from the heat for 6 minutes, turning once, or until no longer pink. Remove to a plate and keep warm.

Place ½ slice cheese on the bottom half of each bun. Place, cheese side up, on the rack and grill or broil for 1 minute, or until the cheese melts. Top each with lettuce, a burger, and a slice of pineapple.

Makes 4 servings
Per serving: 354 calories, 42 g protein, 29 g carbohydrates, 6 g fat, 2 g saturated fat, 71 mg cholesterol, 2 g dietary fiber, 570 mg sodium

plate power

pair with . . .

asian slaw, page 123

or

broccoli soup, page 116

penne with salmon and roasted vegetables

12	ounces penne
2	pounds leeks
1	red bell pepper, cut into strips
¼	cup chicken broth
2	tablespoons lemon juice
1	tablespoon olive oil
2	teaspoons dried thyme, crushed
¼	teaspoon freshly ground black pepper
1	yellow summer squash, halved and cut into ¼" slices
¼	cup pitted kalamata olives
1	salmon fillet (½ pound), skinned

Preheat the oven to 400°F. Prepare the pasta according to package directions.

Meanwhile, cut the leeks into 2" lengths and quarter them lengthwise. Rinse the leeks completely. Place the leeks and bell pepper in a 13" × 9" baking dish. Add the broth, lemon juice, 2 teaspoons of the oil, thyme, and black pepper. Cover with foil and bake for 15 minutes.

Add the squash, olives, and salmon to the baking dish and drizzle with the remaining 1 teaspoon oil. Cover and bake for 30 minutes, or until the salmon is opaque and the vegetables are tender.

Place the penne in a large serving bowl. Break the salmon into bite-size pieces and add to the penne with the vegetables.

Makes 6 servings
Per serving: 402 calories, 18 g protein, 68 g carbohydrates, 7 g fat, 1 g saturated fat, 21 mg cholesterol, 5 g dietary fiber, 121 mg sodium

plate power

pair with . . .

balsamic tomato and roasted pepper salad, page 143

or

curried sweet potato and apple soup, page 89

plate 2 power

pair
with . . .

*stir-fried
asparagus with
ginger, sesame,
and soy,* page 299

or

asian slaw,
page 123, *and an
orange*

salmon over noodles

4	skinned salmon fillets (6 ounces each)
3	tablespoons reduced-sodium soy sauce
2	tablespoons dry sherry
2	tablespoons canola oil
2	large cloves garlic, minced
3	scallions, thinly sliced on the diagonal
3	tablespoons grated fresh ginger
1	teaspoon dark Asian sesame oil
2	tablespoons chopped fresh cilantro
8	ounces buckwheat noodles, cooked

Preheat the oven to 400°F. Tear off four 14" pieces of foil and coat with cooking spray. Place a salmon fillet in the center of each piece.

In a small bowl, combine the soy sauce and sherry. Spoon 1 tablespoon over each fillet. Crimp the foil and seal into packets. Reserve the remaining soy sauce mixture. Place the packets on a baking sheet and bake for 12 minutes, or until the salmon is just opaque in the thickest part.

Meanwhile, heat the canola oil in a small nonstick skillet over medium heat. Add the garlic, scallions, and ginger and cook, stirring, for 2 minutes, or until the scallions have wilted. Add the sesame oil and the remaining soy sauce mixture and bring just to a boil. Stir in the cilantro.

Divide the hot noodles among 4 plates. Open the packets and place the salmon and juices over the noodles. Top with the scallion mixture.

Makes 4 servings
Per serving: 530 calories, 43 g protein, 46 g carbohydrates, 19 g fat, 3 g saturated fat, 94 mg cholesterol, 3 g dietary fiber, 979 mg sodium

pesto salmon

1¼	cups loosely packed fresh basil
1	clove garlic
3	tablespoons chicken broth
1	tablespoon blanched slivered almonds
1	tablespoon lemon juice
2	teaspoons freshly grated Parmesan cheese
2	teaspoons extra-virgin olive oil
¼	teaspoon salt
¼	teaspoon freshly ground black pepper
1	pound skinned salmon fillet, cut into 4 pieces
	Lemon wedges (optional)
	Basil sprigs (optional)

Place the basil, garlic, broth, almonds, lemon juice, cheese, oil, salt, and pepper in a blender. Process until pureed.

Place the salmon on a plate. Spoon 3 tablespoons of the pesto over the salmon and turn to coat both sides. Cover with plastic wrap and let stand for 15 minutes. Reserve the remaining pesto.

Meanwhile, preheat the broiler. Spray a jelly-roll pan with cooking spray.

Place the salmon in the prepared pan. Spread the pesto remaining on the plate on top of each piece. Broil the salmon 4" to 5" from the heat for 6 to 8 minutes, or just until opaque.

Place the salmon pieces on 4 plates and top each piece with some of the reserved pesto. Garnish with lemon wedges and basil sprigs, if using.

Makes 4 servings
Per serving: 203 calories, 24 g protein, 2 g carbohydrates, 11 g fat, 2 g saturated fat, 63 mg cholesterol, 1 g dietary fiber, 242 mg sodium

plate power

pair with . . .

wheat berry salad,
page 263

or

kamut, orange, and fennel salad,
page 252, *and stewed vegetables,*
page 302

orange roughy vera cruz

(quick)

4	orange roughy or red snapper fillets (5 ounces each)
1	tablespoon lime juice
1	teaspoon dried oregano, crushed
1	tablespoon olive oil
1	onion, chopped
1	clove garlic, minced
1	can (15 ounces) Mexican-style diced tomatoes
12	pimiento-stuffed olives, coarsely chopped
2	tablespoons chopped parsley

Preheat the oven to 350°F. Coat a 9" × 9" baking dish with cooking spray. Place the fillets in the baking dish. Sprinkle with the lime juice and oregano.

Heat the oil in a medium skillet over medium heat. Add the onion and garlic and cook, stirring occasionally, for 5 minutes, or until soft. Add the tomatoes (with juice), the olives, and the parsley. Cook, stirring occasionally, for 5 minutes, or until thickened. Spoon over the fillets. Cover tightly with foil.

Bake for 15 minutes, or until the fish flakes easily.

Makes 4 servings
Per serving: 185 calories, 22 g protein, 11 g carbohydrates, 6 g fat, 1 g saturated fat, 28 mg cholesterol, 2 g dietary fiber, 510 mg sodium

plate power

pair with . . .

garden bounty salad, *page 126,* **and** *cilantro and tomato rice, page 249*

or

botana, page 257, ½ *cup steamed broccoli, and* 1 *baked sweet potato mashed with a chipotle chili and* 1 *tablespoon adobo sauce.*

plate ↲ power

pair with . . .

strawberry and red onion salad, page 121, and orzo pasta

or

barley with spring greens, page 265, and the sauce described below

COOKING TIP
In a food processor, combine 1 can (14½ ounces) stewed tomatoes, 1 tablespoon chopped fresh oregano, and 1 tablespoon balsamic vinegar. Process until the mixture is chunky. Warm before serving.

pan-seared (quick) red snapper with olive crust

1⅓	cups fresh bread crumbs
¼	cup chopped fresh oregano, basil, or thyme
16	pitted and finely chopped kalamata olives
2	tablespoons freshly grated Parmesan cheese
½	teaspoon freshly ground black pepper
4	red snapper fillets (5 ounces each)

In a shallow bowl, combine the bread crumbs; oregano, basil, or thyme; olives; cheese; and pepper. Firmly press the fillets into the mixture to coat evenly on both sides. Coat the top of the fillets with cooking spray.

Heat a large cast-iron skillet coated with cooking spray over medium-high heat. Add the fillets and cook, turning once, for 6 minutes, or until the fish flakes easily.

Makes 4 servings
Per serving: 204 calories, 31 g protein, 6 g carbohydrates, 6 g fat, 1 g saturated fat, 54 mg cholesterol, 1 g dietary fiber, 295 mg sodium

cod steaks *quick* sicilian style

1	tablespoon extra-virgin olive oil
1	medium onion, halved and thinly sliced
1	cup thinly sliced fennel
2	cloves garlic, minced
½	teaspoon dried thyme, crushed
¼	teaspoon salt
¼	teaspoon freshly ground black pepper
1	tablespoon balsamic vinegar
1	can (16 ounces) crushed tomatoes
½	cup orange juice
4	cod steaks (1¼ pounds)

Preheat the oven to 425°F.

Heat the oil in a large nonstick skillet over medium-high heat. Add the onion, fennel, garlic, thyme, salt, and pepper and cook, stirring frequently, for 4 minutes, or until the vegetables are tender-crisp. Add the vinegar and cook for 30 seconds.

Stir in the tomatoes and orange juice and bring to a boil. Reduce the heat to medium-low and simmer for 5 minutes, or until the sauce is slightly thickened.

Place the cod steaks in a 9" × 9" baking dish. Spoon the sauce over the fish. Bake for 12 minutes, or until the fish flakes easily.

Makes 4 servings
Per serving: 221 calories, 28 g protein, 15 g carbohydrates, 6 g fat, 1 g saturated fat, 61 mg cholesterol, 3 g dietary fiber, 592 mg sodium

plate power

pair with . . .

pesto pasta, page 260, *and small garden salad with tomato vinaigrette,* page 133

or

baked stuffed potato with spinach and beans, page 283

pair with . . .

roasted carrots and parsnips, page 293, *and millet pilaf,* page 250,

or

cauliflower with red pepper and garlic, page 307, *and a plain baked sweet potato*

blackened snapper

1	teaspoon paprika
½	teaspoon dried oregano, crushed
¼	teaspoon garlic powder
¼	teaspoon onion powder
¼	teaspoon salt
¼	teaspoon ground black pepper
⅛	teaspoon ground red pepper
4	red snapper fillets (5 ounces each)
2	teaspoons olive oil

In a small bowl, combine the paprika, oregano, garlic powder, onion powder, salt, black pepper, and red pepper.

Coat a large cast-iron skillet with cooking spray and heat over high heat. Brush both sides of the snapper with the oil and rub with the spice mixture. Place in the skillet and cook, turning once, for 6 minutes, or until the fish flakes easily.

Makes 4 servings
Per serving: 175 calories, 30 g protein, 1 g carbohydrates, 6 g fat, 1 g saturated fat, 53 mg cholesterol, 0 g dietary fiber, 266 mg sodium

the power of

FISH
Adding more fish to our meals is an easier task these days since most supermarkets now offer a selection of fine fresh fish. Try to eat fish at least twice a week. The protein in fish is lower in fat than most meat dishes, and the fat it contains is the healthy omega-3 variety. Try fresh or canned salmon (not smoked), mackerel, rainbow trout, tuna, whitefish (fresh, not smoked), sardines, and pickled Atlantic herring. Also choose canned white (albacore) tuna packed in water.

COOKING TIP
Almost any firm, white-fleshed fish can be used in the blackened snapper recipe (opposite). Try grouper, sea bass, redfish (red drum), or pompano in place of the snapper.

fish stew (quick) with couscous

2	cloves garlic, minced
1	onion, halved and thinly sliced
1	teaspoon ground cumin
¼	teaspoon ground cinnamon
1	can (15 ounces) chopped tomatoes
1	can (14–19 ounces) chickpeas, rinsed and drained
1	cup chicken broth
⅓	cup pitted prunes, chopped
¼	cup pitted halved kalamata olives
4	orange roughy or halibut fillets (4 ounces each)
1	box (10 ounces) couscous

Coat a large nonstick skillet with cooking spray. Add the garlic, onion, cumin, and cinnamon. Coat lightly with cooking spray and place over medium heat. Cook, stirring, for 8 minutes, or until soft.

Add the tomatoes, chickpeas, broth, prunes, and olives. Cook, stirring occasionally, for 5 minutes. Push the mixture to the edges of the skillet. Add the fish. Spoon the chickpea mixture over the fish. Cover, reduce the heat to low, and cook for 10 minutes, or until the fish flakes easily.

Meanwhile, cook the couscous according to package directions. Fluff with a fork. Evenly divide among 4 plates and top with the fish and chickpea mixture.

Makes 6 servings
Per serving: 371 calories, 22 g protein, 62 g carbohydrates, 4 g fat, 1 g saturated fat, 16 mg cholesterol, 7 g dietary fiber, 485 mg sodium

plate power

pair with . . .

roasted beet salad, page 147

or

morrocan carrot salad with toasted cumin, page 135

grilled swordfish with blueberry salsa

1	cup blueberries, chopped
1	cup chopped watermelon
1	small tomato, seeded and chopped
½	small red onion, minced
½	yellow bell pepper, minced
⅓	cup chopped roasted red peppers
1	jalapeño chile pepper, seeded and minced
2	tablespoons chopped fresh basil
2	tablespoons orange juice
2	limes
1	orange
6	scallions, chopped
1	clove garlic, minced
1	tablespoon olive oil
4	swordfish fillets (5 ounces each)

In a bowl, combine the blueberries, watermelon, tomato, onion, peppers, basil, and juice. Cover, refrigerate for at least 2 hours.

Grate 1 teaspoon lime rind and 2 teaspoons orange rind into a 9" × 9" baking dish. Squeeze ¼ cup lime juice and ⅓ cup orange juice into the dish. Add the scallions, garlic, and oil. Add the fish, turning to coat. Cover, marinate in the refrigerator for 1 hour, turning once. Remove 15 minutes before cooking.

Coat a grill rack with cooking spray. Preheat the grill. Remove the fish from the marinade; discard the marinade. Cook, turning once, for 8 minutes, or until the fish flakes easily. Serve with the salsa.

Makes 4 servings
Per serving: 294 calories, 30 g protein, 23 g carbohydrates, 10 g fat, 2 g saturated fat, 55 mg cholesterol, 5 g dietary fiber, 232 mg sodium

five-alarm shrimp

¼	cup cornstarch
½	teaspoon salt
1	pound jumbo shrimp, peeled and deveined
1	tablespoon canola oil
4	scallions, coarsely chopped
2	red or yellow bell peppers, cut into thin strips
2	tablespoons chopped fresh cilantro or parsley
2	cloves garlic, minced
1	serrano chile pepper, seeded and chopped (wear plastic gloves when handling)
1	tablespoon lime juice
3	tablespoons water
¾	teaspoon crushed black peppercorns

In a shallow bowl, combine the cornstarch and salt. Add the shrimp and toss to coat well.

Heat the oil in a large nonstick skillet over medium-high heat. Add the shrimp and cook for 3 minutes, or until just opaque. Add the scallions, bell peppers, cilantro or parsley, garlic, and chile pepper and cook, stirring often, for 1 minute. Add the lime juice, water, and peppercorns. Cook, stirring constantly, for 1 minute, or until the shrimp are opaque.

Makes 4 servings
Per serving: 203 calories, 24 g protein, 14 g carbohydrates, 6 g fat, 1 g saturated fat, 172 mg cholesterol, 2 g dietary fiber, 464 mg sodium

plate power

pair with . . .

cool greens and tomatoes with creamy dill dressing, page 120, *and ½ cup garlic-flavored rice*

or

cauliflower with red pepper and garlic, page 307, *and southwestern quinoa and chickpea salad,* page 272

shrimp with chard and red beans

4	cloves garlic, minced
1½	teaspoons paprika
1	teaspoon dried thyme, crushed
½	teaspoon freshly ground black pepper
¼	teaspoon salt
¼	teaspoon ground red pepper
1	pound large shrimp, peeled and deveined, tails left on
2	tablespoons olive oil
2	ribs celery, thinly sliced
1	large onion, chopped
1	large green bell pepper, chopped
¾	cup chicken broth
3	cups green or red Swiss chard, thinly sliced
1	can (14–19 ounces) red kidney beans

In a medium bowl, combine the garlic, paprika, thyme, black pepper, salt, and red pepper. Remove about half of the mixture to a small bowl. Add the shrimp to the medium bowl and toss to coat well.

Heat 1 tablespoon of the oil in a large saucepot or Dutch oven over medium heat. Add the celery, onion, and bell pepper. Cook, stirring frequently, for 6 minutes, or until tender-crisp.

Add the reserved spice mixture and cook, stirring frequently, for 2 minutes. Add ¼ cup of the broth. Cover and cook, stirring often, for 5 minutes.

Add the chard and cook, stirring frequently, for 2 minutes, or until wilted. Stir in the beans, shrimp, and the remaining ½ cup broth and bring to a boil over high heat. Reduce the heat to low, cover, and simmer for 4 minutes, or until the shrimp are opaque.

Makes 4 servings
Per serving: 306 calories, 31 g protein, 26 g carbohydrates, 9 g fat, 1 g saturated fat, 172 mg cholesterol, 9 g dietary fiber, 733 mg sodium

linguine with clams

12	ounces linguine
1	tablespoon olive oil
2	shallots, chopped
1	clove garlic, minced
1	cup chopped plum tomatoes
1	cup dry white wine or alcohol-free wine
1½	cups chicken broth
¼	cup + 2 tablespoons chopped Italian parsley
3	dozen littleneck clams, scrubbed

Prepare the linguine according to package directions.

Meanwhile, heat the oil in a large saucepot or Dutch oven over medium-high heat. Add the shallots and garlic and cook, stirring often, for 4 minutes, or until soft. Add the tomatoes and cook for 1 minute. Add the wine and bring to a boil. Cook for 2 minutes. Add the broth and parsley. Bring to a boil.

Add the clams, cover, and cook for 5 minutes, or until the clams open. (Discard any unopened clams.)

Remove the clams to a bowl with a slotted spoon. Return the broth mixture to the heat and bring to a boil. Boil for 4 minutes, or until reduced by one-third. Remove 24 of the clams from their shells and mince; discard those shells. Keep the remaining 12 clams in their shells.

Add the minced clams and pasta to the pot. Toss to combine. Add the clams in the shells.

Makes 6 servings
Per serving: 318 calories, 19 g protein, 44 g carbohydrates, 5 g fat, 1 g saturated fat, 30 mg cholesterol, 2 g dietary fiber, 307 mg sodium

plate power

pair with . . .

minestrone verde, page 94

or

grilled portobellos, peppers, and onions, page 296, *and summer squash with walnuts and parmesan,* page 313

plate ⌇ power

pair
with . . .

broccoli soup,
page 116, **and ½ cup**
long grain and
wild rice pilaf

or

artichoke gratin,
page 303, **and a**
slice of french
bread

baked scallops newburg

¼	cup whole wheat bread crumbs
2	teaspoons butter, melted
1	pound bay scallops, rinsed, drained, and patted dry
8	ounces mushrooms, sliced
3	scallions, sliced
2	tablespoons chopped fresh tarragon or 2 teaspoons dried, crushed
2	tablespoons whole wheat or whole grain pastry flour
¼	teaspoon salt
⅛	teaspoon ground red pepper
1½	cups 1% milk
1	egg yolk

Preheat the oven to 400°F. Place 4 small baking dishes (8 ounces each) on a baking sheet. Coat the dishes with cooking spray.

In a small bowl, combine the bread crumbs and butter.

Heat a large skillet coated with cooking spray over medium heat. Add the scallops and cook, stirring, for 3 minutes, or until opaque. Remove to a plate with a slotted spoon and keep warm.

Add the mushrooms and cook, stirring occasionally, for 3 minutes, or until they release liquid. Add the scallions and tarragon and cook for 1 minute, or until the mushrooms are soft. Remove to the plate with the scallops.

Add the flour, salt, and pepper and cook, stirring constantly, for 1 minute. Gradually whisk in the milk until blended.

Cook, stirring often, for 5 minutes, or until thickened. Add the egg yolk and cook, stirring constantly, for 2 minutes, or until the mixture bubbles. Add the scallops and mushroom mixture and stir to coat well. Spoon the mixture into the prepared baking dishes. Sprinkle with the reserved bread crumb mixture.

Bake for 8 minutes, or until golden and bubbly.

Makes 4 servings
Per serving: 226 calories, 25 g protein, 13 g carbohydrates, 9 g fat, 2 g saturated fat, 98 mg cholesterol, 1 g dietary fiber, 707 mg sodium

grains and legumes

Whole grains and beans pack a powerful weight-loss punch. And they're low in fat and sodium. Whole grains are more readily available than ever, and they're inexpensive and easy to use. Experiment with grains ranging from the familiar brown rice to the out-of-the-ordinary quinoa. Fill your shelves with a large selection of canned or dried legumes such as quick-cooking lentils or slower but exciting dried selections like adzuki beans. Try to include these plant foods in your meals daily.

In this chapter . . .

tabbouleh with fruit

1	cup orange juice
½	cup medium-grain bulgur
1	large tomato, seeded and finely chopped
½	small cantaloupe, finely chopped
1	cup finely chopped hulled fresh strawberries
½	pint fresh blueberries
½	pint fresh raspberries
¼	cup chopped flat-leaf parsley
½	small red onion, finely chopped
1	tablespoon chopped fresh mint
2	tablespoons lemon juice
1	tablespoon extra-virgin olive oil
¾	teaspoon ground cumin
½	teaspoon ground cinnamon
¼	teaspoon salt
¼	teaspoon freshly ground black pepper

In a medium bowl, combine the orange juice and bulgur. Let stand for 30 minutes, or until tender and softened.

Drain the bulgur and place in a large bowl. Add the tomato, cantaloupe, strawberries, blueberries, raspberries, parsley, onion, mint, lemon juice, oil, cumin, cinnamon, salt, and pepper and toss to coat well. Let stand for at least 15 minutes to allow the flavors to blend.

Makes 4 servings
Per serving: 193 calories, 4 g protein, 37 g carbohydrates, 5 g fat, 1 g saturated fat, 0 mg cholesterol, 9 g dietary fiber, 162 mg sodium

plate power

pair with . . .

jerk chicken with mango, page 206

or

1 ounce of goat cheese or brie on rye crackers

plate ᴗ power

pair with . . .

curried sweet potato soup, page 89, *and lamb kebabs,* page 188

or

curried cauliflower and carrots with beans, page 308, *and ½ a grilled chicken breast*

spiced brown rice with cashews

½	tablespoon olive oil
1	medium onion, chopped
1	cup brown basmati or long-grain brown rice
3–4	whole cardamom pods or ½ teaspoon ground cardamom
1	stick cinnamon (4"), broken in half, or ¼ teaspoon ground cinnamon
2	cups chicken broth
⅓	cup unsalted cashews, toasted

Heat the oil in a large saucepan over medium heat. Add the onion and cook, stirring frequently, for 4 minutes, or until soft. Add the rice, cardamom, and cinnamon and cook, stirring, for 2 minutes, or until the rice just starts to brown lightly. Add the broth and bring to a boil over high heat. Reduce the heat to low, cover, and simmer for 50 minutes, or until the liquid is absorbed and the rice is very tender. Stir in the cashews. Remove from the heat and let stand for 5 minutes. Remove and discard the cardamom pods and cinnamon stick.

Makes 8 servings
Per serving: 141 calories, 3 g protein, 22 g carbohydrates, 5 g fat, 1 g saturated fat, 1 mg cholesterol, 2 g dietary fiber, 253 mg sodium

cilantro and tomato rice

1	cup short-grain brown rice
2	cups water
½	teaspoon salt
1	pound tomatoes, coarsely chopped
⅓	cup chopped fresh cilantro
1	tablespoon extra-virgin olive oil
1	tablespoon lime juice or lemon juice
1	clove garlic, minced
1	teaspoon ground cumin
¼	teaspoon freshly ground black pepper
1	can (14–19 ounces) chickpeas, rinsed and drained
¼	cup slivered almonds, toasted

Place the rice, water, and ¼ teaspoon of the salt in a medium saucepan. Bring to a boil over high heat. Reduce the heat to low, cover, and simmer for 50 minutes, or until the rice is tender and the liquid is absorbed.

Meanwhile, in a medium bowl, combine the tomatoes, cilantro, oil, lime juice or lemon juice, garlic, cumin, pepper, and the remaining ¼ teaspoon salt. Cover and let stand at room temperature. Stir in the rice and chickpeas and top with the almonds.

Makes 8 servings
Per serving: 199 calories, 6 g protein, 33 g carbohydrates, 5 g fat, 0 g saturated fat, 0 mg cholesterol, 4 g dietary fiber, 303 mg sodium

plate 〵
power

pair
with . . .

garden-bounty salad, page 126, *and orange roughy vera cruz,* page 227

or

southwestern chicken sauté, page 212, *and ½ cup of steamed broccoli*

plate ⟲ power

pair
with . . .

spaghetti squash casserole, page 314

or

blackened snapper, page 230, **with roasted carrots and parsnips**, page 293

millet pilaf

1	cup millet
1½	cups water
1	cup chicken broth
¼	teaspoon salt
½	cup golden raisins
2	tablespoons dry sherry
1	tablespoon extra-virgin olive oil
⅓	cup natural almonds, coarsely chopped
1½	teaspoons chopped fresh rosemary
2	tablespoons chopped flat-leaf parsley

In a medium saucepan over medium-high heat, cook the millet, stirring frequently, for 4 minutes, or until the grains are fragrant, browned in spots, and just beginning to crackle.

Add the water, broth, and salt. Bring to a boil over high heat. Reduce the heat to low, cover, and simmer for 25 minutes, or until the millet is tender, some grains have burst, and the water has evaporated. Remove from the heat and let stand, covered, for 10 minutes.

Meanwhile, in a small bowl, soak the raisins in the sherry.

Heat the oil in a small skillet over medium heat. Add the almonds and cook, stirring frequently, for 4 minutes, or until lightly toasted. Stir in the rosemary and raisins and cook, stirring, for 30 seconds. Remove from the heat.

Fluff the millet with a fork. Stir in the almond mixture and sprinkle with the parsley.

Makes 4 servings
Per serving: 359 calories, 8 g protein, 55 g carbohydrates, 11 g fat, 1 g saturated fat, 0 mg cholesterol, 7 g dietary fiber, 299 mg sodium

kasha with onions

1	egg
1	cup medium-grain kasha
1	tablespoon extra-virgin olive oil
4	scallions, thinly sliced
3	large shallots, thinly sliced
1	large onion, chopped
1	medium leek, white and green parts, halved lengthwise, rinsed, and sliced ¼" thick
2	cloves garlic, minced
1	tablespoon coarsely chopped fresh thyme or 1 teaspoon dried
½	teaspoon salt
¼	teaspoon freshly ground black pepper
2	cups vegetable or chicken broth
¼	cup coarsely chopped pecans or walnuts

In a medium bowl, beat the egg with a fork. Add the kasha and stir until the grains are coated. Heat a large nonstick skillet over medium heat. Add the kasha and cook, stirring frequently, for 4 minutes, or until the grains are dry and separate. Place in a bowl; set aside. Wipe the skillet with a paper towel.

Heat the oil in the same skillet over medium-high heat. Add the scallions, shallots, onion, leek, and garlic. Cook, stirring frequently, for 6 minutes, or until tender. Stir in the thyme, salt, and pepper and remove from the heat.

Stir the kasha and broth into the onion mixture. Bring to a boil over medium-high heat. Reduce the heat to low, cover, and simmer for 15 minutes, or until the liquid is absorbed.

Sprinkle the kasha with the nuts.

Makes 6 servings
Per serving: 182 calories, 7 g protein, 27 g carbohydrates, 7 g fat, 1 g saturated fat, 35 mg cholesterol, 4 g dietary fiber, 437 mg sodium

plate power

pair with . . .

root vegetable soup, *page 91*

or

barbecued butterflied leg of lamb, *page 187,* **and roasted beet salad,** *page 147*

plate ↄ power

pair
with . . .

baked chicken with prunes, page 202

or

lamb kebabs, page 188

kamut, orange, and fennel salad

1	cup whole grain kamut, spelt, or wheat berries
2½	cups water
1	cup chicken or vegetable broth
3	medium navel oranges
2	tablespoons extra-virgin olive oil
1	tablespoon balsamic vinegar
½	teaspoon salt
¼	teaspoon freshly ground black pepper
1	medium bulb fennel, chopped
1	large red bell pepper, chopped
1	small red onion, chopped
¼	cup sliced pitted kalamata olives

Place the kamut, spelt, or wheat berries in a sieve and rinse until the water runs clear. Place in a bowl with 2 cups of the water. Let stand for 8 hours or overnight. Drain.

Place the kamut, spelt, or wheat berries, the remaining ½ cup water, and the broth in a medium saucepan and bring to a boil over high heat. Reduce the heat to low, cover, and simmer for 45 minutes, or until tender and some of the grains have burst.

Drain in a colander and place in a medium bowl. Let stand for 30 minutes, or until cooled.

Cut off the peel and most of the white membrane from 2 of the oranges. Cut each orange in half through the top end and place the half flat on a cutting board. Cut the half lengthwise into ½" slices. Juice the remaining orange. In a small bowl, whisk together the orange juice, oil, vinegar, salt, and black pepper.

Add the fennel, bell pepper, onion, and olives to the kamut, spelt, or wheat berries. Add the orange juice mixture and toss to coat well. Add the oranges and toss gently.

Serve immediately or cover and chill to serve later.

Makes 6 servings
Per serving: 243 calories, 6 g protein, 41 g carbohydrates, 8 g fat, 1 g saturated fat, 11 mg cholesterol, 5 g dietary fiber, 487 mg sodium

pair
with . . .

minestrone verde,
page 94, **and**
barbecued
butterflied leg of
lamb, page 187

or

grilled portobellos,
peppers, and
onions, page 296
and chicken
piccata with
escarole, page 204

polenta with
fresh tomato sauce

6	*cups water*
¾	*teaspoon salt*
2	*cups coarse yellow cornmeal*
½	*cup (2 ounces) freshly grated Parmesan cheese*
1	*tablespoon extra-virgin olive oil*
1	*large clove garlic, minced*
¼	*teaspoon dried oregano, crushed*
¼	*teaspoon fennel seeds, crushed*
8	*plum tomatoes, coarsely chopped*
⅛	*teaspoon freshly ground black pepper*
2	*tablespoons tomato paste*

Preheat the oven to 400°F. Coat a 9" × 9" baking dish with cooking spray.

Bring the water to a boil in a large saucepan over high heat. Stir in ½ teaspoon of the salt. Add the cornmeal in a slow, steady stream, whisking constantly. Bring to a boil. Stir in the cheese.

Remove from the heat and pour into the prepared baking dish. Bake for 35 minutes, or until firm.

Meanwhile, heat the oil in a large nonstick skillet over medium heat. Add the garlic, oregano, and fennel seeds and cook, stirring, for 3 minutes, or until fragrant.

Stir in the tomatoes, the remaining ¼ teaspoon salt, and pepper. Increase the heat to high and bring to a boil. Reduce the heat to medium-low and simmer, stirring frequently, for 8 minutes, or until the tomatoes are cooked down and juicy. Add the tomato paste and cook, stirring, for 2 minutes, or until the sauce is slightly thickened. Cover and keep warm.

Serve the polenta with the sauce.

Makes 8 servings
Per serving: 176 calories, 6 g protein, 28 g carbohydrates, 5 g fat, 2 g saturated fat, 6 mg cholesterol, 3 g dietary fiber, 229 mg sodium

plate ∿ power

pair with . . .

grilled flank steak with chile tomato salsa, page 170

or

spicy pork strips with garlic greens, page 180

garlic and red pepper grits

3¾	cups water
½	teaspoon salt
¾	cup quick-cooking grits
1	tablespoon canola oil
3	cloves garlic, minced
2	large red bell peppers, chopped
½	teaspoon paprika
½	teaspoon dried thyme, crushed
¼	teaspoon freshly ground black pepper
⅓	cup (1½ ounces) shredded Monterey Jack cheese

Bring the water to a boil in a medium saucepan over high heat. Add the salt and slowly stir in the grits. Reduce the heat to medium-low and cook, stirring occasionally, for 20 minutes, or until the grits are creamy and thickened. Remove from the heat.

Meanwhile, heat the oil in a medium nonstick skillet over medium-low heat. Add the garlic and cook, stirring, for 2 minutes, or until fragrant. Add the bell peppers, paprika, thyme, and black pepper and cook, stirring frequently, for 8 minutes, or until very tender. (Add a tablespoon of water to the pan if it gets dry.)

Stir the bell pepper mixture and the cheese into the grits, stirring until the cheese melts.

Makes 4 servings
Per serving: 185 calories, 6 g protein, 27 g carbohydrates, 7 g fat, 2 g saturated fat, 10 mg cholesterol, 3 g dietary fiber, 358 mg sodium

botana

1	tablespoon olive oil
5	cloves garlic, minced
3/4	teaspoon ground cumin
3/4	teaspoon dried oregano, crushed
2	cans (14–19 ounces each) black beans; rinse and drain 1 can, use both beans and liquid from other can
1	can (15 ounces) diced tomatoes with green chiles
1/4–1/2	cup water
1/2	cup (2 ounces) shredded reduced-fat sharp Cheddar cheese
	Baked tortilla chips or warmed corn tortillas
	Red bell pepper wedges, cucumber spears, and celery sticks for dipping

Heat the oil in a large nonstick skillet over medium heat. Add the garlic, cumin, and oregano and cook, stirring frequently, for 2 minutes, or until fragrant.

Stir in the drained beans and the beans with their liquid and bring to a boil. Remove from the heat. Mash the beans with a potato masher to a coarse-textured puree.

Return to medium heat and stir in the tomatoes and 1/4 cup of the water. Bring to a boil, stirring. Reduce the heat to medium-low and cook, stirring frequently, for 5 minutes, or until the beans are heated through and the flavors are blended. Stir in up to 1/4 cup additional water if the mixture is too thick.

Place in a serving bowl and sprinkle with the cheese. Serve with the chips or tortillas and vegetables.

Makes 8 servings
Per serving: 103 calories, 6 g protein, 16 g carbohydrates, 3 g fat, 1 g saturated fat, 5 mg cholesterol, 5 g dietary fiber, 494 mg sodium

plate power

pair with . . .

tamale pie, page 258

or

cilantro-tomato rice, page 249, **and** *orange roughy vera cruz*, page 227, **and 1/2 cup mango slices**

plate ~ power

pair
with . . .

botana, page 257

or

*½ cup corn tossed
with 1 tablespoon
salsa*

tamale pie

3	tablespoon olive oil, divided
2	large red and/or green bell peppers, chopped
4–5	teaspoons chili powder
2	cans (14–19 ounces each) kidney beans, rinsed and drained
1	can (14½ ounces) diced tomatoes with green chiles
1	can (14½ ounces) diced tomatoes, drained
1	cup yellow cornmeal
¾	cup whole grain pastry flour
1	teaspoon baking powder
½	teaspoon baking soda
¼	teaspoon salt
1	cup (8 ounces) fat-free plain yogurt
1	cup (4 ounces) shredded reduced-fat Cheddar cheese
1	egg

Preheat the oven to 375°F. Coat an 11" × 7" baking dish with cooking spray.

Heat 1 tablespoon of the oil in a large nonstick skillet over medium-high heat. Add the bell peppers and cook, stirring frequently, for 7 minutes, or until tender. Stir in the chili powder, beans, tomatoes with chiles, and diced tomatoes. Bring to a boil. Place in the prepared baking dish.

Meanwhile, in a large bowl, combine the cornmeal, flour, baking powder, baking soda, and salt. Add the yogurt, cheese, egg, and the remaining oil and combine just until blended.

Spoon the cornmeal mixture in spoonfuls over the filling, gently spreading it to cover. Place the baking dish on a baking pan to catch any spillover.

Bake for 25 minutes, or until the crust is lightly browned and firm and the filling is bubbly.

Let stand for 10 minutes before serving.

Makes 6 servings
Per serving: 415 calories, 20 g protein, 57 g carbohydrates, 13 g fat, 4 g saturated fat, 14 mg cholesterol, 13 g dietary fiber, 690 mg sodium

plate ~
power

pair
with . . .

*cod steaks sicilian
style, page 229,
and a small garden
salad with tomato
vinaigrette,
page 133*

or

*½ a grilled chicken
breast, and
½ cup summer
squash sautéed
with chopped
garlic and
1 teaspoon olive
oil*

pesto pasta

8	ounces linguine
2½	cups packed fresh basil
¾	cup packed parsley
2	tablespoons olive oil
3	cloves garlic
2	tablespoons toasted pine nuts or walnuts
¼	cup freshly grated Parmesan cheese
¼	cup chicken broth

Prepare the pasta according to package directions.

Meanwhile, in a food processor or blender, combine the basil, parsley, oil, garlic, and nuts. Pulse to finely chop. Sprinkle with the cheese. With the machine running, add the broth, 1 tablespoon at a time, until the mixture is the consistency of prepared mustard.

Toss the pesto with the pasta and serve.

Makes 4 servings
Per serving: 286 calories, 11 g protein, 34 g carbohydrates, 12 g fat, 2 g saturated fat, 5 mg cholesterol, 3 g dietary fiber, 365 mg sodium

8 ways to pump up pasta while you pare down

Pasta has become a favorite fast food in many households, and why not? It's delicious, low in fat, and can often be ready in just 10 minutes. Here are 8 simple ways to healthfully plate your pasta. Be sure to use whole wheat pasta for these dishes.

1. Stir 2 cups broccoli florets into the pasta water during the last 5 minutes of cooking. Drain with the pasta and top with your favorite sauce.

2. Heat your favorite tomato sauce (even if it's out of a jar) to a simmer, remove from the heat, and let cool for 1 minute. Stir in plain yogurt, reduced-fat sour cream, or part-skim ricotta cheese. A calcium-rich substitute for your usual red sauce.

3. Rinse and drain a can of fiber-full beans (chickpeas or cannellini beans work well with Italian dishes) and add to the simmering sauce just before tossing with the pasta.

4. Bathe your pasta in a flavorful, high-iron sauce. Sauté minced garlic in olive oil until fragrant. Add fresh spinach and sauté just until wilted (be sure to use enough; spinach shrinks to about one-quarter of its volume when wilted). Toss with hot cooked pasta and top with freshly grated Romano cheese.

5. Add red bell peppers to your favorite sauce. Or, make a red pepper sauce. Sauté red bell pepper strips and some shallots in olive oil until browned. Add some vegetable broth and simmer until very tender. Puree in the blender and toss over hot pasta.

6. Dice firm or smoked tofu into bits and adding to a vegetable sauce.

7. Toss a light pasta dish with grilled or broiled salmon.

8. Forgo long-cooking brown rice when you're in a rush and top whole wheat spaghetti with stir-fried veggies and fish or chicken.

plate ↄ power

pair with . . .

chopped millet salad, page 124

or

cauliflower with red pepper and garlic, page 307

whole grain caprese pasta

1	pound whole wheat pasta shapes, such as twists
1	cup (8 ounces) fat-free plain yogurt
1	tablespoon + 1 teaspoon extra-virgin olive oil
½	teaspoon salt
1	large clove garlic
1	cup packed fresh basil + additional for garnish
2	large tomatoes, chopped
1	teaspoon balsamic or red wine vinegar
6	ounces reduced-fat mozzarella cheese, cubed

Prepare the pasta according to package directions.

Meanwhile, place the yogurt, oil, salt, and garlic in a blender. Puree until smooth. Add the basil and puree until completely blended.

Place the tomatoes in a small bowl. Toss with the vinegar and add the cheese.

Place the pasta in a large serving bowl. Top with the basil sauce and tomato mixture. Garnish with additional basil.

Makes 8 servings
Per serving: 301 calories, 16 g protein, 48 g carbohydrates, 7 g fat, 3 g saturated fat, 12 mg cholesterol, 5 g fiber, 284 mg sodium

wheat berry salad

1	cup wheat berries or whole grain spelt
3½	cups water
2	cups chicken or vegetable broth
3	cups small broccoli florets
2	tablespoons extra-virgin olive oil
2	cloves garlic, minced
1	tablespoon fresh herb, such as basil, rosemary, or marjoram, or 1 teaspoon dried, crushed
2	cups halved red and yellow cherry tomatoes
1	cup fresh, drained canned, or frozen corn kernels
¼	teaspoon salt
¼	teaspoon freshly ground black pepper

Place the wheat berries or spelt in a sieve and rinse until the water runs clear. Place in a bowl with 2 cups of the water. Let stand for 8 hours or overnight. Drain.

Place the remaining 1½ cups water and broth in a medium saucepan and bring to a boil over high heat. Add the wheat berries or spelt and return to a boil. Reduce the heat to low, cover, and simmer for 45 minutes, or until tender, adding the broccoli during the last 5 minutes. Drain and place in a large bowl.

Meanwhile, heat the oil in a skillet over medium-high heat. Add the garlic and herb and cook, stirring, for 1 minute. Add the tomatoes, corn, salt, and pepper and cook, stirring frequently, for 3 minutes, or until the tomatoes begin to collapse. Serve over the wheat berries or spelt.

Makes 6 servings
Per serving: 256 calories, 11 g protein, 47 g carbohydrates, 9 g fat, 1 g saturated fat, 0 mg cholesterol, 12 g dietary fiber, 460 mg sodium

plate power

pair with . . .

pesto salmon, page 225

or

barbecued butterflied leg of lamb, page 187

barley with spring greens

1½	cups chicken or vegetable broth
½	cup pearl barley
1	tablespoon extra-virgin olive oil
1	bunch scallions, thinly sliced
3	cloves garlic, slivered
10	cups loosely packed torn mixed greens, such as escarole, Swiss chard, watercress, and arugula
¼	teaspoon salt
⅛	teaspoon freshly ground black pepper

Bring the broth to a boil in a medium saucepan over high heat. Add the barley and return to a boil. Reduce the heat to low, cover, and simmer for 45 minutes, or until tender.

Meanwhile, heat the oil in a large saucepot or Dutch oven over medium-high heat. Add the scallions and garlic and cook, stirring frequently, for 3 minutes, or until the scallions are wilted.

Add the greens, salt, and pepper. Cook, stirring, for 3 minutes, or until just wilted.

Fluff the barley with a fork and stir into the greens.

Makes 4 servings
Per serving: 143 calories, 5 g protein, 24 g carbohydrates, 4 g fat, 1 g saturated fat, 0 mg cholesterol, 7 g dietary fiber, 391 mg sodium

plate power

pair with . . .

grilled swordfish with blueberry salsa, page 234

or

soybeans with sesame and scallions, page 298, *and ½ cup pineapple*

plate ᘒ power

pair
with . . .

**spicy pork strips
with garlic greens,**
page 180

or

**pot roast with
dried fruit and red
wine,** page 172

baked barley with mushrooms and carrots

1	tablespoon butter
3	large carrots, halved lengthwise and thinly sliced
1	large onion, halved and thinly sliced
1¼	cups vegetable or chicken broth
10–12	ounces cremini, baby portobello, or white button mushrooms, sliced
2	cups water
1	cup pearl barley
1	teaspoon dried thyme, crushed
½	teaspoon salt
¼	teaspoon freshly ground black pepper

Preheat the oven to 350°F.

Melt the butter in an ovenproof Dutch oven over medium-high heat. Add the carrots, onion, and 1 tablespoon of the broth. Cook, stirring frequently, for 8 minutes, or until tender, adding another 1 tablespoon broth halfway through cooking.

Add the mushrooms and 2 tablespoons of the remaining broth and cook, stirring frequently, for 4 minutes, or until tender.

Stir in the remaining 1 cup broth, the water, barley, thyme, salt, and pepper. Bring to a boil over high heat. Cover the pot and place in the oven. Bake for 45 minutes, or until the barley is tender and the liquid is absorbed.

Makes 6 servings
Per serving: 176 calories, 7 g protein, 33 g carbohydrates, 3 g fat, 1 g saturated fat, 5 mg cholesterol, 8 g dietary fiber, 392 mg sodium

barley risotto

4	cups chicken or vegetable broth
2½	cups water
2	tablespoons extra-virgin olive oil
1	medium leek, both white and green parts, halved, rinsed, and very thinly sliced, or 1 large onion, chopped
1	clove garlic, minced
¾	cup medium pearl barley
½	teaspoon dried tarragon, crushed
¼	teaspoon freshly ground black pepper
½	cup frozen peas, thawed
¼	cup (1 ounce) freshly grated Parmesan cheese
1	tablespoon chopped fresh chives (optional)

Combine the broth and water in a medium saucepan and bring to a boil over high heat. Reduce the heat to low, cover, and simmer.

Heat the oil in a large saucepan over medium heat. Add the leek or onion and garlic. Cook, stirring, for 4 minutes. Add the barley, tarragon, and pepper; stir until the barley is coated.

Begin adding the hot broth mixture, about ½ cup at a time, stirring frequently after each addition and cooking until the liquid is nearly evaporated. Continue adding the broth mixture, ½ cup at a time, until all has been added and the barley is very tender and creamy, about 55 minutes.

Stir in the peas, cheese, and chives, if using. Cook, stirring, for 5 minutes, or until heated through.

Makes 4 servings
Per serving: 250 calories, 8 g protein, 35 g carbohydrates, 9 g fat, 2 g saturated fat, 5 mg cholesterol, 7 g dietary fiber, 719 mg sodium

plate power

pair with . . .

california chicken, page 200

or

straciatelle with escarole and chickpeas, page 98

plate ~ power

pair with . . .

chicken piccata with escarole, page 204

or

3 ounces grilled beef sirloin and spinach salad with tomato vinaigrette, page 133

quinoa with peperonata

1	cup quinoa (see cooking tip on next page)
2	cups water
1/4	teaspoon salt
2	tablespoons extra-virgin olive oil
3	large red bell peppers, cut into 1/2" squares
3	cloves garlic, minced
2	inner stalks celery with leaves, thinly sliced
1	medium red onion, chopped
1/4	teaspoon salt
1/4	teaspoon freshly ground black pepper
1	can (14 1/2 ounces) diced tomatoes, drained, with 2 tablespoons of the liquid reserved
2	strips orange peel (each 2" long), removed with a vegetable peeler
1	tablespoon drained capers, chopped

Place the quinoa in a fine-mesh strainer and rinse under cold running water until the water runs clear.

Place the water in a medium saucepan and bring to a boil over high heat. Add the quinoa and salt and return to a boil. Reduce the heat to low, cover, and simmer for 20 minutes, or until the quinoa is tender and the water is absorbed.

Meanwhile, heat the oil in a large skillet over medium heat. Add the bell peppers, garlic, celery, onion, salt, and black pepper and cook, stirring frequently, for 8 minutes, or until tender-crisp.

Stir in the tomatoes and the reserved 2 tablespoons tomato liquid, the orange peel, and capers. Bring to a boil over high heat. Reduce the heat to low, cover, and simmer, stirring occasionally, for 12 minutes, or until the vegetables are very tender. Remove and discard the orange peel.

Fluff the quinoa with a fork and spoon into a shallow serving dish. Top with the pepper mixture.

Makes 4 servings
Per serving: 262 calories, 7 g protein, 39 g carbohydrates, 10 g fat, 1 g saturated fat, 0 mg cholesterol, 5 g dietary fiber, 605 mg sodium

the power of

BEANS
Beans contain a healthy dose of fiber—approximately 7 grams per ½ cup. When you increase the amount of fiber in your diet, you feel full more quickly so you eat less.

Although dried beans have negligible amounts of sodium, the easy-to-use canned varieties are packed in a salt brine. Because salt draws water out of your cells, it makes you feel bloated, and may add several unwelcome pounds of "water weight," Look for low-sodium canned beans and always rinse the beans to reduce the sodium content.

To prevent the gas that often follows a bean dish, toss the beans with summer savory, ginger, or cumin. These spices have been shown to reduce beans' gas-producing effects.

Here are some delicious ways to get more beans into your diet.

- Toss into soup or salads.
- Add to stir-fry dishes.
- Add to vegetable dishes during the last 3 minutes of cooking.
- Make guacamole with half mashed beans and half avocado.
- Stir into stews.
- Add to salsa for a hearty dip.
- Mash with minced vegetables and slather on bread topped with lettuce, tomato, and another bread slice.

COOKING TIP
You must thoroughly rinse the quinoa to remove the saponin, a naturally occurring coating on the grain that has a bitter flavor.

quinoa with peppers and beans

1	cup quinoa (see tip on page 269)
2½	cups vegetable broth
2	tablespoons extra-virgin olive oil
3	cloves garlic, minced
1	tablespoon finely chopped peeled fresh ginger
¾	teaspoon whole cumin seeds
2	medium red bell peppers, cut into thin strips
1	large onion, cut into thin wedges
1	can (14–19 ounces) black beans, rinsed and drained
¼	cup chopped fresh cilantro

Place the quinoa in a fine-mesh strainer and rinse under cold running water until the water runs clear.

Bring 2 cups of the broth to a boil in a medium saucepan over high heat. Add the quinoa and return to a boil. Reduce the heat to low, cover, and simmer for 20 minutes, or until tender.

Meanwhile, heat the oil in a large nonstick skillet over medium heat. Add the garlic, ginger, and cumin seeds and cook, stirring, for 2 minutes, or until fragrant. Add the bell peppers and onion and cook, stirring, for 8 minutes, or until tender. Stir in the beans and the remaining ½ cup broth and cook for 2 minutes.

Fluff the quinoa with a fork and stir in the cilantro. Place in a serving bowl and top with the pepper mixture.

Makes 4 servings
Per serving: 307 calories, 14 g protein, 50 g carbohydrates, 10 g fat, 1 g saturated fat, 0 mg cholesterol, 9 g dietary fiber, 637 mg sodium

plate ⸱ power

pair with . . .

cinnamon carrot coins, page 304

or

curried sweet potato and apple soup, page 89

plate ⌒ power

pair with . . .

tortilla soup, with lime, page 106

or

cauliflower with red pepper and garlic, page 307, and five-alarm shrimp, page 237

southwestern quinoa and chickpea salad

1	*cup quinoa (see tip on page 269)*
1¾	*cups water*
⅛	*teaspoon salt*
1	*cup rinsed and drained canned chickpeas*
1	*medium tomato, seeded and chopped*
1	*clove garlic, minced*
3	*tablespoons lime juice*
2	*tablespoons finely chopped fresh cilantro*
4	*teaspoons extra-virgin olive oil*
½	*teaspoon ground cumin*

Place the quinoa in a fine-mesh strainer and rinse under cold running water until the water runs clear.

Bring the water to a boil in a medium saucepan over high heat. Add the quinoa and salt and return to a boil. Reduce the heat to low, cover, and simmer for 20 minutes, or until tender and the liquid is absorbed.

Meanwhile, in a large bowl, combine the chickpeas, tomato, garlic, lime juice, cilantro, oil, and cumin. Add the quinoa and toss to coat well.

Makes 6 servings
Per serving: 141 calories, 4 g protein, 23 g carbohydrates, 4 g fat, 0 g saturated fat, 0 mg cholesterol, 3 g dietary fiber, 144 mg sodium

adzuki beans
with miso dressing

1 1/4	cups dried adzuki beans, small red beans, or black beans, picked over and rinsed
1/4	teaspoon freshly ground black pepper
2	tablespoons mellow white miso
3	tablespoons orange juice
2	tablespoons lemon juice
2	tablespoons olive oil
1/2	teaspoon grated fresh ginger
3	scallions, diagonally sliced
2	medium cucumbers, peeled, halved, seeded, and cut into thin diagonal slices
1	small carrot, shredded
1/4	cup coarsely chopped walnuts

Place the beans in a bowl. Add water to cover by 2". Cover and let stand overnight.

Drain the beans and place in a medium saucepan. Add water to cover by 2" and bring to a boil over high heat. Stir in the pepper. Reduce the heat to low, cover, and simmer, stirring, for 30 minutes, or until very tender.

Drain the beans and place in a serving bowl for 20 minutes.

Meanwhile, in a large bowl, whisk together the miso, orange juice, lemon juice, oil, and ginger. Stir in the scallions, cucumbers, carrot, walnuts, and beans.

Let stand for 15 minutes to blend the flavors.

Makes 4 servings
Per serving: 351 calories, 15 g protein, 49 g carbohydrates, 12 g fat, 2 g saturated fat, 0 mg cholesterol, 10 g dietary fiber, 327 mg sodium

plate ⸑
power

pair
with . . .

a medium orange or small bunch of grapes

or

salad of shredded cabbage and radishes tossed in the same miso dressing

bahamian bean and corn stew with sweet potatoes

1	cup dried appaloosa, calypso, pinto, or cranberry beans, sorted and rinsed
½	teaspoon dried thyme, crushed
2	tablespoons canola oil
5	cloves garlic, minced
1	large onion, chopped
1	large red bell pepper, chopped
1	habanero or Scotch bonnet chile pepper or 2 jalapeño chile peppers, seeded and minced (optional); wear plastic gloves when handling
3	cups chicken or vegetable broth
1	large sweet potato, peeled and cut into 1" chunks
1	tablespoon minced fresh ginger
2	teaspoons turmeric
1	teaspoon paprika
1	teaspoon ground coriander
¼	teaspoon salt
2	cups fresh or frozen corn kernels
1	can (5½ ounces) pineapple tidbits packed in juice
	Lime wedges (optional)

Place the beans in a bowl. Add water to cover by 2", cover, and let stand overnight. Drain and rinse the beans.

Place the soaked beans in a medium saucepan. Add water to cover by 2". Bring to a boil over high heat. Skim off the foam and stir in the thyme. Reduce the heat to low, cover, and simmer, stirring occasionally, for 1¼ hours, or until tender. Drain the beans, return to the pot, and set aside. (This may be done 1 to 3 days ahead. Store in the refrigerator.)

Heat the oil in a Dutch oven over medium-high heat. Add the garlic, onion, bell pepper, and chile pepper (if using) and cook, stirring occasionally, for 6 minutes, or until the vegetables are tender.

Stir in the broth, sweet potato, beans, ginger, turmeric, paprika, coriander, and salt. Bring to a boil over high heat. Reduce the heat to low, partially cover, and simmer for 25 minutes, or until the sweet potatoes are tender.

Stir in the corn, cover, and simmer for 5 minutes longer, or until tender. Remove from the heat and stir in the pineapple (with juice).

Ladle the stew into bowls and serve with lime wedges, if using.

Makes 4 servings
Per serving: 435 calories, 15 g protein, 81 g carbohydrates, 8 g fat, 1 g saturated fat, 0 mg cholesterol, 17 g dietary fiber, 597 mg sodium

plate ↻ power

pair
with . . .

*garden bounty
salad,* page 126

or

*chopped millet
salad,* page 124

mediterranean baked beans

1	cup great Northern beans, picked over and rinsed
1	cup red kidney beans, picked over and rinsed
2	cups chicken broth
1½	cups water
6	cloves garlic, minced
2	tablespoons extra-virgin olive oil
1	large sprig fresh sage or ½ teaspoon dried, crushed
½	teaspoon freshly ground black pepper

Place the great Northern and kidney beans in a bowl. Add cold water to cover by 2". Cover and let stand overnight.

Preheat the oven to 325°F.

Drain the beans and place in an ovenproof Dutch oven. Add the broth, water, garlic, oil, sage, and pepper.

Cover and bake for 1 hour and 45 minutes, or until the beans are very creamy and tender. (Add a little more water during baking, if needed.)

Makes 4 servings
Per serving: 292 calories, 15 g protein, 42 g carbohydrates, 8 g fat, 1 g saturated fat, 0 mg cholesterol, 16 g dietary fiber, 408 mg sodium

lentils with tomatoes

1½	cups brown lentils, picked over and rinsed
3½	cups water
¼	teaspoon ground allspice
½	teaspoon freshly ground black pepper
¾	teaspoon salt
2	tablespoons extra-virgin olive oil
2	cloves garlic, minced
3	medium tomatoes, cut into 1½" chunks
½	cup (4 ounces) fat-free plain yogurt
2	tablespoons snipped fresh chives or scallion greens

In a large saucepan, combine the lentils, water, allspice, and ¼ teaspoon of the pepper. Bring to a boil over high heat. Reduce the heat to low, cover, and simmer for 25 minutes, or until the lentils are tender but still hold their shape. Remove from the heat and stir in ½ teaspoon of the salt.

Meanwhile, heat the oil in a large nonstick skillet over medium-high heat. Add the garlic and cook, stirring, for 30 seconds, or until fragrant. Add the tomatoes, the remaining ¼ teaspoon salt, and the remaining ¼ teaspoon pepper. Cook, stirring occasionally, for 2 minutes, or until the tomatoes just start to release their juices. Remove from the heat.

Drain the lentils and place in a shallow serving dish. Spoon the tomato mixture over the lentils, top with the yogurt, and sprinkle with the chives or scallion greens.

Makes 4 servings
Per serving: 344 calories, 23 g protein, 49 g carbohydrates, 8 g fat, 1 g saturated fat, 1 mg cholesterol, 23 g fiber, 482 mg sodium

plate ﹀
power

pair
with . . .

small salad comprised of baby spinach, red onions, and mushrooms, with mustard vinaigrette, page 133

or

turnip and carrot soup with parmesan, page 90

vegetables

From artichokes to zucchini, vegetables are a weight-loss powerhouse. They are high in fiber, vitamins, minerals, and complex carbohydrates. Providing a burst of color on your plate, they're easy to prepare, and versatile enough that you can enjoy them every night of the week. Fresh veggies contain lots of nutrients, but don't forget the frozen option. Flash-frozen soon after the vegetables are picked at the peak of their season, they are a great substitute, especially in the winter months.

In this chapter . . .

plate power

pair with . . .

roasted beet salad, *page 147,* ***and turkey-sage cutlets with mushrooms,*** *page 218*

or

spaghetti squash casserole, *page 314*

rosemary-roasted potatoes

1	*very large sweet potato (1 pound), peeled and cut into ¾" chunks*
4	*small red or white new potatoes, scrubbed and cut into ¾" chunks*
4	*teaspoons extra-virgin olive oil*
2	*teaspoons chopped fresh rosemary or ½ teaspoon dried, crushed*
½	*teaspoon grated orange peel*
¼	*teaspoon salt*
⅛	*teaspoon freshly ground black pepper*

Preheat the oven to 425°F. Coat a 13" × 9" baking pan with cooking spray.

Place the sweet potatoes, potatoes, oil, rosemary, orange peel, salt, and pepper in the prepared baking pan. Toss to coat well. Spread the potatoes in a single layer.

Roast, turning the potatoes several times, for 45 minutes, or until very tender and browned.

Makes 4 servings

Per serving: 222 calories, 4 g protein, 41 g carbohydrates, 5 g fat, 1 g saturated fat, 0 mg cholesterol, 5 g dietary fiber, 163 mg sodium

spicy oven fries

2	medium russet potatoes, scrubbed and cut into long ¼"-thick strips
1	tablespoon canola oil
1	tablespoon roasted garlic and red pepper spice blend
¼	teaspoon salt
¼	teaspoon freshly ground black pepper

Preheat the oven to 425°F. Coat a 13" × 9" baking pan with cooking spray.

Place the potatoes in a mound in the prepared baking pan and sprinkle with the oil, spice blend, salt, and pepper. Toss to coat well. Spread the potatoes in a single layer.

Bake, turning the potatoes several times, for 40 minutes, or until crisp and lightly browned.

Makes 4 servings
Per serving: 115 calories, 3 g protein, 18 g carbohydrates, 4 g fat, 0 g saturated fat, 0 mg cholesterol, 2 g dietary fiber, 144 mg sodium

plate ʂ
power

pair
with . . .

**grilled tomato and
cheese sandwiches,**
page 155

or

**roast beef and
charred vegetable
sandwiches,**
page 153

baked stuffed potatoes with spinach and beans

4	large russet potatoes, pricked several times with a fork
4	ounces low-fat goat cheese
1/4	cup (2 ounces) reduced-fat sour cream
1	tablespoon extra-virgin olive oil
2	teaspoons fat-free milk
1/2	teaspoon salt
1/2	teaspoon freshly ground black pepper
1	package (10 ounces) frozen chopped spinach, thawed and squeezed dry
2	scallions, thinly sliced
1	can (14–19 ounces) cannellini beans, rinsed and drained

Preheat the oven to 425°F.

Place the potatoes directly on the oven rack and bake for 1 hour, or until soft when squeezed (wear an oven mitt).

Remove the potatoes from the oven and cut each lengthwise in half. Let stand until easily handled but still warm.

Scoop out the potato pulp into a large bowl, leaving a 1/4"-thick shell. Place the potato shells in a 13" × 9" baking pan.

With a potato masher, mash the pulp with the cheese, sour cream, oil, milk, salt, and pepper. Fold in the spinach, scallions, and beans. Spoon into the potato shells. Bake for 20 minutes, or until lightly browned.

Makes 8 servings
Per serving: 227 calories, 11 g protein, 31 g carbohydrates, 7 g fat, 4 g saturated fat, 14 mg cholesterol, 6 g dietary fiber, 368 mg sodium

plate power

pair with . . .

manhattan clam chowder, page 107

or,

grilled flank steak with chile-tomato salsa, page 170

plate ᵕ power

pair
with . . .

lamb kebabs,
page 188

or

*chicken breasts
arrabbiata,*
page 203

thyme and rosemary potatoes

2	pounds potatoes, scrubbed and sliced
1	tablespoon extra-virgin olive oil
1	tablespoon chopped fresh rosemary or 1 teaspoon dried, crushed
1	tablespoon chopped fresh thyme or 1 teaspoon dried, crushed
2	cloves garlic, minced
¼	teaspoon salt
¼	teaspoon freshly ground black pepper

Preheat the oven to 425°F.

Place the potatoes in a 13" × 9" baking dish. Add the oil, rosemary, thyme, garlic, salt, and pepper and toss to coat well.

Bake for 40 minutes, or until golden and tender.

Makes 8 servings
Per serving: calories, 3 g protein, 29 g carbohydrates, 2 g fat, 0 g saturated fat, 0 mg cholesterol, 3 g dietary fiber, 82 mg sodium

sherried squash bake

2	pounds butternut squash, peeled, seeded, and cut into cubes
½	cup fat-free milk
2	tablespoons unbleached or all-purpose flour
1	egg
2	tablespoons cream sherry or apple juice
⅓	packed brown sugar
½	teaspoon salt
¼	teaspoon ground white or black pepper
⅛	teaspoon ground cinnamon

In a covered saucepan, heat 1" of lighted salted water to boiling. Place the squash in a steamer basket and insert into the saucepan. Cover and simmer 7 minutes, or until very tender.

Preheat the oven to 325°F. Coat a 9" × 9" baking dish with nonstick spray.

In a large bowl with a mixer at medium speed, beat the squash, milk, eggs, sherry or apple juice, brown sugar, salt, and pepper. Spoon the mixture into the prepared baking dish. Sprinkle with the cinnamon.

Bake for 30 minutes, or until a wooden pick inserted in the center comes out clean.

Makes 4 servings
Per serving: 97 calories, 3 g protein, 20 g carbohydrates, 1 g fat, 27 mg cholesterol, 0 g fiber, 155 mg sodium

plate power

pair with . . .

turkey-sage cutlets with mushrooms, page 218, and thyme and rosemary roast potatoes, (opposite page)

or

pork tenderloin with vegetables, page 184

pair
with . . .

*spiced pork
scallops with fruit
chutney,* page 176

or

*spicy chicken with
cool green dipping
sauce,* page 214, *and
sliced cucumbers*

indian-spiced potatoes and spinach

2	medium russet potatoes, scrubbed and cut into ½" chunks
2	tablespoons canola oil
3	large cloves garlic, minced
1	medium onion, chopped
1¾	teaspoons ground cumin
¾	teaspoon ground coriander
½	teaspoon ground turmeric
¼	teaspoon ground ginger
¼	teaspoon salt
¼	teaspoon freshly ground black pepper
⅛	teaspoon ground cinnamon
2	cups frozen cut leaf spinach (from a bag)
2–4	tablespoons water
½	cup (4 ounces) fat-free plain yogurt

Place a steamer basket in a large saucepan with ½" of water. Place the potatoes in the steamer. Bring to a boil over high heat. Reduce the heat to medium, cover, and cook for 20 minutes, or until the potatoes are very tender.

Place the potatoes in a bowl and keep warm. Drain and dry the saucepan.

Heat the oil in the same saucepan over medium heat. Add the garlic and onion and cook, stirring frequently, for 5 minutes, or until soft. Add the cumin, coriander, turmeric, ginger, salt, pepper, and cinnamon and cook, stirring, for 30 seconds to cook the spices.

Add the potatoes and cook, stirring frequently, for 5 minutes, or until crisp and golden.

Add the spinach and 2 tablespoons water. Cover and cook, tossing gently, adding additional water 1 tablespoon at a time, if needed, for 5 minutes, or until heated through.

Place in a serving bowl. Spoon the yogurt on top, but don't stir it in, and serve hot.

Makes 4 servings
Per serving: 195 calories, 8 g protein, 24 g carbohydrates, 7 g fat, 1 g saturated fat, 1 mg cholesterol, 6 g dietary fiber, 350 mg sodium

sweet potato stew

1½	cups brown rice
1	tablespoon olive oil
3	cloves garlic, minced
2	red bell peppers, cut into 1" chunks
1	large onion, chopped
1	tablespoon minced fresh ginger
½	teaspoon ground allspice
¼	teaspoon ground red pepper
4	cups vegetable broth
2	large sweet potatoes, peeled and cut into 1" chunks
½	cup natural peanut butter
1	cup boiling water
⅓	cup tomato paste
1	can (10½–15 ounces) chickpeas, rinsed and drained
1	pound spinach, coarsely chopped

Prepare the rice according to package directions.

Meanwhile, heat the oil in a Dutch oven over medium-high heat. Add the garlic, bell peppers, and onion; cook for 3 minutes. Add the ginger, allspice, and ground red pepper; cook for 1 minute.

Add the broth and potatoes; bring to a boil. Reduce the heat to low, cover, and simmer for 15 minutes, or until tender.

In a bowl, whisk the peanut butter and water. Add to the pan with the tomato paste, chickpeas, and spinach. Cook for 10 minutes, or until heated through. Serve over the rice.

Makes 6 servings
Per serving: 426 calories, 19 g protein, 61 g carbohydrates, 16 g fat, 3 g saturated fat, 0 mg cholesterol, 16 g dietary fiber, 669 mg sodium

fluffy garlic mashed potatoes

4	medium russet or Yukon gold potatoes, cut into 1" chunks
8	cloves garlic
½	cup buttermilk
1	tablespoon butter
½	teaspoon salt
¼	teaspoon freshly ground black pepper
1	tablespoon snipped fresh chives, dill, or scallion greens

Place a steamer basket in a large saucepan with ½" of water. Place the potatoes and garlic in the steamer. Bring to a boil over high heat. Reduce the heat to medium, cover, and cook for 20 minutes, or until the potatoes are very tender.

Place the potatoes and garlic in a bowl and mash with a potato masher. Add the buttermilk, butter, salt, pepper, and chives, dill, or scallion greens; mash until well-blended.

Makes 4 servings
Per serving: 172 calories, 6 g protein, 30 g carbohydrates, 4 g fat, 2 g saturated fat, 9 mg cholesterol, 3 g dietary fiber, 360 mg sodium

plate power

pair with . . .

pot roast with dried fruit and red wine, page 172, and ½ cup steamed green beans

or

chicken breasts arrabiata, page 203, and a side of broccoli rabe

root vegetable mash

3	pounds sweet potatoes, peeled and cut into small chunks
1	pound celery root, peeled and cut into small chunks
2	cloves garlic
1	small onion, peeled and chopped
⅓	cup 1% milk, warmed
1½	tablespoons olive oil
½	teaspoon salt

Place a steamer basket in a large saucepan with ½" of water. Place the sweet potatoes, celery root, and garlic in the steamer. Bring to a boil over high heat. Reduce the heat to medium, cover, and cook for 10 minutes. Add the onion, cover, and cook for 10 minutes longer, or until the onion and celery root are very tender.

Place the vegetables in a bowl and mash with a potato masher. Add the milk, oil, and salt. Mash to blend.

Makes 8 servings
Per serving: 221 calories, 4 g protein, 45 g carbohydrates, 3 g fat, 1 g saturated fat, 0 mg cholesterol, 6 g dietary fiber, 207 mg sodium

plate power

pair with . . .

rosemary roast chicken with pan gravy, page 210, and roasted beet salad, page 147

or

orange and sage roast turkey breast with pan gravy, page 216, stuffed vidalia onion, page 294, and ½ cup brussels sprouts glazed with 1 teaspoon maple syrup

plate ∿
power

pair
with . . .

*rosemary roast
chicken with pan
gravy,* page 210, *and
root vegetable
mash,* page 291

or

kasha with onions,
page 251, *and
barbecued
butterflied leg of
lamb,* page 187

roasted beets
with herbs and garlic

2	*pounds small beets, scrubbed*
2	*tablespoons chicken or vegetable broth*
1	*tablespoon extra-virgin olive oil*
2	*cloves garlic, minced*
1	*large shallot, finely chopped*
½	*teaspoon dried sage, crushed*
	Pinch of ground allspice
⅛	*teaspoon salt*
⅛	*teaspoon freshly ground black pepper*

Preheat the oven to 400°F.

Cut each beet into 8 wedges. Place the beets, broth, oil, garlic, shallot, sage, allspice, salt, and pepper in an 11" × 7" baking dish. Toss to coat well.

Cover tightly with foil and bake, stirring occasionally, for 1 hour, or until the beets are very tender.

Makes 4 servings
Per serving: 132 calories, 4 g protein, 23 g carbohydrates, 4 g fat, 1 g saturated fat, 0 mg cholesterol, 5 g dietary fiber, 288 mg sodium

roasted carrots
and parsnips

1	pound carrots, cut into 1" chunks
1	pound parsnips, cut into 1" chunks
4	small red onions, cut into wedges
6	cloves garlic
½	tablespoon extra-virgin olive oil
½	teaspoon salt
½	teaspoon grated lemon peel

Preheat the oven to 375°F. Coat a medium baking pan with cooking spray. Add the carrots, parsnips, onions, garlic, oil, salt, and lemon peel. Toss to coat well.

Bake, stirring occasionally, for 40 minutes, or until golden and tender.

Makes 6 servings
Per serving: 113 calories, 2 g protein, 24 g carbohydrates, 2 g fat, 0 g saturated fat, 0 mg cholesterol, 7 g dietary fiber, 229 mg sodium

plate ᔈ power

pair with . . .

one-pot chicken and rice, page 196

or

beef stroganoff, page 165

COOKING TIP
If serving with one-pot chicken and rice, start the vegetables during the last 15 min of the chicken/rice cooking. Turn the heat up to 375° and roast for ½ hour longer.

pair
with . . .

*orange and sage
roast turkey breast
with pan gravy,
page 216, root
vegetable mash,
page 291, and ½ cup
brussels sprouts
glazed with
1 teaspoon maple
syrup*

or

*pork tenderloin
with vegetables,
page 184*

stuffed vidalia onions

4	Vidalia or sweet onions
½	teaspoon olive oil
2	medium zucchini, shredded
3	cloves garlic, minced
1	teaspoon dried thyme, crushed
1	teaspoon dried basil, crushed
3	tablespoons plain dry bread crumbs
1½	tablespoons chopped toasted pine nuts
3	tablespoons freshly grated Parmesan cheese
¼	teaspoon salt
¼	teaspoon freshly ground black pepper

Preheat the oven to 400°F. Line a small baking pan with foil.

Cut ½" off the top of each onion; slightly trim the bottoms so that the onions stand upright. Place the onions, cut side up, in the prepared baking pan and coat with cooking spray. Bake for 1 hour, or until soft. Set aside for 15 minutes, or until cool enough to handle.

Reduce the oven temperature to 350°F.

Remove and discard the onion peels. Using a spoon, scoop out the onion centers, leaving a ½" shell. Chop the centers and reserve 1 cup for the stuffing; save the remainder for another use.

Heat the oil in a large nonstick skillet over medium heat. Add the zucchini, garlic, thyme, basil, and the 1 cup chopped onions. Cook for 6 minutes, or until the zucchini is softened and most of the liquid has evaporated. Remove from the heat and stir in the bread crumbs, pine nuts, 2½ tablespoons of the cheese, salt, and pepper.

Divide the filling among the onion shells. Place the onion shells in the same baking pan and top with the remaining ½ tablespoon cheese.

Bake for 20 minutes, or until golden.

Makes 4 servings
Per serving: 122 calories, 6 g protein, 18 g carbohydrates, 4 g fat, 1 g saturated fat, 3 mg cholesterol, 4 g dietary fiber, 262 mg sodium

pair
with . . .

linguine with clams, page 241, *and summer squash with walnuts and parmesan,* page 313

or

polenta with fresh tomato sauce, page 254, *and chicken piccata with escarole,* page 204

COOKING TIP
To cook this dish indoors, coat a broiler-pan rack with cooking spray and preheat the broiler. Place the vegetables on the rack and broil, turning often, for 10 minutes, or until browned.

grilled portobellos, peppers, and onions

¼	cup chopped flat-leaf parsley
3	tablespoons lemon juice
2	tablespoons extra-virgin olive oil
3	cloves garlic, minced
1	teaspoon dried Italian herb seasoning, crushed
½	teaspoon freshly ground black pepper
¼	teaspoon salt
2	large red bell peppers, cut into strips
6	ounces portobello mushrooms, sliced
1	large sweet white onion, halved and cut into 1"-thick slices

Coat a grill rack with cooking spray. Preheat the grill to medium-hot.

In a large bowl, combine the parsley, lemon juice, oil, garlic, Italian seasoning, black pepper, and salt. Add the bell peppers, mushrooms, and onion and toss to coat well. (The mixture can be prepared ahead to this point and refrigerated up to 2 days.)

Place a vegetable basket or grill screen on the grill rack and place the vegetables on the basket or screen. Grill, turning often, for 15 minutes, or until very tender and lightly charred.

Makes 4 servings
Per serving: 110 calories, 3 g protein, 10 g carbohydrates, 7 g fat, 1 g saturated fat, 0 mg cholesterol, 3 g dietary fiber, 155 mg sodium

braised italian peppers with onions and thyme

1	tablespoon olive oil
6–8	Italian frying peppers, cut into 2" chunks
1	large red onion, cut into wedges
1	tablespoon balsamic vinegar
2	teaspoons coarsely chopped fresh thyme or 1/4 teaspoon dried, crushed
1/8	teaspoon salt
1/8	teaspoon freshly ground black pepper
2	plum tomatoes, cut into 1/2" chunks
3	tablespoons chicken or vegetable broth or water

Heat the oil in a large skillet over medium heat. Add the frying peppers and onion and cook, stirring occasionally, for 5 minutes, or until the onion starts to soften.

Add the vinegar, thyme, salt, and black pepper and cook for 1 minute. Add the tomatoes and broth or water. Reduce the heat to low, cover, and simmer, stirring occasionally, for 8 minutes, or until the vegetables are very tender.

Makes 4 servings
Per serving: 90 calories, 2 g protein, 14 g carbohydrates, 4 g fat, 1 g saturated fat, 0 mg cholesterol, 3 g dietary fiber, 134 mg sodium

plate 、
power

pair
with . . .

shrimp with chard and red beans,
page 238

or

serve on a slice of italian bread with chicken breasts arrabbiata,
page 203

pair
with . . .

stir-fried asparagus with ginger, sesame, and soy, opposite page, *and 2 ounces cooked soba noodles*

or

½ cup steamed brown rice and 1 cup broccoli stir-fried with 1 tablespoon low sodium soy sauce, 1 clove garlic, and 1 teaspoon ginger.

soybeans with sesame and scallions

1	bag (12 ounces) frozen shelled green soybeans (edamame)
1	tablespoon soy sauce
½	cup water
1½	teaspoons sesame oil
	Dash of hot-pepper sauce (optional)
2	tablespoons minced scallions
⅛	teaspoon freshly ground black pepper

In a medium saucepan over high heat, bring the soybeans, soy sauce, and water to a boil, stirring occasionally. Reduce the heat to low and simmer for 12 minutes, or until tender. If any liquid remains, cook, stirring occasionally, over medium-high heat until the liquid has evaporated.

Remove from the heat. Stir in the oil, hot-pepper sauce (if using), scallions, and black pepper.

Makes 4 servings
Per serving: 132 calories, 9 g protein, 11 g carbohydrates, 5 g fat, 0 g saturated fat, 0 mg cholesterol, 5 g dietary fiber, 280 mg sodium

stir-fried asparagus with ginger, sesame, and soy

1½	pounds thin asparagus, cut diagonally into 2" pieces
2	teaspoons canola oil
½	large red bell pepper, cut into thin strips
1	tablespoon chopped fresh ginger
1	tablespoon reduced-sodium soy sauce
⅛	teaspoon crushed red-pepper flakes
1	teaspoon toasted sesame oil
1	teaspoon sesame seeds, toasted

Bring ¼" water to a boil in a large nonstick skillet over high heat. Add the asparagus and return to a boil. Reduce the heat to low, cover, and simmer for 5 minutes, or until tender-crisp. Drain in a colander and cool briefly under cold running water. Wipe the skillet dry with a paper towel.

Heat the canola oil in the same skillet over high heat. Add the bell pepper and cook, stirring constantly, for 3 minutes, or until tender-crisp. Add the asparagus, ginger, soy sauce, and red-pepper flakes and cook for 2 minutes, or until heated through. Remove from the heat and stir in the sesame oil and sesame seeds.

Makes 4 servings
Per serving: 79 calories, 5 g protein, 7 g carbohydrates, 5 g fat, 0 g saturated fat, 0 mg cholesterol, 4 g dietary fiber, 157 mg sodium

plate power

pair with . . .

chinese barbecued pork chops, page 173, *and steamed brown rice*

or

soybeans with sesame and scallions, opposite page, *and steamed brown rice*

stir-fried broccoli and mushrooms with tofu

1/3	cup chicken or vegetable broth
1	tablespoon apricot all-fruit spread
1	tablespoon reduced-sodium soy sauce
1	tablespoon dry sherry
2	teaspoons cornstarch
1	tablespoon canola oil
1	large bunch broccoli, cut into small florets
4	cloves garlic, minced
1	tablespoon finely chopped fresh ginger
4	ounces mushrooms, sliced
1	cup halved cherry and/or yellow pear tomatoes
8	ounces firm tofu, drained and cut into 1/4" cubes

In a cup, whisk together the broth, all-fruit spread, soy sauce, sherry, and cornstarch. Set aside.

Heat the oil in a large nonstick skillet over medium-high heat. Add the broccoli, garlic, and ginger and cook, stirring constantly, for 1 minute. Add the mushrooms and cook, stirring frequently, for 3 minutes, or until tender-crisp and lightly browned.

Add the tomatoes and tofu and cook, stirring frequently, for 2 minutes, or until the tomatoes begin to collapse.

Stir the cornstarch mixture and add to the skillet. Cook, stirring, for 2 minutes, or until the mixture boils and thickens.

Makes 4 servings
Per serving: 147 calories, 9 g protein, 15 g carbohydrates, 7 g fat, 1 g saturated fat, 0 mg cholesterol, 4 g dietary fiber, 230 mg sodium

plate power

pair with . . .

1/2 cup steamed brown rice

or

2 ounces cooked soba noodles

pair
with . . .

pesto salmon,
page 225, *and*
kamut, orange,
and fennel salad,
page 252

or

maple squash
with cardamom,
page 312, *and*
½ a roast chicken
breast

stewed vegetables

2	teaspoons olive oil
1	large onion, halved and thinly sliced
3	cloves garlic, thinly sliced
1	can (16 ounces) whole tomatoes
½	teaspoon dried thyme, crushed
¼	teaspoon salt
1	pound green beans, halved
1	medium zucchini, halved lengthwise and thinly sliced
½	cup fresh basil leaves, cut into thin strips

Heat the oil in a large nonstick skillet over medium heat. Add the onion and garlic and cook, stirring occasionally, for 4 minutes, or until tender.

Add the tomatoes (with juice), thyme, and salt, stirring to break up the tomatoes. Bring to a boil over high heat. Add the green beans. Reduce the heat to low, cover, and simmer, stirring occasionally, for 10 minutes, or until the beans are tender.

Add the zucchini and cook, stirring occasionally, for 5 minutes, or until tender. Remove from the heat and stir in the basil.

Makes 6 servings
Per serving: 73 calories, 3 g protein, 13 g carbohydrates, 2 g fat, 0 g saturated fat, 0 mg cholesterol, 5 g dietary fiber, 211 mg sodium

artichoke gratin

2	packages (9 ounces each) frozen artichoke hearts
1	tablespoon lemon juice
3	tablespoons plain dry bread crumbs
1	tablespoon freshly grated Parmesan cheese
1	teaspoon dried Italian herb seasoning, crushed
1	clove garlic, minced
1	teaspoon extra-virgin olive oil

Preheat the oven to 375°F. Coat a 9" glass pie plate with cooking spray.

Place the artichokes in a colander and rinse well with cold water to separate. Drain well, then pat dry with paper towels. Place in the prepared pie plate and sprinkle with the lemon juice.

In a small bowl, combine the bread crumbs, cheese, Italian seasoning, garlic, and oil. Sprinkle the mixture evenly over the artichokes.

Bake for 15 minutes, or until the topping is golden.

Makes 4 servings
Per serving: 102 calories, 6 g protein, 18 g carbohydrates, 2 g fat, 0 g saturated fat, 1 mg cholesterol, 7 g dietary fiber, 184 mg sodium

plate power

pair with . . .

beef stroganoff, page 165

or

one-pot chicken and rice, page 196

plate power

pair with . . .

spiced brown rice with cashews, *page 248,* ***and spiced pork scallops with fruit chutney,*** *page 176*

or

quinoa with peppers and beans, *page 271*

cinnamon carrot coins

6	*medium carrots, thinly sliced*
6	*tablespoons orange juice*
1½	*teaspoons unsalted butter*
¾	*teaspoon ground cinnamon*
⅛	*teaspoon freshly ground black pepper*

Place the carrots and orange juice in a medium saucepan. Cover and cook over medium-low heat for 6 minutes, or until the carrots are tender-crisp.

Add the butter, cinnamon, and pepper. Cook for 1 minute, stirring to coat.

Makes 6 servings

Per serving: 51 calories, 1 g protein, 10 g carbohydrates, 1 g fat, 1 g saturated fat, 3 mg cholesterol, 2 g dietary fiber, 40 mg sodium

sweet-and-sour red cabbage and apples

(quick)

1	tablespoon butter
1	tablespoon canola oil
1	large onion, chopped
½	medium head red cabbage, cored and shredded
½	teaspoon salt
¼	teaspoon freshly ground black pepper
¼	teaspoon ground allspice
3	medium sweet-tart apples (such as Golden Delicious), peeled, cored, and cut into thin wedges
¼	cup frozen apple juice concentrate
2	tablespoons red wine vinegar

In a large saucepot or Dutch oven, heat the butter and oil over medium heat until the butter melts. Add the onion and cook, stirring frequently, for 6 minutes, or until soft.

Add the cabbage, salt, pepper, and allspice. Cook, stirring frequently, for 4 minutes, or until the cabbage begins to wilt and the color starts to change.

Add the apples, apple juice concentrate, and vinegar. Bring to a boil. Reduce the heat to low, cover, and simmer, stirring frequently, for 15 minutes, or until the cabbage is very tender.

Makes 6 servings
Per serving: 124 calories, 2 g protein, 21 g carbohydrates, 5 g fat, 1 g saturated fat, 5 mg cholesterol, 4 g dietary fiber, 235 mg sodium

plate power

pair with . . .

pork tenderloin with vegetables, page 184

or

maple squash with cardamom, page 312, **and 3 ounces roast chicken or turkey**

cauliflower with red pepper and garlic

1	large head cauliflower, cut into small florets
1	large red bell pepper, cut into 1" squares
2	tablespoons extra-virgin olive oil
4	cloves garlic, minced
1	tablespoon red wine vinegar
2	teaspoons chopped fresh thyme or ¼ teaspoon dried, crushed
¾	teaspoon paprika
½	teaspoon salt

Place a steamer basket in a large saucepan with ½" of water. Place the cauliflower and pepper in the steamer. Bring to a boil over high heat. Reduce the heat to medium, cover, and cook for 4 minutes, or until tender-crisp. Place in a serving bowl.

Heat the oil in a small skillet over medium heat. Remove from the heat and stir in the garlic. When the sizzling stops, stir in the vinegar, thyme, paprika, and salt. Add to the vegetables and toss to coat well.

Makes 4 servings
Per serving: 122 calories, 4 g protein, 12 g carbohydrates, 7 g fat, 1 g saturated fat, 0 mg cholesterol, 5 g dietary fiber, 345 mg sodium

plate power

pair with . . .

five-alarm shrimp, page 237, *and southwestern quinoa and chickpea salad,* page 272

or

blackened snapper, page 230, *and a baked sweet potato*

pair
with . . .

spiced brown rice with cashews, page 248, and ½ a grilled chicken breast marinated in low-fat yogurt for ½ an hour

or

fish stew with couscous, page 233

curried cauliflower and carrots with beans

1	large head cauliflower, cut into small florets
2	large carrots, cut into ½"-thick diagonal slices
2	tablespoons olive oil
1	medium onion, chopped
1	tablespoon finely chopped fresh ginger
2	cloves garlic, minced
1	tablespoon unbleached or all-purpose flour
1½–2	teaspoons curry powder
1	cup chicken or vegetable broth
2	tablespoons dry white wine
1	can (14–19 ounces) black beans or chickpeas, rinsed and drained
½	cup chopped fresh cilantro or flat-leaf parsley

Place a steamer basket in a large saucepan with ½" of water. Place the cauliflower and carrots in the steamer. Bring to a boil over high heat. Reduce the heat to medium, cover, and cook for 10 minutes, or until tender. Place in a bowl and keep warm. Rinse and dry the saucepan.

Heat the oil in the same saucepan over medium heat. Add the onion, ginger, and garlic and cook, stirring frequently, for 3 minutes, or until soft.

In a cup, combine the flour and curry powder. Add to the saucepan and cook, stirring, for 1 minute.

Gradually stir in the broth and wine and bring to a boil. Reduce the heat to low and simmer, stirring frequently, for

5 minutes, or until the sauce is lightly thickened.

Add the beans or chickpeas and cook, stirring, for 3 minutes, or until heated through. Add to the vegetables in the bowl and toss gently just until combined. Sprinkle with the cilantro or parsley.

Makes 8 servings
Per serving: 129 calories, 6 g protein, 17 g carbohydrates, 5 g fat, 1 g saturated fat, 1 mg cholesterol, 6 g dietary fiber, 322 mg sodium

plate ꞯ power

pair with . . .

rosemary roast chicken with pan gravy, page 210

or

orange and sage roast turkey breast with pan gravy, page 216

stuffed acorn squash

3	acorn squash, halved lengthwise and seeded
2/3	cup quick-cooking barley
2	teaspoons vegetable oil
1	small onion, chopped
1	rib celery, chopped
1	clove garlic, chopped
3	ounces mushrooms, sliced
1/4	cup chopped fresh parsley and/or thyme or sage or 2 teaspoons dried, crushed
1	cup coarse fresh bread crumbs
2/3	cup dried cranberries
1	teaspoon grated lemon peel
1/4	teaspoon salt
1/4–1/2	cup vegetable broth or apple juice

Preheat the oven to 400°F.

Place the squash, cut side up, on a baking sheet. Coat the cut sides lightly with cooking spray. Bake for 30 minutes, or until fork-tender.

Meanwhile, prepare the barley according to package directions.

Heat the oil in a medium nonstick skillet over medium heat. Add the onion, celery, and garlic and cook for 2 minutes. Add the mushrooms and parsley and/or thyme or sage and cook for 4 minutes, or until the mushrooms are soft. Remove from the heat. Stir in the bread crumbs, cranberries, lemon peel, salt, and barley. Add up to 1/2 cup broth or apple juice to moisten and bind the stuffing.

Reduce the oven temperature to 350°F. Spoon the stuffing into the squash halves. Bake for 10 minutes, or until heated through.

Makes 6 servings
Per serving: 198 calories, 4 g protein, 44 g carbohydrates, 3 g fat, 0 g saturated fat, 0 mg cholesterol, 6 g dietary fiber, 190 mg sodium

COOKING TIP

Ingredients for savory recipes should be considered options, not dictates. If you don't care for an ingredient in the list, feel free to make substitutions. Any number of grains can take the place of barley in Stuffed Acorn Squash, for example. Try quinoa, millet, cracked wheat berries, or even chunks of whole grain bread. Instead of cranberries, use dried cherries, dried apricots, diced apples, diced pears, or another fresh or dried fruit of your choice. By tailoring recipes to suit your tastes, your healthy eating plan is sure to succeed.

plate ~ power

pair with . . .

stewed vegetables, page 302, and ½ a roast chicken breast

or

sweet-and-sour red cabbage and apples, page 305, and 3 ounces roast chicken or turkey

maple squash with cardamom

1	tablespoon butter, melted
1	tablespoon maple syrup
1	teaspoon ground cardamom
¼	teaspoon salt
1	large butternut squash (3¼ pounds)

Preheat the oven to 400°F. Coat a 13" × 9" baking pan with cooking spray.

In a large bowl, combine the butter, maple syrup, cardamom, and salt.

Pierce the squash in several places with a fork. Place in the microwave and cook for 4 minutes, or until softened. Peel and seed the squash and cut into 1" chunks. Add to the bowl with the butter mixture and toss to coat well. Place the squash mixture in the prepared baking pan.

Bake, tossing occasionally, for 45 minutes, or until browned and tender.

Makes 4 servings
Per serving: 207 calories, 4 g protein, 47 g carbohydrates, 3 g fat, 2 g saturated fat, 8 mg cholesterol, 6 g dietary fiber, 192 mg sodium

summer squash with walnuts and parmesan

quick

2	teaspoons butter
2	large cloves garlic, minced
1	medium zucchini, cut into 3"-long spears
1	medium yellow summer squash, cut into 3"-long spears
2	tablespoons chicken or vegetable broth or water
1/8	teaspoon salt
1/8	teaspoon freshly ground black pepper
1/3	cup chopped walnuts, toasted
1/4	cup (1 ounce) shredded Parmesan cheese

Melt the butter in a large nonstick skillet over medium-low heat. Add the garlic and cook, stirring constantly, for 1 minute, or until soft.

Add the zucchini, yellow squash, broth or water, salt, and pepper. Bring to a simmer over medium heat. Cover and simmer, stirring occasionally, for 6 minutes, or until the squash are tender. Remove from the heat. Sprinkle with the walnuts and cheese.

Makes 4 servings
Per serving: 145 calories, 6 g protein, 7 g carbohydrates, 11 g fat, 3 g saturated fat, 10 mg cholesterol, 2 g dietary fiber, 251 mg sodium

plate power

pair with . . .

linguine with clams, page 241, and grilled portobellos, peppers, and onions, page 296

or

quinoa with peppers and beans, page 271

plate ↵ power

pair with . . .

slice of garlic bread

or

rosemary-roasted potatoes, page 280

spaghetti squash casserole

1	spaghetti squash, halved lengthwise and seeded
1	tablespoon vegetable oil
2	cloves garlic, chopped
1	small onion, chopped
1	teaspoon dried basil, crushed
2	plum tomatoes, chopped
8	ounces 1% cottage cheese
1/2	cup (2 ounces) shredded low-fat mozzarella cheese
1/4	cup chopped parsley
1/4	teaspoon salt
1/4	cup (1 ounce) freshly grated Parmesan cheese
3	tablespoons seasoned dry bread crumbs

Preheat the oven to 400°F. Coat a 13" × 9" baking dish and a baking sheet with cooking spray.

Place the squash, cut side down, on the prepared baking sheet. Bake for 30 minutes, or until tender. With a fork, scrape the squash strands into a large bowl.

Meanwhile, heat the oil in a medium skillet over medium heat. Add the garlic, onion, and basil and cook for 4 minutes, or until soft. Add the tomatoes and cook for 3 minutes, or until the mixture is dry.

To the bowl with the squash, add the cottage cheese, mozzarella, parsley, salt, and the tomato mixture. Toss to coat. Place in the prepared baking dish. Sprinkle with the Parmesan and bread crumbs.

Bake for 30 minutes, or until hot and bubbly.

Makes 6 servings
Per serving: 219 calories, 12 g protein, 28 g carbohydrates, 7 g fat,
3 g saturated fat, 10 mg cholesterol, 4 g dietary fiber, 528 mg sodium

COOKING TIP

Spaghetti squash can also be prepared in the microwave oven. Pierce the squash in
several places with a knife. Place on a microwaveable plate and cover loosely with a
piece of plastic wrap. Cook on high power, turning twice, for 20 minutes, or until
tender when pierced. Remove and let stand until cool enough to handle.

desserts

Most people don't think of desserts as weight-loss foods. However, balance is an important part of a healthy diet, and all of these recipes are prepared using the healthiest cooking methods and the highest-quality ingredients. For example, whole grain pastry flour is used because it is unprocessed, so the tummy-trimming fiber remains in the flour. It is important that you enjoy good-quality desserts now and then to reduce cravings for less-nutritious, empty-calorie sweets.

In this chapter . . .

oatmeal cookies with cranberries and chocolate chips

quick

2	cups rolled oats (not quick-cooking)
½	cup whole grain pastry flour
¾	teaspoon baking soda
½	teaspoon ground cinnamon
¼	teaspoon salt
½	cup packed brown sugar
⅓	cup canola oil
3	egg whites
2	teaspoons vanilla extract
¾	cup dried sweetened cranberries
½	cup mini semisweet chocolate chips

Preheat the oven to 350°F. Coat 2 large baking sheets with cooking spray.

In a large bowl, combine the oats, flour, baking soda, cinnamon, and salt. In a medium bowl, whisk the brown sugar, oil, egg whites, and vanilla extract until smooth. Stir in the cranberries and chocolate chips. Add to the flour mixture; stir just until blended.

Drop the batter by scant tablespoons onto the prepared baking sheets. Bake for 10 minutes, or until the cookies are golden brown.

Cool the cookies on racks. Store in an airtight container.

Makes 18 cookies
Per serving: 157 calories, 3 g protein, 23 g carbohydrates, 6 g fat, 1 g saturated fat, 0 mg cholesterol, 2 g dietary fiber, 97 mg sodium

almond coffee drops

²/₃	cup almonds
2	egg whites, at room temperature
1	teaspoon vanilla extract
¼	teaspoon cream of tartar
¼	teaspoon salt
½	cup granulated sugar
½	teaspoon instant coffee granules

Preheat the oven to 350°F. Coat 2 baking sheets with cooking spray.

Finely chop the almonds in a food processor or by hand.

Reduce the oven temperature to 325°F.

Place the egg whites, vanilla extract, cream of tartar, and salt in a large bowl. With an electric mixer on high speed, beat until the whites are frothy. Gradually add the sugar, beating until stiff glossy peaks form.

Using a rubber spatula, gently fold in the nuts and coffee granules just until blended.

Drop the batter by rounded teaspoons onto the prepared baking sheets, spacing them about 1" apart. Bake for 20 minutes, or until lightly browned.

Place the cookies on racks and let cool completely. Store in an airtight container.

Makes 10 servings
Per serving: 99 calories, 3 g protein, 12 g carbohydrates, 5 g fat, 0 g saturated fat, 0 mg cholesterol, 1 g dietary fiber, 69 mg sodium

almond and chocolate flourless cake

2	tablespoons unsalted butter
3	tablespoons unsweetened cocoa powder
½	cup blanched almonds
2	tablespoons + ¾ cup sugar
3	ounces bittersweet chocolate
½	cup (4 ounces) reduced-fat sour cream
2	egg yolks
1	teaspoon vanilla extract
¼	teaspoon almond extract (optional)
5	egg whites, at room temperature
¼	teaspoon salt
1	tablespoon toasted slivered almonds (optional)

Preheat the oven to 350°F. Generously coat a 9" springform pan with 2 teaspoons of the butter and dust with 1 tablespoon of the cocoa (don't tap out the excess cocoa; leave it in the pan).

In a food processor, combine the blanched almonds with 2 tablespoons of the sugar. Process until finely ground.

In the top of a double boiler over barely simmering water, melt the chocolate and the remaining 4 teaspoons butter, stirring occasionally, until smooth. Remove from the heat. Place the chocolate mixture in a large bowl. Add the almond mixture, sour cream, egg yolks, vanilla extract, almond extract (if using), ½ cup of the remaining sugar, and the remaining 2 tablespoons cocoa. Stir until well-blended.

In a large bowl, with an electric mixer on high speed, beat the egg whites and salt until frothy. Gradually add the remaining ¼ cup sugar, beating until stiff glossy peaks form.

Stir one-quarter of the beaten whites into the chocolate mixture to lighten it. Gently fold in the remaining whites until no white streaks remain. Place in the prepared pan. Gently smooth the top.

Bake for 30 minutes, or until the cake has risen, is dry on the top, and a wooden pick inserted in the center comes out with a few moist crumbs.

Place in the pan on a rack and cool until warm. The cake will fall dramatically. Loosen the edges of the cake with a knife and remove the pan sides. Sprinkle with the toasted almonds, if using.

Makes 12 servings
Per serving: 184 calories, 5 g protein, 21 g carbohydrates, 10 g fat, 4 g saturated fat, 45 mg cholesterol, 1 g dietary fiber, 81 mg sodium

carrot cake with cream cheese frosting

Cake

2	cups whole grain pastry flour
2	teaspoons baking powder
2	teaspoons baking soda
1	teaspoon ground cinnamon
¼	teaspoon salt
1	cup granulated sugar
2	eggs
2	egg whites
⅓	cup canola oil
2	teaspoons vanilla extract
1	cup buttermilk or fat-free plain yogurt
2	cups finely shredded carrots
½	cup golden raisins
½	cup well-drained crushed pineapple

Frosting

2	ounces reduced-fat cream cheese, at room temperature
2	tablespoons unsalted butter, at room temperature
1¼	cups confectioners' sugar
½	teaspoon vanilla extract
3	tablespoons chopped walnuts or pecans

To make the cake: Preheat the oven to 350°F. Coat two 8" round cake pans with cooking spray.

In a medium bowl, combine the flour, baking powder, baking soda, cinnamon, and salt.

In a large bowl, using a wire whisk, beat the granulated sugar, eggs, egg whites, oil, and vanilla extract until well-blended and frothy. Whisk in the buttermilk or yogurt. Stir in the carrots, raisins, and pineapple. Add the flour mixture and stir just until blended.

Evenly divide the batter between the prepared cake pans. Bake for 25 minutes, or until a wooden pick inserted in the center comes out clean.

Cool the cakes in the pans on racks for 30 minutes. Loosen the edges and turn the cakes out onto the racks to cool completely.

To make the frosting: In a medium bowl, with an electric mixer on medium-high speed, beat the cream cheese and butter just until blended. Beat in the confectioners' sugar and vanilla extract until light and fluffy.

Place one cake layer on a plate. Spread the top of the layer with frosting, but not the sides. Place the other cake layer on top. Spread the top of the layer with the remaining frosting. Sprinkle with the walnuts or pecans.

COOKING TIP
If you don't have buttermilk or yogurt, you can use soured milk instead. To make soured milk, pour the desired amount of 1% milk into a measuring cup. Add 1 tablespoon lemon juice or cider vinegar. Let stand for 10 minutes.

Makes 16 servings
Per serving: 237 calories, 4 g protein, 38 g carbohydrates, 9 g fat, 2 g saturated fat, 33 mg cholesterol, 2 g dietary fiber, 291 mg sodium

olive oil–cornmeal cake with blueberry and red wine sauce

Cake

1	cup yellow cornmeal
¾	cup sugar
½	cup whole grain pastry flour
1¼	teaspoons baking powder
½	teaspoon baking soda
¼	teaspoon salt
2	eggs
2	egg whites
½	cup (4 ounces) fat-free plain yogurt
¼	cup extra-virgin olive oil
1	tablespoon freshly grated orange peel
2	tablespoons orange juice
1	tablespoon confectioners' sugar (optional)

Sauce

1	pint fresh or frozen blueberries
¼	cup dry red wine
1	tablespoon orange juice
	Pinch of ground nutmeg

To make the cake: Preheat the oven to 350°F. Coat an 8" round cake pan with cooking spray. Line the pan bottom with a round of waxed paper and coat the waxed paper with cooking spray.

In a large bowl, combine the cornmeal, sugar, flour, baking powder, baking soda, and salt.

In a medium bowl, using a wire whisk, beat the eggs, egg whites, yogurt, oil, orange peel, and orange juice. (The mixture may look curdled.) Add to the cornmeal mixture and stir just until blended. Place in the prepared pan.

Bake for 25 minutes, or until browned, firm, and a wooden pick inserted off-center comes out clean.

Cool in the pan on a rack for 30 minutes. Loosen the edges and turn the cake out onto the rack. Peel off the waxed paper and let cool completely.

To make the sauce: In a medium saucepan, combine the blueberries, wine, orange juice, and nutmeg. Bring to a boil over medium-high heat, stirring constantly. Boil for 1 minute.

Reduce the heat to low, cover, and simmer, stirring frequently, for 5 minutes, or until the blueberries are tender and the sauce is thickened.

Place the sauce in a bowl, partially cover, and let cool. Dust the cake with confectioners' sugar, if using, and serve with the sauce.

Makes 10 servings
Per serving: 212 calories, 4 g protein, 34 g carbohydrates, 7 g fat, 1 g saturated fat, 43 mg cholesterol, 2 g dietary fiber, 219 mg sodium

lemon cheesecake

1¼	cups graham cracker crumbs
¼	cup pecans, toasted and ground
2¼	cups sugar
3	tablespoons butter, melted
3	egg whites, divided
2	packages (8 ounces each) fat-free cream cheese
1	package (8 ounces) reduced-fat cream cheese
¼	cup all-purpose flour
½	cup lemon juice
2	eggs
2	cups (16 ounces) fat-free sour cream

Preheat the oven to 350°F. Coat a 9" springform pan with cooking spray.

In a large bowl, combine the cracker crumbs, pecans, ¼ cup of the sugar, and butter. Lightly beat 1 of the egg whites in a cup. Add half of the egg white to the bowl; reserve the remainder for another use or discard. Mix well. Press the mixture into the bottom and 1" up the sides of the prepared pan.

Bake for 10 minutes, or until lightly browned. Cool on a rack.

Meanwhile, place the fat-free cream cheese and reduced-fat cream cheese in a food processor. Process for 1 minute, or until smooth. Add the flour and 1½ cups of the remaining sugar. Process for 3 minutes, or until light and fluffy; stop and scrape the sides of the bowl as necessary. Add the lemon juice and process briefly. Add the eggs and the remaining 2 egg whites, one at a time, and process until just incorporated.

Place the mixture in the prepared crust. Bake for 1 hour. Remove from the oven; do not turn off the oven.

In a small bowl, combine the sour cream and the remaining ½ cup sugar. Spread over the hot cheesecake. Bake for 10 minutes. Place on a rack and let cool to room temperature. Cover and refrigerate for at least 8 hours.

Makes 16 servings
Per serving: 268 calories, 9 g protein, 41 g carbohydrates, 8 g fat, 4 g saturated fat, 43 mg cholesterol, 0 g dietary fiber, 314 mg sodium

COOKING TIP
This cheesecake is equally delicious served with a fresh fruit topping. Omit the sour-cream topping. Toss 3 cups berries, sliced peaches, or orange segments with 2 tablespoons melted jam or jelly. Decoratively arrange the fruit on top of the cooled cheesecake.

rich 'n' creamy brown rice pudding

3	cups low-fat milk
½	cup uncooked brown rice
½	teaspoon salt
¼	teaspoon freshly grated nutmeg
2	eggs, lightly beaten
½	cup dried cherries

In a medium saucepan, combine the milk, rice, salt, and nutmeg. Bring to a boil over high heat. Reduce the heat to low, cover, and simmer for 45 minutes. Remove from the heat and let cool for 5 minutes.

Stir ½ cup of the rice mixture into the eggs, stirring constantly. Gradually stir the egg mixture into the saucepan. Stir in the cherries.

Place over medium-low heat and cook, stirring constantly, for 5 minutes, or until thickened. Serve warm or refrigerate to serve cold later.

Makes 6 servings
Per serving: 173 calories, 8 g protein, 27 g carbohydrates, 3 g fat, 1 g saturated fat, 76 mg cholesterol, 2 g dietary fiber, 279 mg sodium

chocolate-zucchini loaf

1 1/3	cups whole grain pastry flour
1/2	cup soy flour
1 1/2	teaspoons baking powder
1 1/2	teaspoons ground cinnamon
1/2	teaspoon baking soda
1/4	teaspoon salt
2	eggs
1/2	cup packed brown sugar
1/2	cup (4 ounces) fat-free plain yogurt
1/3	cup canola oil
2	teaspoons vanilla extract
1 1/2	cups shredded zucchini
1/2	cup mini semisweet chocolate chips

Preheat the oven to 350°F. Coat a 9" × 5" loaf pan with cooking spray.

In a large bowl, combine the pastry flour, soy flour, baking powder, cinnamon, baking soda, and salt.

In a medium bowl, using a wire whisk, beat the eggs, brown sugar, yogurt, oil, and vanilla extract until smooth. Stir in the zucchini and chocolate chips. Add to the flour mixture and stir just until blended. Place in the prepared loaf pan.

Bake for 40 minutes, or until the cake is springy to the touch and a wooden pick inserted in the center comes out clean. Cool in the pan on a rack for 30 minutes. Remove from the pan and cool completely on the rack.

Makes 12 servings
Per serving: 209 calories, 5 g protein, 27 g carbohydrates, 10 g fat, 2 g saturated fat, 36 mg cholesterol, 2 g dietary fiber, 175 mg sodium

ginger pumpkin pie

1¼	cups whole grain pastry flour
¼	teaspoon + ⅛ teaspoon salt
3	tablespoons canola oil
2	tablespoons cold butter, cut into small pieces
2–4	tablespoons ice water
½	cup packed brown sugar
1	egg
2	egg whites
1½	teaspoons vanilla extract
½	teaspoon ground cinnamon
½	teaspoon ground ginger
¼	teaspoon ground nutmeg
1	can (15 ounces) plain pumpkin
1	cup fat-free evaporated milk

In a food processor, combine the flour and ¼ teaspoon of the salt. Pulse until blended. Add the oil and butter. Pulse until the mixture resembles a fine meal. Add the water, 1 tablespoon at a time, as needed, and pulse just until the dough forms large clumps. Form into a ball and flatten into a disk. Cover and refrigerate for at least 1 hour.

Preheat the oven to 425°F. Coat a 9" pie plate with cooking spray.

Place the dough between 2 pieces of waxed paper and roll into a 12" circle. Remove the top piece of paper and invert the dough into the pie plate. Peel off the second piece of paper. Press the dough into the pie plate and up onto the rim, patching where necessary. Turn under the rim and flute. Chill in the refrigerator.

Meanwhile, in a large bowl, whisk the brown sugar, egg, egg whites, vanilla extract, cinnamon, ginger, nutmeg, and the remaining ⅛ teaspoon salt until well-blended. Whisk in the pumpkin and milk. Pour into the chilled crust. Bake for 15 minutes. Reduce the temperature to 350°F. Bake for 25 minutes, or until a knife inserted off-center comes out clean. Cool on a rack.

Makes 8 servings
Per serving: 252 calories, 7 g protein, 36 g carbohydrates, 9 g fat, 3 g saturated fat, 36 mg cholesterol, 4 g dietary fiber, 217 mg sodium

COOKING TIP
To save time on baking day, you can make the dough for this pie 1 to 3 days ahead. Wrap in plastic wrap and refrigerate until ready to use.

strawberry tart with oat-cinnamon crust

COOKING TIP
For a flavor-rich calcium boost, serve the tart with a scoop of fat-free vanilla frozen yogurt on the side.

Crust

⅔	cup rolled oats
½	cup whole grain pastry flour
1	tablespoon sugar
1	teaspoon ground cinnamon
¼	teaspoon baking soda
2	tablespoons canola oil
2–3	tablespoons fat-free plain yogurt

Filling

¼	cup strawberry all-fruit spread
½	teaspoon vanilla extract
1½	pints strawberries, hulled

To make the crust: Preheat the oven to 375°F. Coat a baking sheet with cooking spray.

In a medium bowl, combine the oats, flour, sugar, cinnamon, and baking soda. Stir in the oil and 2 tablespoons of the yogurt to make a soft, slightly sticky dough. If the dough is too stiff, add the remaining 1 tablespoon yogurt.

Place the dough on the prepared baking sheet and pat evenly into a 10" circle. If the dough sticks to your hands, coat them lightly with cooking spray.

Place a 9" cake pan on the dough and trace around it with a sharp knife. With your fingers, push up and pinch the dough around the outside of the circle to make a 9" circle with a rim ¼" high.

Bake for 15 minutes, or until firm and golden. Remove from the oven and set aside to cool.

T*o make the filling:* Meanwhile, in a small microwaveable bowl, combine the all-fruit spread and vanilla extract. Microwave on high power for 10 to 15 seconds, or until melted.

Brush a generous tablespoon evenly over the cooled crust. Arrange the strawberries evenly over the crust. Brush the remaining spread evenly over the strawberries, making sure to get some of the spread between the strawberries to secure them.

Refrigerate for at least 30 minutes, or until the spread has jelled.

Makes 6 servings
Per serving: 187 calories, 4 g protein, 31 g carbohydrates, 6 g fat,
0 g saturated fat, 0 mg cholesterol, 3 g dietary fiber, 65 mg sodium

apple crumble with toasted-oat topping

6	medium Jonagold or Golden Delicious apples, cored and thinly sliced
½	cup unsweetened applesauce
¾	cup rolled oats
3	tablespoons toasted wheat germ
3	tablespoons packed light brown sugar
1	teaspoon ground cinnamon
1	tablespoon canola oil
1	tablespoon unsalted butter, cut into small pieces

Preheat the oven to 350°F. Coat a 13" × 9" baking dish with cooking spray.

Combine the apples and applesauce in the prepared baking dish.

In a small bowl, combine the oats, wheat germ, brown sugar, and cinnamon. Add the oil and butter. Mix with your fingers to form crumbs. Sprinkle the oat mixture evenly over the apples.

Bake for 30 minutes, or until the topping is golden and the apples are bubbling.

Makes 8 servings
Per serving: 132 calories, 2 g protein, 25 g carbohydrates, 4 g fat, 1 g saturated fat, 4 mg cholesterol, 5 g dietary fiber, 4 mg sodium

COOKING TIP
Although you can make this recipe with peeled apples, leaving the peels on ensures that you get more of the slimming benefits of fiber.

summer fruit compote

1	cup water
1	package (6 ounces) mixed whole dried fruit
3	tablespoons frozen orange juice concentrate
2	tablespoons packed brown sugar
3	whole allspice berries
1	bay leaf
1	stick cinnamon or a pinch of ground cinnamon
3	medium peaches, cut into ¾" wedges
3	medium plums, cut into ¾" wedges
1	cup pitted sweet white or red cherries (optional)

COOKING TIP
Once you've added the fresh fruit, don't let the mixture boil. Let the heat of the liquid gently cook the fruit. Boiling will make it break up.

In a large saucepan, combine the water, dried fruit, orange juice concentrate, brown sugar, allspice berries, bay leaf, and cinnamon stick or ground cinnamon. Bring to a boil over high heat. Reduce the heat to low, cover, and simmer, stirring occasionally, for 10 minutes, or until the fruit is very tender.

Add the peaches and plums. Cover and simmer for 5 minutes, or until the peaches and plums are tender but not mushy. Stir in the cherries, if using, and cook for 3 minutes. Remove from the heat and place in a serving bowl. Let stand for at least 1 hour, or until the fruit has cooled and the flavors have blended. Remove and discard the bay leaf and cinnamon stick before serving.

Makes 6 servings
Per serving: 217 calories, 3 g protein, 56 g carbohydrates, 1 g fat, 0 g saturated fat, 0 mg cholesterol, 7 g dietary fiber, 5 mg sodium

the power of
ORANGES

So often consumed as a breakfast drink, intensely-flavored oranges tend to satisfy cravings more than bland foods.

Be sure not to peel off the white spongy layer just beneath the skin; it contains half of the fruit's pectin which helps control blood sugar. And stock up on juice concentrate because it's as nutritious as fresh juice. Try these simple tips to use more juice concentrate in your meals.

- Replace your sugary frostings with a glaze for cakes or brownies by blending with confectioners' sugar.
- Decrease the fat in homemade full-fat salad dressings by replacing half the oil with OJ concentrate.
- Use as a base for fruit salad and toss with a variety of chopped fruits and minced fresh mint.
- Make a marinade for chicken or fish by combining with a touch of oil and vinegar and your favorite minced herb.

fresh berry shortcakes *quick*

2	cups whole grain pastry flour
3	tablespoons + ⅓ cup sugar
2	teaspoons baking powder
¼	teaspoon baking soda
¼	cup butter, cut into small pieces
⅔	cup + 2 tablespoons buttermilk (see tip on page 323)
1½	pints assorted berries
2	tablespoons orange juice
2	cups (16 ounces) fat-free frozen vanilla yogurt

Preheat oven to 400°F. Coat a baking sheet with cooking spray.

In a large bowl, combine the flour, 2 tablespoons of the sugar, baking powder, and baking soda. Cut in the butter until the mixture resembles cornmeal. Add ⅔ cup of the buttermilk, stirring with a fork until the dough comes together.

Turn the dough out onto a lightly floured surface. Pat to ½" thickness. Using a 3" round cutter, cut 8 biscuits. (Pat the dough scraps together to cut out all the biscuits.) Place on the prepared baking sheet. Brush with the remaining 2 tablespoons buttermilk. Sprinkle with 1 tablespoon of the remaining sugar. Bake for 12 minutes, or until golden brown. Remove to a rack to cool.

Meanwhile, in a large bowl, combine the berries, orange juice, and the remaining ⅓ cup sugar. Let stand for 10 minutes.

Split the biscuits crosswise in half. Place a biscuit bottom on each of 8 dessert plates. Top with the berry filling and a scoop of frozen yogurt. Cover with the biscuit tops.

Makes 8 servings
Per serving: 302 calories, 7 g protein, 54 g carbohydrates, 7 g fat, 4 g saturated fat, 19 mg cholesterol, 5 g dietary fiber, 259 mg sodium

pear and almond crisp

4	large pears, cored and sliced ½" thick
2	tablespoons maple syrup
1	tablespoon lemon juice
1	teaspoon vanilla extract
½	teaspoon freshly grated nutmeg
1	cup rolled oats (not quick-cooking)
⅓	cup sliced natural almonds
¼	cup packed brown sugar
2	tablespoons whole grain pastry flour
2	tablespoons cold butter, cut into small pieces
2	tablespoons canola oil

Preheat the oven to 350°F.

Combine the pears, maple syrup, lemon juice, vanilla extract, and nutmeg in an 11" × 7" baking dish.

In a medium bowl, combine the oats, almonds, brown sugar, flour, butter, and oil and mix with your fingers to form crumbs. Sprinkle the topping over the pear mixture.

Bake for 40 minutes, or until the pears are tender and bubbly and the topping is lightly browned.

Makes 10 servings
Per serving: 182 calories, 3 g protein, 27 g carbohydrates, 8 g fat, 2 g saturated fat, 6 mg cholesterol, 3 g dietary fiber, 26 mg sodium

broiled peaches and strawberries

5	medium peaches, cut into 1" wedges
1½	pints strawberries, hulled and quartered
2	tablespoons honey
½	teaspoon ground cinnamon
⅛	teaspoon ground allspice or cloves
1	tablespoon butter, cut into small pieces
3	tablespoons slivered fresh mint, lemon verbena, or cinnamon basil (optional)

Preheat the broiler. Coat a large baking sheet with sides with cooking spray.

In a large bowl, combine the peaches, strawberries, honey, cinnamon, and allspice or cloves and toss to coat well. Place the fruit on the prepared baking sheet. Dot with the butter.

Broil, turning the pan 2 or 3 times (no need to turn the fruit), for 4 minutes, or until the fruit is glazed, bubbly, and golden brown in spots. Remove from the oven and let cool slightly.

Sprinkle with the mint, lemon verbena, or cinnamon basil, if using. Serve warm or at room temperature.

Makes 6 servings
Per serving: 111 calories, 1 g protein, 23 g carbohydrates, 3 g fat, 1 g saturated fat, 5 mg cholesterol, 4 g dietary fiber, 23 mg sodium

plate index

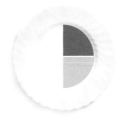

Index

Note: <u>Underscored</u> page references indicate boxed text or cooking tips. **Boldfaced** page references indicate photographs.

O

P

Conversion Chart

These equivalents have been slightly rounded to make measuring easier.

Volume Measurements

U.S.	Imperial	Metric
¼ tsp	–	1 ml
½ tsp	–	2 ml
1 tsp	–	5 ml
1 Tbsp	–	15 ml
2 Tbsp (1 oz)	1 fl oz	30 ml
¼ cup (2 oz)	2 fl oz	60 ml
⅓ cup (3 oz)	3 fl oz	80 ml
½ cup (4 oz)	4 fl oz	120 ml
⅔ cup (5 oz)	5 fl oz	160 ml
¾ cup (6 oz)	6 fl oz	180 ml
1 cup (8 oz)	8 fl oz	240 ml

Weight Measurements

U.S.	Metric
1 oz	30 g
2 oz	60 g
4 oz (¼ lb)	115 g
5 oz (⅓ lb)	145 g
6 oz	170 g
7 oz	200 g
8 oz (½ lb)	230 g
10 oz	285 g
12 oz (¾ lb)	340 g
14 oz	400 g
16 oz (1 lb)	455 g
2.2 lb	1 kg

Length Measurements

U.S.	Metric
¼"	0.6 cm
½"	1.25 cm
1"	2.5 cm
2"	5 cm
4"	11 cm
6"	15 cm
8"	20 cm
10"	25 cm
12" (1')	30 cm

Pan Sizes

U.S.	Metric
8" cake pan	20 × 4 cm sandwich or cake tin
9" cake pan	23 × 3.5 cm sandwich or cake tin
11" × 7" baking pan	28 × 18 cm baking tin
13" × 9" baking pan	32.5 × 23 cm baking tin
15" × 10" baking pan	38 × 25.5 cm baking tin (Swiss roll tin)
1½ qt baking dish	1.5 liter baking dish
2 qt baking dish	2 liter baking dish
2 qt rectangular baking dish	30 × 19 cm baking dish
9" pie plate	22 × 4 or 23 × 4 cm pie plate
7" or 8" springform pan	18 or 20 cm springform or loose-bottom cake tin
9" × 5" loaf pan	23 × 13 cm or 2 lb narrow loaf tin or pâté tin

Temperatures

Fahrenheit	Centigrade	Gas
140°	60°	–
160°	70°	–
180°	80°	–
225°	105°	¼
250°	120°	½
275°	135°	1
300°	150°	2
325°	160°	3
350°	180°	4
375°	190°	5
400°	200°	6
425°	220°	7
450°	230°	8
475°	245°	9
500°	260°	–